5/23/9

THE FOX AND THE WHIRLWIND

Dedicated to all free spirits
and their pursuit to follow
the wind. May you never
break wind.

Geronimo

The Fox and the Whirlwind

General George Crook and Geronimo

A Paired Biography

Peter Aleshire

John Wiley & Sons, Inc.
New York • Chichester • Weinheim • Brisbane • Singapore • Toronto

Published by John Wiley & Sons, Inc.
Published simultaneously in Canada

This publication is designed to provide accurate and authoritative information in
regard to the subject matter covered. It is sold with the understanding that the pub-
lisher is not engaged in rendering professional services. If professional advice or
other expert assistance is required, the services of a competent professional person
should be sought.

Library of Congress Cataloging-in-Publication Data:

Aleshire, Peter.
    The fox and the whirlwind : General George Crook and Geronimo : a
paired biography / Peter Aleshire.
        p.   cm.
    Includes bibliographical references and index.
    ISBN 0-471-32575-9 (acid-free paper)
    1. Geronimo, 1828–1909. 2. Apache Indians—Kings and rulers
Biography. 3. Crook, George, 1829–1890. 4. Generals—United States
Biography. 5. Apache Indians—Wars, 1883–1886.   I. Title.
E99.A6G3224   2000
979'.004972'0092—dc21
    [B]   99-36279

Printed in the United States of America

10 9 8 7 6 5 4 3 2 1

To Frank and Fran Aleshire,
the authors of my history

CONTENTS

PREFACE

GERONIMO and General George Crook were born to destroy each other.

And they did—the perfect enemies, perfectly capturing the tragic strengths and weaknesses of their respective cultures. Their terrible battles, relentless pursuits, and futile victories provide a fascinating insight into the merciless, decades-long clash between their two sharply contrasting worlds. And yet their remarkable similarities as warriors suggest unexpected resonance in their lives and characters. They each seemed cast for their tragic roles, with complementary strengths and perfectly matched weaknesses. Shakespeare could not have conceived more admirable, and tragically flawed protagonists. Geronimo, an Apache war shaman, made a religion of revenge and fought on long past hope and reason so that he ultimately became both the whites' most hated foe and a romanticized symbol of Indian resistance. Crook, the nation's most successful Indian fighter, combined a paradoxical sympathy with a relentless antipathy. He became both the Apaches' best friend and their worst enemy. He labored all of his life to destroy the cultures and warriors he admired in the service of the men and the system that ultimately disregarded and disrespected him.

Crook and Geronimo each embodied the essence of their respective cultures. Crook was professional, honorable, courageous, racist, righteous, remorseless, just, and a brilliant strategist; Geronimo was indomitable, cunning, courageous, racist, religious, merciless, vengeful, and a brilliant strategist. Crook never questioned the right of whites to destroy native cultures and seize their land;

ix

Geronimo never questioned the right of a warrior to extract his revenge, torment his enemies, and defend his homeland. Their overlapping stories provide a compelling way to explain some of the most important events in U.S. history while providing unexpected insight into the mind-set of their warring cultures.

However, telling the two stories in an evenhanded way presents certain difficulties. The story on the white side is wonderfully documented through firsthand sources. Crook left an uncompleted autobiography, which has been strongly edited and annotated by Martin F. Schmitt. In addition, Captain John Bourke wrote a series of absorbing accounts of his service in Crook's command, and left diaries that remain a priceless documentary source. That era's professional officer corps was filled with literate, insightful observers, and a number of them also left firsthand accounts of their service with Crook. Moreover, newspaper reporters on key occasions accompanied Crook's units in the field, leaving additional accounts. Finally, the officers wrote many official dispatches and reports of the events as they took place. I also got some help from military historian Tom Cutrer, who made some valuable suggestions concerning my description of events during the Civil War. I'm also indebted to Kathy Khoury for her editing and suggestions. Unfortunately, presenting the Apache version of the story in a way that satisfies the conventions of historiography presents greater problems. Geronimo did dictate his autobiography to a sympathetic white man late in his life, relying on his memory to recount events that occurred decades earlier. In addition, historian Eve Ball, who lived for years on the Mescalero Reservation in New Mexico, set down the recollections of various leading men on the reservation who had been boys in the bands of Geronimo, Juh, Victorio, and other leading Chiricahua and Warm Springs Apache leaders. Anthropologist Grenville Goodwin performed a similar service among the White Mountain Apache, gathering up the firsthand accounts of several old warriors who served as scouts for the army. Anthropologist Morris Opler also wrote a detailed, insightful, and sympathetic account of the lifeway of the Chiricahua Apache. Other writers have drawn on all of these primary sources to offer an account of Apache history, most notably Angie

Debo in her impressive biography of Geronimo. Any attempt to tell the story from the Apache viewpoint is fraught with hard choices, even down to the spelling of names. Of course, nineteenth-century writers were creative in their rendering of standard English, and differed dramatically in their rendering of the tongue-twisting Apache names. I have usually settled for the spellings used by Eve Ball and other writers whose work was reviewed by Apache informants. However, in these pages you will find variations in spelling in quotes or notes taken from other primary sources. For all of these reasons, it has proved difficult and frustrating to write history from the Apache viewpoint without betraying its cadence, outlook, and perspective.

I have settled on my own solution to the problem, by telling this story with two distinct voices. I have employed a more conventional approach for Crook's story, but have attempted to tell Geronimo's story in a manner more consistent with the oral accounts of the Apaches themselves. In this, I was inspired by the tone of Maria Sandoz's brilliant biography of Crazy Horse. I adopted a narrative voice, avoided the use of direct quotation marks, and took the liberty of probing interior thoughts when I had a basis to do so in firsthand accounts. I also accepted at face value Geronimo's claim to supernatural powers, which have been testified to by Apache witnesses. I do this, in part, because most other accounts have given insufficient weight to Geronimo's role as a religious leader and a possessor of Power. I also chose which versions of events to believe based on the facts and on the information Geronimo would have had available to him. In each case where I selected one version of the truth over another, I provided a trail of footnotes. But at most points in the narrative, I tried not to introduce information that Geronimo did not have. It is possible to do this while still giving the reader a complete picture by shifting back and forth from Geronimo's world to Crook's world. In the end, I hope the reader will see the conflict from both viewpoints at the same time.

Part of the point of this shifting of voices, and of the intertwining of these two lives, is to underscore the lesson that history is not a certain set of facts that constitute the truth. History remains, rather, the stories that we tell. Each generation tells different stories to satisfy different needs. Each writer chases truth, which appears always shimmering at the horizon, drawing us on. But we never quite catch up. It's a bit like chasing a small band of Apache warriors through the wilderness, seeking signs of their passage.

Part One

PROLOGUE

1

Geronimo
THE PRICE OF POWER

GERONIMO WATCHED the dancers circle the bonfire, their long shadows flung, flickering outward by the flames. The old man listened to the singers, their long voices rising to a wail and falling to a moan. All this while the once-terrible warrior stared wordlessly at the chanting shaman Lot Eyelash, who was now seeking out the evil that had dogged Geronimo's family, his band, his life.

Who could doubt that Geronimo had been witched?

Were not all of the eight wives of his life dead or gone away? Had not five of his children died already, from the bullets of the Mexicans or the diseases of the White Eyes? And was not his beloved Eva now sick herself—dwindling toward death like all the others? Had he not wielded Power all of his life, protecting his life, and the lives of his warriors, but come nonetheless to this place, lost to even the most distant call of a single coyote—from whence Geronimo's Power came? Geronimo had lifted up his knife, struck down his enemies, and fulfilled the obligation of revenge. He had gone where his Power directed him—even through the bullets of his enemies. He had healed the sick, held back the sun from rising, and looked into the fatal future, like holding coals in his open palm. Even when the warriors had so little hope that they called themselves "the Dead"—still he fought on. He had done everything asked of him, and still his children died, and still The People died. So it seemed only reasonable to wonder who had called so much evil down on him.

Geronimo posed kneeling and holding his rifle for this studio photo by Ben Wittick in 1887. It is perhaps the most famous photo of a Native American. (*Courtesy National Archives*)

After all, Geronimo had earned many enemies. The Mexicans still frightened their children with his name in the dark, and the White Eyes still thrilled with the fear of him although he was an old man far from the warpath. Even many among his own people spoke against him, blaming their long imprisonment and exile on his war against all hope, and against all reason, and against all other people.

Knowing this, Geronimo had gone to Lot Eyelash. He had gone in his pain and his humility to this other shaman, and asked for the dance, and the songs, and the whispering of the Power which cupped Lot Eyelash in its palm. Geronimo wanted to know finally who had done this thing. Who had witched him so that everyone he loved sickened and died as with the ghost sickness?

So Geronimo listened—waiting to learn the name of his enemy.

Lot Eyelash sang the first song his Power had taught him—as Geronimo had learned his Coyote songs, and his Ghost songs, and all the other songs by which an honorable man might live his life even in times that made no sense.

Lot Eyelash sang his second song on into the night, as the dancers shuffled, and the singers chanted.

Lot Eyelash sang the third song as the night grew long, and the legs of the dancers trembled.

And Lot Eyelash sang the fourth song—which was the sacred number.

So Geronimo waited then for the name of his enemy, his warrior face held perfectly expressionless.

Suddenly, Lot Eyelash fell silent, as though a voice had broken into his song. The shaman turned about, and flung his arm out, pointing at Geronimo.

You did it! cried Lot Eyelash, into the sudden silence of The People. You did it so that you could live on.[1]

Some of those who heard it drew back from Geronimo—for those who wield Power are both admired and feared. Power seeks its price for the gifts it barters. You might charm it, or cajole it, or placate it—but Power must have its own way. No one could know which was the hand, and which was the knife. Geronimo's Power had stopped the sun in its path, taken the gunpowder from the cartridges of the enemy, showed him the future, and saved him from more wounds than you could count—some of the healed bullet holes deep enough to hide pebbles. Who could say what such a Power might ask, or offer?

But others of those who heard Lot Eyelash dismissed the claim, knowing weaker men had always feared Geronimo. These weak men resented the rebuke of his refusal to surrender. Geronimo had used his great Power on behalf of The People for all of his long life—and now he pulled his grandson in the little red wagon, and urged the children to their lessons, and played with the babies with perfect happiness. He would not do such a thing—trading Eva for a few years added to a life already heavy with regret.

As for Geronimo, he did not speak, but sat staring still at Lot Eyelash, his black eyes glittering in the firelight. Geronimo held the reins of his expression tight, as he had when the White Eyes put the shackles on him, as he had when they loaded him on the train, as he did through all the death, and loss, and futile triumph of his long life.

And who can say what long, dark thoughts enfolded him in that moment.

Perhaps, looking back on his terrible journey, he wondered whether it might be true after all. For he had tried to do right, but had called down great wrongs on his people. Loss had haunted him all his life—like a ghost called back by the reckless use of the name of one who has gone. Surely he had earned a warrior's death—not this long burning down to ash in the midst of his enemies.

Had he somehow earned the great punishment of his life? Or had he merely lived in the wrong season, the last leaf clinging to the last branch in foolish defiance of winter?

2

Crook

THE COST OF DUTY

GENERAL GEORGE CROOK, whose command covered a vast sprawl of the West he had struggled all his life to pacify, fumed. General Nelson A. Miles's lies had once again strained Crook's famous restraint. It was maddening, the twists of truth and the slights on character inflicted on Crook in his honorable struggle to win the release of the imprisoned Chiricahua—who were winnowed more severely by disease with each passing year.

Crook had devoted much of the past year to this question. He could not let it go, seeing it now as a question of honor. He had devoted the best and hardest years of his life to breaking the Apache resistance. He had convinced the great majority of the Apache—even the redoubtable Chiricahua—to live peacefully on the reservation. In the end, only a handful of bloodthirsty, unreconstructed troublemakers inspired by the damnable Geronimo had treacherously and persistently refused to accept the inevitable. Geronimo's repeated broken promises and his final drunken bolt into the wilderness had led to Crook's resignation from that command and Miles's appointment. Miles had then proceeded to make a grand fool of himself, calling for more and more troops until he had a quarter of the U.S. Army chasing a handful of savages without result. Miles had disdained the use of scouts, which had been the mainstay of Crook's long, successful campaign against the Apache—a campaign that had stretched with some interruptions from 1870 to 1885. In this, Miles comforted Crook's

legions of harsh critics, who insisted the scouts had actually prevented the capture of the renegades. Some of those same former
scouts had finally found Geronimo and the last of his warriors in
Mexico, and convinced them to talk with General Miles, who had
promised them a two-year exile on a reservation in the East with
their families, followed by a return to the reservation. But the government had betrayed that promise, imprisoning the renegades
along with the former scouts for years. Crook had served on a
commission to investigate and recommended settling the Chiricahua prisoners at the Mount Vernon, Alabama, military barracks,
to which they had been transferred from a disease-ridden prison
camp in Florida. Crook had found them at Mount Vernon still
dispirited and subject to disease, and had recommended their
removal to a much more suitable reservation in the Indian Territory in Oklahoma.

But Crook's recommendation had borne with it the implication
that General Miles had dealt treacherously with the Chiricahua—
punishing the innocent along with the guilty and violating his own
promises to the surrendering warriors.

Miles had vigorously defended his position as a bill authoriz-
ing the relocation of the Chiricahua came before Congress. By
sending the scouts and the peaceful Chiricahua into exile with
Geronimo, Miles had betrayed Crook's own promises to the Chiricahua and so made a liar of a man who had spent his entire life
living by his own stern code of honor and integrity. Miles had
imprisoned even the loyal scouts like Chato. Crook maintained
the scouts had made possible every single success against the hostiles. They had saved his life many a time, and proven unflinching,
honorable, and unswerving—once their loyalty could be won.

Miles had betrayed that loyalty by imprisoning nearly four
hundred peaceful Chiricahua. Miles wrote, "In July of 1886 I
found at Fort Apache over 400 men and women and children
belonging to the Chiricahua and Warm Springs Indians, and a
more turbulent, desperate, disreputable band of human beings I
had never seen before, and hope never to see again. When I visited their camp they were having their drunken orgies every night,
and it was a perfect pandemonium. One of the most prominent

General George Crook, seen here with rifle in hand standing on a bearskin, was an avid hunter all his life—once killing a charging grizzly at nearly point-blank range with a single shot through the beast's open mouth. (*Courtesy National Archives*)

among the Indians was Chato, who at one time had led what was perhaps the bloodiest raid ever made in that country. The young men were insolent, violent, and restless, and anxious to go on the warpath. I received reliable information that another outbreak was contemplated by the Indians, and was then being arranged amongst them."[1]

Captain John G. Bourke, who had served loyally as Crook's chief aide through these battles, responded.

> Crook was not the man to lie to anyone or deal treacherously by him. If there was one point in his character which shone more resplendent than any other, it was his absolute integrity in his deal- ings with representatives of inferior races. . . . For Geronimo and those with him, any punishment that could be inflicted without incurring the imputation of treachery would not be too severe; but the incarceration of Chato and the three-fourths of the band who had remained faithful for years and had rendered such signal service in pursuit of the renegades can never meet with the approval of honorable soldiers and gentlemen. . . . Not a single Chiricahua had been killed, captured, or wounded throughout the entire campaign— with two exceptions—unless by Chiricahua-Apache scouts, who, like Chato, had kept pledges given to General Crook in the Sierra Madre in 1883 . . . There is no more disgraceful page in the history of our relations with the American Indians than that which conceals the treachery visited upon the Chiricahua who remained faithful in their allegiance to our people.[2]

Crook had also fired off a volley in response to Miles's claims that the scouts had proved treacherous. "This is all false. These stories are being circulated for a purpose. Chato was not only faithful, but it was due entirely to the efforts of his Indian scouts that the hostiles under Nachez and Geronimo surrendered to me in March 1886. It is true that General Miles did discharge the Apache scouts and after operating against thirty-three Indians for over five months without killing or capturing a single one of them, he sent Lieutenant [Charles] Gatewood and two of Chato's scouts, who succeeded in securing the surrender of the renegades upon the promise that they should not be harmed, and should be sent to join their families in Florida."[3]

Maddening. Crook had worn himself out in the service of his country—four decades of almost continuous fighting—only to have his honor, and his judgment, and his integrity impugned by place-holders, politicians, and wretched journalists.

Galling. The savages themselves sometimes seemed exemplars of honor and courage, next to the thieving, drunken wretches who had persistently foiled peace—and frustrated his efforts. Repeatedly, his superior officers had undone his promises and rebuffed his recommendations. Corrupt civil officials had defrauded, debased, and abused the Indians—driving them to war and then calling in the army for the killing. The wretched contractors had sold whiskey and ammunition, and done everything possible to keep the Indians stirred up—seizing their share of graft and provender even at the expense of the lives of innocent women and children. The worst elements among the settlers had murdered wantonly, then heaped infamy on Crook. And in the final indignity, that lying old murderer Geronimo had snatched the victory he had earned away from him—casting a shadow across Crook's career and bringing this unjust doom down on the Chiricahua.

But Crook could do so little, really. The end was inevitable. The savages must give way to civilization. He had done everything he could in his life to hasten the transformation—and to save individual Indians by convincing them to submit. Still, he wondered sometimes at the way things had worked out.

As he had said to the class at West Point in 1884: "With all his faults, and he has many, the American Indian is not half so black as he has been painted. He is cruel in war, treacherous at times, and not overly cleanly. But so were our forefathers. His nature, however, is responsive to a treatment which assures him that it is based on justice, truth, honesty and common sense; it is not impossible that with a fair and square system of dealing with him the American Indian would make a better citizen than many who neglect the duties and abuse the privileges of that proud title."[4]

But on the morning of March 21, 1890, after his customary exercise, Crook felt a sudden pressure on his chest—a slow, choking sensation. He staggered to the sofa, and fell down upon it, crying out to his wife, "Mary! Mary! I can't breathe."

She came to him quickly, and found him on the couch gasping for breath. He had spent his life in the most arduous service on the frontier. He had been shot, pierced by arrows, and endured sickness—and now lay dying at the age of sixty-two, the most successful Indian fighter in the nation's history.

"I am choking," he said quietly. A short time later he was dead.

When the news reached the Sioux leader Red Cloud that "Three Stars" was dead, he said, "When Three Stars came; he, at least, had never lied to us. His words gave the people hope. He died. Their hope died again. Despair came again."[5]

When news of Crook's death reached the camps of the Apaches living around Camp Apache they "let their hair down, bent their heads forward on their bosoms, and wept and wailed like children"[6] for the man they had known as Gray Fox.

But when the news reached Geronimo—Crook's greatest enemy among the Indians—Geronimo grunted in satisfaction. Gray Fox had earned many deaths, said Geronimo, with his lies.

But Geronimo should have mourned him, because Crook's death killed the chances for the relocation of the Chiricahua. Miles triumphed and the Chiricahua remained prisoners for another twenty years.

A terrible question had haunted Crook's life—just as it did Geronimo's.

All his life, Crook labored to do right. He had lived by a code of honor, and acted with fierce determination, justice, and compassion.

But had the achievement of his life been a terrible injustice? Had he done his best and most enduring work in destroying men whose courage resembled his own, on behalf of the weak and the corrupt? Had he helped to destroy everything he loved best?

Part Two

1828–1861

Early Conflicts

3

Geronimo

The Making of a Warrior

In the beginning times, terrible monsters and many beasts occupied the world. Human beings could not live in such a world, which was divided between two tribes of creatures—the birds, whose chief was Eagle, and the beasts, among whom was a terrible dragon. The two tribes quarreled often. The birds wished to admit light into the world, while the beasts loved the darkness. Finally, the birds made war against the beasts.

The birds won this war, and so brought light, and the moon, and the sun, and the stars into the world. Even so, they did not kill all of the beasts. Many terrible monsters remained—including Dragon, with his four thick coats of horny scales.[1]

White Painted Woman lived on the earth then, and she had many children. But the dragon came along every time and ate up her children. One day Rain fell down on her, and got her pregnant. When the child was born, she dug a hole under her campfire and hid him there. She called her baby "Child of Waters." When Dragon came, he saw the footprints of the child, but he could not find the baby. It went on like this for a time, but when the child grew larger he would not stay in the cave and hide under the fire. One day he told his mother that he would go hunting. She pleaded with him not to go. She warned him about Dragon, and the bears, and the serpent, and all the other monsters. But he would not listen. Instead he went to his uncle—Slayer of Enemies—who was then the only other man living.[2]

15

So Child of Waters and Slayer of Enemies went out hunting, and killed a deer. But after they had set the meat out to dry, Dragon came. Slayer of Enemies was struck dumb with fear, but Child of Waters was not afraid—and faced Dragon boldly. Dragon took the deer and seated himself beside it, saying to the boy, This is the child I have been seeking. Boy, you are nice and fat, so when I have eaten this venison I shall eat you. But the boy said, No, you shall not eat me, and you shall not eat that meat. He walked right up to Dragon and took the meat back. Dragon said, as he took the meat back again, I like your courage. But you are foolish; what do you think you could do? Well, said the boy, taking the meat back again in his turn; I can do enough to protect myself, as you may find out. Four times Dragon took the meat; and four times the boy took it back again. Then the boy asked, Dragon, will you fight me?

So they agreed to fight. Child of Waters said that Dragon could shoot his bow four times, and then Child of Waters would do the same. Dragon laughed, and took up his bow, each arrow as large as a small tree. He fired the first shot at Child of Waters, but the boy made a peculiar sound and leaped up into the air just before the giant arrow reached him. The arrow splintered into a thousand pieces and the boy was standing on top of a rainbow, above where Dragon had aimed his shot. Four times this happened the same way. Then it was the turn of Child of Waters to shoot. All right, said Dragon. Your arrows cannot pierce my first coat of horn, and I have three other coats. So Child of Waters fired his first arrow. It struck Dragon just over the heart, and immediately his first coat of armor shattered and fell away. Child of Waters shot four times and Dragon stood very still, trembling with fear, but unable to move. The last arrow penetrated Dragon's heart—and with a terrible roar he rolled down the mountainside, over four precipices into a canyon below. Immediately storm clouds swept the mountains, lightning flashed, thunder rolled, and the rain poured.

Child of Waters went out then into the world, and killed all of the monsters. He and his uncle sometimes hunted together, but sometimes quarreled as well. Slayer of Enemies would eventually become the father of the White Eyes—picking for them the gun and obtaining for them cattle and horses from the Crows. Child of Waters was father to The People.[3] He killed the most terrible of monsters by his courage, and his cleverness—and by calling on the protection of his Power, which came from his father, who was Rain, Sun, and Wind. Child of Waters picked for his people the bow and arrow and also obtained for them the best place to live— among the sacred mountains where the rocks, and the trees, and the canyons, and the sky all knew them. Child of Waters taught The People how they should live, how they should hunt, the prayers that they should pray, and how they should conduct themselves in all things. And from that time on down to this, each man must spend his life walking in the footprints of Child of Waters. Each life remembers him—so that every warrior's story should start with the story of Child of Waters, so that every warrior should follow along in his footsteps in the great round of life and do all things in a right manner.

And so Goyathlay, whose boyhood name meant "Shrewd,"[4] was born[5] in No-doyohn Canyon near the headwaters of the great Gila River, among the sacred red-and-gold colored mountains, during the last good times of a once-free people. He was born into the very place that Usen, the creative spirit who had ordered the world, had made for The People, and from which Child of Waters had driven all the monsters. The rocks knew them, and the rivers knew them, and the wind knew them. The generations that had gone before were buried in its secret places; their seeds were scattered in the good soil, and the deep canyons knew all of their songs.

Goyathlay was the grandson of Chief Mahko of the Bedonkohe, a great warrior who lived in peaceful times. Mahko taught his people to value farming, and tend to their own quiet business. He was also a man of great Power, who walked in the right way, and spoke in the right way, and followed after Child of Waters, stepping in his tracks. Mahko's son, Taklishim, the Gray One, was the father of Goyathlay and an important man also among the Bedonkohe—in the days when they were a strong people.

The Bedonkohe had strong friends. They were closest to the Chokonen, the true Chiricahua led in times to come by Cochise.

They were close also to the Mimbreno and Chihenne,[6] led by Mangas Coloradas, who was the greatest leader The People had ever known. The Bedonkohe also often married with and fought with the Nednai, the wildest of all The People, who lived deep in the Sierra Madre. The Bedonkohe also knew the White Mountain people, but although linked by clans and kinship, they did not often raid together or turn to each other in trouble. The same would be said of the Mescaleros—who lived way off to the east near the Lipan, who hunted buffalo out where the earth ran off to be with the sky beyond the reach of the eyes.

The rest of the world consisted mostly of enemies. Some were only sometime enemies, like the Tontos[7] and the Navajo. Others they raided when they needed things, like the home-staying Pima and the Papago. But the great enemies of all The People were first the Spanish and then the Mexicans. These were slow, frightened people whose only advantage lay in their great numbers and their guns and their bullets. Man to man, they could hardly fight at all— and one Mexican cut off from his friends, and horses, and wagons, and supplies could hardly even stay alive. But they clustered in great numbers in their towns, and sent out soldiers in great numbers, and forever schemed with the enemies of The People. Sometimes the Mexicans would even pay out rewards for the scalp of any of The People who could be trapped and killed, or shot from ambush. But mostly The People held the Mexicans in great contempt, and let them stay alive so they would raise the sheep, and the cattle, and the horses, and the other things they needed for the long winters and the great ceremonials.

The parents of Goyathlay, Juanita and Taklishim (the Gray One), neglected nothing in his birth and in his training.[8] They rolled the baby on the floor of the shelter in which he was born— rolled him to the east, and the west, and the north, and the south. Even so would he roll himself, east, west, north, and south, each time in the years to come that he passed by that place—at least until he was sent away beyond all hope of seeing it ever again.[9] His parents made a cradle of oak, with yucca stalks for the crosspiece, and oak for the footrest, and wild mustard for the bedding and buckskin to cover the frame—each piece made just so, in the old way. They hung bags of sacred pollen from the crosspieces, and beads of turquoise, and bits of lightning-riven wood, to bless and amuse the baby. When they held the ceremony to bless the cradle, they marked Goyathlay's face with four dots of pollen. Everyone who came to the feast that followed said that everything had been done in the right way—and the baby, who already seemed so alert, and shrewd, and aware, would walk quickly along a right path. His parents also did everything in the old way when they held the moccasin ceremony for him when he was seven, amid much feasting and celebration, and the sound of the men shouting as they played hoop and pole in the sacred way. His parents made for Goyathlay the shirt and the moccasins from flawless buckskin. At dawn, the Medicine Man who knew all the old songs right back to Child of Waters's time, sang the right songs in the right way—then he lifted the boy to the east, and the west, and the north, and the south. He made the footprints on a piece of white buckskin, just as White Painted Woman had done for Child of Waters when he prepared to go out and kill the monsters. The Medicine Man led Goyathlay to the buckskin, so that he walked perfectly in the four footprints of pollen while the Medicine Man sang a prayer for each step. Then the boy took four steps himself, so that his feet would learn the journey that Child of Waters had taken. The Medicine Man led him around in a circle four times clockwise, singing four songs, saying four prayers. He beat on the drum and everyone joined in, singing about Life Giver, and White Painted Woman, and Child of Waters, and how the earth was made, and how the fruit grew, and how Child of Waters was born and hidden under the fire, and how he killed all the monsters—the boy dancing all the time with the rest. Finally the Medicine Man picked up the moccasins that had been made for the boy in the old, sacred way. He lifted the moccasins to the four directions, and marked them with pollen, and then he put pollen on Goyathlay's foot. He put the moccasins on the boy's feet—first the right, then the left, saying, Now you can run.[10]

It had always been thus.

But who could have known then how far the boy would have to run.

Goyathlay grew up in the usual way. From the very first, he played at being a warrior—at following Child of Waters's path. He played hide-and-seek all through the camp. He practiced stealing things—so that he could return them in triumph. Along with the other boys, he often went off and hid in the trees, in the rocks, in the bushes—which learned his name with the long, slow patience of rocks, and trees, and growing things. Mostly he played with his relatives—especially with the eight boys who were his brothers because they were the sons of his parents, and of his parents' brothers and sisters. No one would think to punish the boys for running away thus, and for hiding—only to ridicule them if they hid so carelessly that they could be found.

Goyathlay spent his days playing, and exploring, and practicing for the responsibilities of manhood. He hunted rats in their woodpiles. He practiced endlessly with the small bow he made for himself—and wagered his arrows, and anything else that came to hand, in unending contests with the other boys. He learned to wrestle, and to dodge stones thrown by the other boys, and even arrows. His parents never struck him—but they had no need of it. Ridicule and silence cut more deeply than any blow. Fighting, and going off alone, and playing jokes—these were all lessons that a boy had to learn, not matters for punishment. So he and his brothers made slings of willow branches and practiced flicking mud at birds. They made popguns out of hollow reeds. They built fires at night and threw their moccasins at the bats that fluttered toward the flame out of the darkness and chased birds. They also played many pranks on one another—like slipping nettles into one another's bedding and then laughing at the itching and scratching and long, red welts that resulted. They played hide-and-seek, and raced, and wrestled with no rules whatever.

Sometimes when he failed to show proper respect to his elders, his parents would warn Goyathlay that they would give him away to a mean old man if he did not behave. Soon after that, an old man with a cruel face would begin to hang around their camp with a sack in his hands so that Goyathlay would promise to behave.

If Goyathlay cried when he was little, and would not stop, sometimes his parents would put a piece of cloth over his head—or dribble a little water on his head—until he stopped. After all, a child who would not stop crying could bring disaster to the whole band when they were hiding from their enemies.[11] Sometimes when he had been bad, his parents would send him to another camp to get something ridiculous. Seeing that he was being punished, his relatives would send him on to someone else, so that he would be running from place to place all day long.

Goyathlay learned how to do all things in the proper manner, knowing that the world was full of dangers, most of which set their snare for a boy or a man through his own disrespect and carelessness. Goyathlay learned to never step on a coyote track, to avoid snakes and fish, to speak respectfully to deer and rats, to say his prayers to the rising sun and to avoid using Bear's name lest he draw to the camp one of the outcast warriors who sometimes became bears. He learned to move carefully, and reverently, and with respect for the spirit of all things. He almost never fell asleep during the great storytellings, especially during the stories about Coyote, the trickster. Goyathlay listened avidly, memorizing them in his turn for the long nights of winter that lay ahead.

Goyathlay began training for his proper role as a warrior when he was seven, as befits the grandson of a chief, and the son of a respected man. He knew that The People had need of warriors to follow in the path of Child of Waters, who had given them the best places, but also many enemies. The warriors went often on raids to take what they needed from weaker peoples. Sometimes, someone would kill a warrior. Then the relatives of the dead man would call upon their clan members, and their relatives, and their leaders to get revenge—as Usen had said they should do. Then they would raise a war party—sometimes hundreds of warriors—and go kill as many of the enemy as they could. Only in this way would their enemies learn the price of a warrior's life. Mostly, they fought the Mexicans to the south, who had good weapons, and lots of cattle and horses. They were like ants—weak, and easy to crush, but strong in numbers and unity of purpose. Perhaps Usen had made these weak and unfinished creatures to provide The People with horses and cattle. These days, you could hardly hold the moccasin ceremony for the boys, or the White Painted Woman coming-of-age ceremony for the girls, or get married, unless you had been on a successful raiding party. Of course, the Mexicans fought back, and organized the enemies of The People, and sent soldiers to chase the raiding parties, and paid for scalps so the war was constant with them.

So the boys like Goyathlay began training when they were small. Every morning, Goyathlay rose before the sun and ran quickly to the top of the mountain near his camp—thinking all the while as he ran that perhaps he would see the Ga'an, the mountain spirits that safeguarded the people and lived in the sacred mountains. The running made his legs strong, so they stretched out longer and longer—but mostly the running strengthened his mind and his heart. In running, as in most things, the mind runs on ahead and brings the body along after.

His father said to him, My son, no one will help you in this world. You must do something. You run to that mountain and back, and that will make you strong. My son, you know that no one is your friend, not even your sister, your father, or your mother. Your legs are your friends, your brain is your friend, your eyesight is your friend, you hair is your friend, your hands are your friends; you must do something with them. When you grow up, you live with these things and think about it. Someday you will be with people who are starving. You will have to get something for them. If you go somewhere, you must beat the enemies who are attacking you before they get over the hill. Before they beat you, you must get in front of them and bring them back dead. Then people will be proud of you. All the camps will talk about you. They will call my name and say my son is fine and does good work. Then we will be proud of you. If you are lazy, people will hate you.[12]

Older, seasoned warriors took on the task of training. Sometimes they made the boys fight each other, even if they were badly matched, so that the boys would learn courage even against hopeless odds. They gave the boys slings and had them throw stones at one another, knowing that the stones posed far less danger than lax training. The boys set off on races, with the trainers running along behind with switches to beat whichever boy ran in the last position. Sometimes, the strongest and bravest boys would drop back and snatch the stick from the trainer's hand—taking the beating to give all the other boys a good start. They learned to ride, controlling their horses with only a rope around the nose. Just at dawn in the winter, they followed the trainer to the stream, where he cracked the surface of the ice and ordered them into the water. They came out at his command, then stood in the snow, trying not to shiver, and never complaining. They plunged into the water again and again. Goyathlay learned to catch the coyote of courage, letting burning sage or the pitch of the sunflower scar his skin without flinching. These things he did to show that he would not yield to the weakness of the body. He could bear any discomfort, any loss, without even a change of his expression.

Goyathlay undertook the four raids of his apprenticeship as a warrior as soon as his father would let him. He waited eagerly for each raid, hoping the leading warrior would select him as an apprentice. Goyathlay observed the rules of the raid with great care. He eagerly followed the instructions of the warriors, tended to their horses, gathered the firewood, sat up through the night to keep watch. He learned the special language of the warpath—with all of its indirect references. Words, after all, had great Power. Saying a thing could make it start wanting to happen. So on the warpath they talked around the edge of things, like a lone warrior scouting an enemy's camp. So instead of saying "heart," he said, "that by which I live." And instead of saying "owl," he said, "he who wanders by night." And instead of saying "pollen," he said, "that which is becoming life." He drank only through the drinking tube, and scratched only with the scratching stick, so that his skin would not soften and the meat in the camp would not spoil. The older men called him Child of Waters while on the warpath, and Goyathlay took care not to turn around quickly—always first looking carefully over his shoulder and then turning only toward the sun. He did not gaze upward, lest he bring rain. He did not eat entrails, so as not to spoil his luck with horses. He learned all the habits of caution that would keep him alive in all the years to follow. He learned to travel across open places only at night; to look for water from a high place by searching for a trace of green; to sleep beneath a little bush or under grass rather than in the shady places that would draw the enemy; to never stand up and look about without holding a bit of grass or a bush in front of himself to frustrate the eyes of his enemies; to remember each day's rendezvous should an attack scatter the party. And most of all, he learned to remain in all things careful, and truthful, and moderate—so that his character would be molded to that frame like buckskin wrapped around a shield.

He also formed his friendship with Juh—which would carry him through his life. Juh was Nednai, who were brothers to the Bedonkohe. Stocky, broad-shouldered, broad-faced, Juh was as powerful and fierce as a badger. Though Juh was confident and powerful, he also stammered so that the other boys were tempted to make fun of him. But a boy would make such a mistake once, because Juh was a powerful fighter, and it seemed clear he would one day lead others in war. Juh was also full of mischief, and sometimes cruel—and in this he was very much like Goyathlay. When the Nednai and the Bedonkohe camped close to each other, Juh would sometimes take his small band of roughneck Nednai boys and stalk the Bedonkohe girls out gathering acorns. Juh would jump out of some hiding place, scattering them, and over-turning their woven baskets full of acorns. Once Juh did this to Ishton, Goyathlay's sister. Ishton complained to her grandmother, the widow of the great chief Makho. The old woman called Goy-athlay to her, and told him that he should get together some boys and teach Juh a lesson. So Goyathlay and Juh fought the first of their many great battles, but this one time on opposite sides.

The easy play of Goyathlay's youth ended abruptly. Soon after the Nednai left for the remote sanctuary of the great mountains to the south, Taklishim died of an illness. It was a sad and unex-pected thing. Back then, not many people got sick in the clean camps of The People. In later days—when they were crowded on the reservations and forced into living near the disease-ridden White Eyes—most people died of illness. But in the old days, sick-ness came as such a surprise that you wondered what had called it down on you. Perhaps you had eaten something that a coyote had urinated upon. Perhaps you had said the name of someone who had gone on to The Happy Place. Perhaps you had been witched. But no one could say what Power Goyathlay's father had offended that he should die so soon. Perhaps that is when Goyathlay resolved to seek Power—so that he might have some defense against a world full of hostile forces. Certainly, both friendly and malevolent forces shaped the world. But the spiteful and malicious Powers paid the most attention to affairs of human beings. Usen had set everything in motion, and given The People great gifts, but then he had gone off to tend to other business. It did little good to pray to Usen. He was busy, off somewhere else. So The People took care not to draw the attention of malevolent Powers who might kill them for no particular reason—like a bored child with a small bird. And even when Power helped you and taught you Its songs and ceremonies, you remained a bird in Its hands.

Goyathlay assumed the position of an adult with the death of his father. He lived in his mother's wickiup, and brought her food. He also provided for his sisters. He was admitted to the council of warriors at the age of seventeen.[13] He was perfectly happy in that moment. He could go wherever he pleased. No one could control him, for even the chiefs of The People can only ask for a warrior's help, with no power to command it. [14]

Soon his other sisters made good marriages, which in their turn helped sustain Goyathlay in all the years to come. Ishton married Juh, who had teased her and chased her and now took her into his heart. Juh should have come then to live with the Bedonkohe, as was the custom. But he was marked already for great things among the Nednai, so Ishton went instead to live with Juh and the Nednai in the Sierra Madre.

Another sister of Goyathlay, Nah-dos-te, married Nana—of the Chihenne band. This was a fortunate thing. Nana was a great man—already old, and wise, and fierce. He had hard eyes that saw a long way. Nana was small, but tough as ironwood, and a good shot with a rifle. He knew every trail and hidden spring, and no man had ever heard him complain or falter. He was soft-spoken and stern, never boasting, but also never failing in his duty. He had great Power and could always find bullets, therefore taking the lead of any war party whose chief goal was to find ammunition. Nana had a face like the mountains, remote and remorseless. He looked out on the world with flat, farseeing eyes, as though he had already seen every possible thing, and was only seeing them happening now all over again. Nana had been wounded a long time ago, so that he limped—but nonetheless he could ride all day, and sit alongside the fire smoking his pipe when the younger, stronger warriors who had ridden all the while with him had fallen onto their grass bedding like dead men. Everyone said that Nana had the Power to be a chief—to mold others to his purpose. But he did not burn with ambition and vanity as did many other great men. His Chihenne usually followed along behind Mangas Coloradas's Mimbrenos band. Many said that Mangas Coloradas was the greatest chief who had ever accepted the responsibility of leadership among The People, and Nana seemed content to defer to him. Because Nana held so important a position among the Chihenne, Nah-dos-te went to live with them, thus once again overlooking the long custom of The People, which said a man should go to live with his wife's family. Still, it was a good match for the Bedonkohe—and for Goyathlay's family.

Of course, times already had begun to change. For as long as anyone could remember, The People had gone among the tribes of the Mexicans,[15] like a man through a field of ripe corn. The Mexicans were a weak and treacherous people, blessed with guns, and crops, and cattle and sheep through the misguided gifts of Slayer of Enemies. This did not disturb The People—for it was easy to take these things from the Mexicans without grubbing in the soil, and living like slaves. The Mexicans were trapped in their ugly lives. The People took what they pleased, making sure to leave the Mexicans enough horses, and sheep, and cattle so that there would be always more to take. The warriors had no great desire to kill Mexicans, since that only made for trouble. Mostly, they wanted only to bring back enough supplies for the winter and for the ceremonials. Any major ceremony could consume the plunder from a year's raiding. It seemed just to The People that the

Mexicans should provide the horses, and the cattle, and the plunder—since they had come unasked into the lands that had always belonged to The People.[16]

But the bands of the Mexicans had made it a larger war, sending out men to kill The People like game. The Mexicans cut away the scalps of the people they killed, mutilating their victims so they would remain scarred and humiliated forever in The Happy Place. Years ago, a great chief of the Mimbreno had learned the folly of trusting the Mexicans. He had made a peace, and took his people to a great feast where the Mexicans gave them whiskey, and then slaughtered them all. Mangas Coloradas had survived that slaughter, and exacted a terrible revenge—which remained a sacred duty for any warrior of The People.

Then a new people had come from the east, unbidden, into the sacred places of The People. They were a strange-talking people, pale as ghosts, with white showing all around the outside of their pale eyes like frightened horses. Goyathlay had heard rumors of their coming from other warriors, who said they always carried good guns. Some of their bands hunted beaver. The People mostly let them pass through the land—taking careful note of their good, far-shooting guns. But then others came, bringing with them soldiers, as the Mexicans used. Mangas Coloradas said that the White Eyes were fighting against the Mexicans, and so offered to help them. The White Eyes refused the help, and went away again. Some said that the White Eyes had won their fight with the Mexicans. Others said that they had simply gone away, when they saw that The People were so strong. Still, they remained a distant threat—like a dream of fire, or flood, or death.[17]

So The People had need of Goyathlay, when he finished his apprenticeship, and rolled his first smoke of sacred tobacco in oak leaves, and for the first time stepped out into the firelight to dance his acceptance of an invitation to raid.

Goyathlay took his mother to visit the Nednai—already missing Ishton, his sister, and Juh, the boisterous friend of his boyhood. They traveled together for weeks, learning the strange country, finding the faint traces of the Nednai, groping deeper into the Sierra Madre. Goyathlay noted how carefully the Nednai lived, like deer that can only sip at the stream where danger gathers. But perhaps that journey was just the dream that shows things that have not yet happened waiting on the trail just ahead.

But Goyathlay had other reasons for his journey.

And better reasons than any of these for becoming a warrior—and a full man.

Alope.

So slender.

So delicate.

She had taken his heart, the way a man with Power makes the wildest horse stand, trembling, for a touch.

She was Nednai, of Juh's band, and Goyathlay's life had twined about hers as honeysuckle from two roots growing along the same branch. He had watched her a long time from a distance. He had crept through the woods, and watched her gather roots, and herbs, and berries. He had lain by the creek, and waited for her to come there, then watched her awhile before stealing away unseen.

She had captured him, and broken him, and gentled him—before they had even spoken.

So he waited and watched her at the social dances. Summoning his courage, he danced around with the young men on the outside of the circle, while the girls danced around about the inside circle. They exchanged glances, and each time she looked away quickly, but smiling, so that his heart lunged like an eagle in a snare.

Finally they had arranged to meet, slipping away from the adults, escaping into their own place. They had even lain down together—although her father, and her brothers, and her male relatives might have done something violent and final, if they had known that Alope had been with this upstart young warrior. True enough—Goyathlay came from a good family. But he had no father, and uncertain prospects, and a mother and a sister already to support.[18]

Nonetheless, soon after Goyathlay finally found the Nednai, he went to No-po-so—Alope's father—and presented his case. No-po-so was not pleased. He looked doubtfully at the stocky warrior—

still little more than a boy, although fulfilling a man's role. Goyathlay had a strong face—a warrior's face—his mouth like the slash
of the knife, his eyes dark and careful. He had about him a
strength touched with arrogance, but arrogance was not a failing
in a warrior. He had also an intensity that was more unsettling. He
did not laugh easily, and did not take well the inevitable jokes and
pranks of the boys, and the young warriors, and the teasing of the
older warriors. The People loved to laugh, and play jokes, and gossip, but none of these things came easily to Goyathlay. Still, he
was the grandson of Makho. No one spoke ill of him. So No-po-so
did not refuse his permission. Instead, he asked for too many
ponies as the bride price. He did not think that so young a warrior, with a mother and a sister to support, could possibly capture
so many ponies.

Goyathlay looked a while at No-po-so, knowing the price was
too high, but too proud to protest. Perhaps No-po-so did not like
Goyathlay. Or perhaps he merely wanted to keep Alope for himself—a comfort to his old age. No matter. Goyathlay said nothing,
but took the words of No-po-so with him on the first raiding party
he could find going south.

And when Goyathlay had all of the horses he needed, he
returned, and tied the horses to a tree in front of No-po-so's wickiup. He stood, wordless and proud, while Alope happily gathered
her things, and hurried after Goyathlay—who had captured her
heart long before he set out after the ponies that would declare
him to the entire band. So Goyathlay left his mother's wickiup,
and nearby made a second wickiup, covered in buffalo skins,
made comfortable with bear robes and lion hides, and hung with
spears and bows and arrows. Alope moved into this home as sunlight moves into the meadow at dawn. She drew pictures as delicate, and graceful, and beautiful as she on the tanned hides. She
beaded his moccasins, and his belt, and his quiver—her regard for
him stitched into them with the tiny motions of her fingers. Later,
when everything had burned down to ash and char, Goyathlay
would remember that time as perfect. She was slender as a flower
stalk—strong in the manner of the grass that yields to the wind,
but then springs back upright. She bore him children, one, and

then another, and then a third—bringing forth this life out of the lithe perfection of her body. Goyathlay went on raids, and brought back horses, and cattle, and everything that Alope needed, that his children needed. He grew in respect. He kept all the old ways. He learned the songs for the joyful times, and the coyote stories for the long nights of winter, and he watched his children growing up, one tumbling after another. He watched them roll in the grass like pups, too big for their feet, playing and loitering, and growing— even as he had done, as Child of Waters had done, as every child of The People had done in these places which remembered them from back before the first memory.

Perhaps it would have been better if she had been lazy, with a sharp tongue, and thick fingers—so that he did not love her so. Perhaps it would have been better if he had never been happy—so that the memory of it could not drive him through all the later times of his life. Or perhaps it could not be helped. Perhaps it was like the boy whose nature is set on the raids of his apprenticeship—so that it can never change afterward.

In any case, Goyathlay stretched his heart out so that it hardened and formed around her. How could he know that once set, his heart could not be altered? How could he know that should he lose her, his heart would remain just so—hollow, and burned, and impossible ever again to fill?

Goyathlay took Alope and his mother and his children and went with other members of his band down into the south, down to Janos,[19] with whose people they were at peace. They camped near the town with families from Mangas Coloradas's Mimbreno band, leaving only a few guards with the women and children. What had they to fear? They had long been friends with the Janos Mexicans. They came often, traded goods, bought the strong Mexican drinks, and lolled in the city square. They touched nothing that belonged to the Janos Mexicans. They did not take their cattle. The Janos Mexicans could come and go as they pleased and graze their sheep far from the town without fear. They smiled, and laughed, and were friendly. Some of their women married warriors of The People.

The warriors felt safe—especially since they had with them Mangas Coloradas, the great chief. Mangas was a giant, towering over other warriors. He had the great head of a lion, fearless and strong, so that all eyes shifted to him when he entered a space, and everyone fell silent when he spoke. He dressed in great splashes of color—and his Power over men glinted from his eyes like the sun off the barrel of a rifle. His daughters had married other leading chiefs—including Cochise, the feared and respected chief of the Chiricahua. Mangas Coloradas had made his reputation as a warrior, leading many successful raids that brought back much plunder, which he shared with the openhanded generosity expected of a leader. He had taken as one of his wives a beautiful Mexican woman, and when the brothers of his first wife objected Mangas Coloradas killed them in a knife fight. So only a foolish man would challenge Mangas Coloradas, or enter within the circle of his knife held at the end of his long arm. But Mangas Coloradas's great Power lay in his voice, in his mind, in his ability to move the council, and bend all others to his will. Even the great chief of the Navajo made an alliance with him, and Mangas Coloradas could sometimes draw together into a single force the Mimbreno, and the Mescalero, and the Bedonkohe, and the Nednai, and the Chiricahua because of his Power, and the force of his personality. A chief could never command, only persuade. He could never call on blind obedience. Each warrior made his own decisions and leaders drew followers only so long as their Power held, only so long as their decisions were strong, only so long as they earned respect.

So Goyathlay had no fear when he left Alope and his mother and his children. He went with the warriors into town, to trade away the goods they had taken in raids on other Mexican towns which had not made peace. They drank freely, and laughed, and joked with the Mexicans.[20]

Returning to camp, they encountered a woman running toward them, scratched and terrified. Mexicans from another town had attacked the camp—killing many, and capturing most of the rest.[21] They had killed the warriors of the guard and also taken all the ponies, their arms, and their supplies. The stunned warriors considered their choices. The woman said that the soldiers had a large force, well armed so the handful of surviving warriors had no hope against them. A warrior does not fear death—and when no choice is left to him he will fight with reckless courage. But a warrior never seeks death. It is not courage to leap into the fire when you could pass it by to the side, and you cannot gain honor— or revenge—by running foolishly into the guns of your enemies. So the warriors did not hurry forward and attack the Mexicans, although they knew the Mexicans would sell the women and children they had taken prisoner into slavery far to the south where escape was nearly impossible, and death a delivery. In fact, the warriors wondered whether more Mexicans were coming along behind them—from Janos—to finish them. So they did the only thing possible—they scattered into the brush, each heading by a different path toward the safe meeting place they had agreed upon that morning. The People always set a place of meeting, even when they had no reason to anticipate attack, so that they could scatter, evade pursuit, and gather together again within a day or two, or three.

Hours later, eighty warriors gathered at the place of meeting. They had no ponies. They had few weapons. They waited through the endless night, starting up again with each rustle of the brush to see if it was their wife, or their child, or their mother stealing through the darkness. But the gloom that had fallen on them with the first news only deepened. So few came. And when the stragglers stopped coming, Goyathlay was alone. He knew then that Alope and his mother and his children were all dead, because they had not come softly in out of the darkness as his heart had yearned for them to do.

So he walked away from the others and stood by the river, looking into the dark water. Back in the camp, the warriors debated what they should do. But Goyathlay paid no attention. He stood so for hours, as though dead himself. He had no weapons. Nothing. Everything was gone. Broken. Dead. He could not fight. He knew it was forbidden even to go get the bodies of his children, of his mother, or of Alope—partly because that would perhaps take him into the trap of the Mexicans, but mostly because all of the Chindi spirits of the dead would linger in that place. In truth, he had no will to do anything. He cared for nothing—not fighting, not praying. He had been emptied out.[22]

After a long while, he heard the sound of the warriors and the few survivors moving away, softly, in the darkness, moccasined feet muffled by grief. No one spoke to him. He spoke to no one. He had nothing to say. But after a time, he turned, numb and empty, and shuffled after them. He scarcely knew where his feet directed him, but sometime in that endless walk he turned aside, drawn irresistibly to the ruins of the camp. Perhaps he hoped that the soldiers could still be there, waiting for him to give him the death that seemed the only escape now. Perhaps he had been killed already, and the Ghost Sickness had him now. No matter. He came then to the camp, alone and empty. He moved among the bodies. He found his mother. He found his children. He found Alope—the ground stained dark with her blood. The Mexicans had cut off their hair, even the children, and the blood crusted their faces.[23] Some said that the Mexicans did this to show their contempt, knowing that the dead would not then have their hair in The Happy Place. Others said that the Mexicans did this for money so they could sell the hair, like beaver pelts. Goyathlay sat for a time among the bodies, not caring that the Chindi must hover still in so terrible a place, not caring that the soldiers might come back, not caring about anything at all. The emptiness grew, like stones piled on his chest, until finally it broke him. Then he sat alone in all the world and wept, his face in his hands.

Then he heard a voice call his name: Goyathlay.

He struggled to master himself.

The voice called him again: Goyathlay.

Now he looked up, peering about in the darkness.

The voice called again: Goyathlay.

Now he sat very still, because the voice seemed so familiar, and because it came from no particular direction, but from all around him.

Then the voice called him again: Goyathlay.

This was the fourth time, the sacred fourth time, so Goyathlay knew that he must answer, and that Power spoke to him now.

I am here, said Goyathlay, empty even of fear.

No gun can ever kill you, said the voice. I will take the bullets from the guns of the Mexicans, so they will have nothing but powder. And I will guide your arrows.[24]

Goyathlay waited, but the voice said nothing further.

Finally, Goyathlay rose, his tears now like the memory of rain in a tumble of desert stones. He knew then as he turned and took the trail back to the north that the Power had chosen him—filling the empty space in him with something else. Goyathlay trudged on through the darkness, sorting everything into its place. He knew he would never again be happy. He could think of only one reason the Power had given him this great gift in this terrible time. He must become revenge. Why else should the Power protect him from bullets? Why else should the Power speak of the Mexicans? So as he walked north, beneath the stars, beneath the glowing path in the sky that Alope and Juanita and his three children followed even then, Goyathlay honed the bitter edge of his resolve with hatred, his duty to the dead—and to the living. Even the memory of happiness must goad him to his purpose, and nothing would ever be the same for him again.

So when he came finally back to the place that had been his home with Alope, others could see the change in him—as though grief and hate had eaten away everything but the white, hard bone of him. He came straight into camp and piled up in his wickiup everything Alope had touched or used—every small, loving, beaded memory of her, every child's toy of twisted twigs, and with them everything that had been his mother's. Then he set the torch to them and watched as they burned—his eyes like chips of obsidian with a light behind them.[25] Goyathlay went then to the grave of his father, on the flanks of the sacred mountain where the Ga'an Mountain Spirits lived. Standing there, Goyathlay swore he would spend his life on revenge.

Then Goyathlay went to the council, which was considering how they should respond to the treachery of the Mexicans, to their great loss, to the sacred duty of revenge. Goyathlay put himself, and his hatred, and his great wrong into the hands of the council. They knew that they had not the strength to seek revenge alone.

Goyathlay spoke quietly. He had never been eloquent in the manner of Mangas Coloradas, or of Cochise, or of the other great leaders whose power rested on eloquence. But now they would feel the power of his loss—and something else, something dangerous behind his eyes. Mangas Coloradas saw it, and knew that others would see it, and knew that Goyathlay carried all the dead women and the dead children with him, behind his eyes, so that no true warrior could refuse should he speak their true names and ask his help. So it was decided that Goyathlay should go to Cochise and his Chokonen, and to Juh and his Nednai, and to any other bands that might help them obtain their revenge.

This Goyathlay did—traveling without stopping all through that fall and into the winter.

Goyathlay knew that Cochise held the reins in his strong hands. Cochise had risen high in the regard of The People—second only to Mangas Coloradas in his Power over men and the respect that he inspired. He held much greater influence over his warriors than most chiefs, so that even the wildest spirits did not defy him. Tall, and graceful, with a face that was calm, and distant, and farseeing, Cochise's wisdom in settling disputes and laying his plans was rarely questioned. His Chokonen were among the most numerous and powerful of all of the bands of the Chiricahua, and were like brothers to the Nednai and the Bedonkohe and the most important allies of the Mimbreno and the Chihenne. Cochise had married the daughter of Mangas Coloradas, so that they were kinsmen now as well. He was like Mangas Coloradas in thinking ahead of the present and in his skillful diplomacy, and subtle thoughts, and ruthless carefulness.

Goyathlay went to the Chokonen, standing alone before the council fire, and spoke to them in this way: Kinsmen, you have heard what the Mexicans have recently done without cause. You are my relatives: uncles, cousins, and brothers. We are men the same as the Mexicans are; we can do to them what they have done to us. Let us go forward and trail them—I will lead you to their city. We will attack them in their homes. I will fight in the front of the battle. I only ask you to follow me to avenge this wrong done by these Mexicans—will you come?[26]

He looked around the circle of warriors—eye, to eye, to eye—and saw assent in each of them.

It is well. You will all come, he said, as though he knew that they must come, as he knew that his Power had filled him up again, as he knew that he could never again have a life as other men. Remember the rule in war, men may return or they may be killed, he added, speaking in such a way that others who heard him began to speak differently of him afterward. If any of those young men are killed, he continued, I want no blame from their kinsmen, for they themselves have chosen to go. If I am killed, no one need mourn me. My people have all been killed in that country and I, too, will die if need be.

So when the summer raiding season returned,[27] a great party of warriors assembled under the leadership of Mangas Coloradas and Cochise and other chiefs. They painted their faces and fastened war bands upon their brows. They came on foot, so they could move quickly and without notice down into the land of their enemies. Each man wore moccasins and carried the tools to make a fresh pair, and each man wrapped a cloth around his waist to serve as clothing, and a blanket. Each carried three days' rations, although the journey would be much longer. Then they set out at the ground-devouring walk of a warrior, covering forty or fifty miles a day on a fourteen-hour march, moving at a pace that would wear out and kill the horse of a Mexican soldier.

They came finally to Arispe, the town that had sent out the soldiers who had killed Alope.[28] They camped near the town, showing themselves, but making no hostile moves. The people of Arispe sent eight men out to talk. The warriors went to these men, and surrounded them, and killed them all. Then they cut away their hair. This was not a thing warriors normally did, but now they did to the men from Arispe the same thing that had been done to their women and children. The warriors did this openly, knowing that the soldiers would come out from Arispe to avenge the eight men.

That night, the warriors waited for the coming fight. They set sentries to watch the town. And they all prayed as they waited for the first flush of dawn. They did not pray for help. Usen did not bother with such things—and each warrior knew that he must look to his feet, and his hands, and his legs, and his arms, and his head, and his heart for his help. But they prayed for health. And they prayed that they might see the deceptions of the enemy in time to turn aside.

Then Mangas Coloradas turned to Goyathlay, giving him the battle although he was no chief, nor yet even a war shaman. Everyone knew Goyathlay had lost everything when the soldiers had attacked. And everyone knew that the Power of his loss had drawn everyone together, to this place, before their enemies. So Mangas Coloradas, and Cochise, and the other chiefs gave him the battle. Goyathlay stood a moment, their eyes on him, quiet under the weight of the honor. Then he made the plan—putting the bands in a hollow circle near the river where they would hide in the trees waiting for the approach of the soldiers. He said that he would attack the soldiers in the center, while most of the warriors remained hidden, so that they would come on into the circle. When enough of the other warriors had stepped forward to volunteer for that position of greatest danger and honor, Goyathlay selected another group of warriors to go around through the trees to attack the soldiers from behind. Everyone saw that it was a good plan, and so they went to their places to wait for the soldiers.

The sun had already risen well above the trees when the soldiers came out, a great many of them, on foot and horseback. The foot soldiers came on first, moving in a ragged rank. The horse soldiers stayed behind. Goyathlay and the others came out of the trees, firing arrows, calling insults, and drawing the soldiers to them. The soldiers stopped about four hundred yards off, and began firing at the warriors who had gone back into the trees. Seeing that the soldiers would not come further forward, Goyathlay led the decoy warriors out into the open—making a dash against the line of soldiers, taunting them with his war Power. Just as the Power had told him, the bullets of the Mexicans could not touch him. All through the battle, Goyathlay kept the image of Alope, and those of his children, before him like a shield. He knew that his Power would see the thought, and so protect him from the bullets of his enemies and give all of the other warriors courage. He ran always in the front line, killing many soldiers by his own hand. He ran at their lines fearlessly, knowing their bullets were useless against him. Other braves, shamed by his courage, ran beside him toward the soldiers. But many had not his Power, and so they fell beside him. Even so, Goyathlay would not stop—could not stop. His Power gripped him, and would not loosen its hold. Even the Mexicans could feel it, and after a time they began calling out in fear when they saw him coming toward them. "Geronimo," they cried. "Geronimo."[29] For two hours they fought, with many dead on both sides.

Finally Goyathlay found himself standing alone among the dead in an open place with three other warriors. They had fired all of their arrows. They had broken off their spears in the bodies of their enemies. They had only their hands and their knives, and were surrounded by their slain foes. Two soldiers, who still had their guns, saw the four warriors—including the one whom they would come to call Geronimo. So the soldiers rode toward them, shooting down two of the warriors as they came on before they put aside their empty guns and drew their sabers. One soldier rode up against the warrior standing beside Goyathlay, and killed him with a sweep of his saber. But Goyathlay dodged to the side, and pulled a spear from the body of a dead man, and turned to face the other soldier's charge. The soldier missed his aim, and Goyathlay ducked under the sword and drove his spear through the soldier's body. Seeing the second soldier coming out of the corner of his eye, Goyathlay sprang forward and seized the dead man's sword before turning to face the second enemy. They ran together, and grappled, the ground slippery with blood. They swayed, and fell, and rolled on the ground. As they rolled, Goyathlay pulled out his knife and plunged it into the body of the soldier. He wrenched the saber out of the hand of the dead man, and stood over the body, waving the saber, making the woods echo with his war cry. He stood alone among the dead, covered in blood, gorged on death. And though he knew vengeance could not call Alope back from The Happy Place, it remained the only joy left to his emptied heart.

But the soldiers had broken. The survivors ran back to the town. The warriors had their revenge, but they had paid a heavy price. They gathered around Goyathlay, whose Power had killed so many soldiers. They praised him and began rehearsing the stories of the battle that they would tell for seasons to come. They even cut away the hair of the dead men, as Goyathlay commanded—as the soldiers themselves had done to Alope.[30]

After this battle, Goyathlay had a new name—for the fear of the Mexicans had changed him from Goyathlay to Geronimo.

And, born in death, Geronimo had only just started.

The Mexicans did not know that his thirst could never be slaked.

They did not know what a price his Power would one day exact from him, and from those he loved, and from The People he had vowed to protect.

4

Crook

Early Years

George Crook was born into a time of destiny made manifest.

But he had no sense of destiny about him.

He was the ninth of ten children born on September 8, 1828, to Elizabeth Matthews Crook and Thomas Crook—a tanner in the quiet farm country of Taylorsville, Ohio. His ancestors came to America from Scotland in the seventeenth century, and so his roots in the fertile topsoil of the young continent went back to the beginnings of the upstart nation. His father had been born in Maryland, and served in a militia company, which defended Fort McHenry in 1814, before he became sick and was discharged. In Ohio Thomas Crook took up farming, the better to feed his burgeoning family. He was practical, industrious, and well-informed, and soon accumulated 340 acres of good land on the banks of the Miami River valued at $13,600 in 1850, thanks in part to the transportation possibilities offered by the Erie Canal. A sober Whig Republican, Thomas Crook also served as a justice of the peace before his death in 1875.

The Crooks were a quiet, prosperous, respectable family—conscientious, hardworking, abstemious. They dressed in homespun and lived mostly on the fruits of the farm, with plenty of meat, and eggs, and butter. The sprawling family lived mostly all together in the single room of their home, until Thomas Crook's laboriously gained prosperity allowed him to expand the house.

George Crook's brothers became serious and respectable professionals—a doctor, a dentist, a tailor, a postmaster, a politician. His sisters married well. Growing up, they rarely left the vicinity of Taylorsville.

In the crowd at the Crooks' dinner table, George gave no early hint of distinction. He seemed painfully shy, strikingly silent. Careful, slow, and self-contained, he observed the bafflement of the world about him with an owlish detachment and restraint. He was an easy child to overlook in the bustle of the Crook household, a stolid, thick, solid farmer's son.

But he had been born into interesting times.

The hurly-burly nation was then barely fifty years old. Thomas Crook had been born but a decade after the Revolution, and had come of age in the midst of the U.S. victory against the British in the War of 1812. Having forged a sense of national identity from these experiences, the country had now turned its formidable energies on the beckoning frontier. The nation's birth had been marked by struggles against the native peoples who had once claimed the eastern seaboard. The generations of conflict had resulted in the destruction and displacement of almost every tribe in the East, laying the foundations for notions of racial superiority that would dominate the history of the 1800s and the expansion into the West.

Crook seemed fated to a quiet life as an Ohio farmer until Whig congressman Robert Schneck began casting about his district for a promising young man to nominate to West Point—then one of the few avenues to an education. Schneck, in a later newspaper interview, recalled that he had remembered that the respected, solidly Whig, squire Crook had a passel of sons and so had inquired of the old farmer whether one of his sons might be interested in a military career. Thomas Crook sent George to the congressman's office. "The boy was exceedingly noncommunicative," Schneck later recalled. "He hadn't a stupid look, but was quiet to reticent. He didn't seem to have the slightest interest or anxiety about my proposal. I explained to him the requirements and labors of the military school, and finally asked him, 'do you think you can conquer all that?' His monosyllabic reply was, 'I'll try.' And so I sent him, and he came through fairly."[1]

Crook's signature attitude of phlegmatic, taciturn self-confidence expressed itself immediately, produced by the combination of his sturdy, self-contained nature and the solid foundations of his upbringing. He remained throughout his life calm, unflappable, emotionally remote, stern, and confident—his nature resting on some interior foundation with little need for exterior support.

Nonetheless, he proved an academically undistinguished recruit. The officer corps at that time remained a bastion of the educated class, and many of Crook's fellow officers showed a quick intelligence and even a literary flair that shines now in the writings they left behind. Crook's intellect did not run along those lines. In June of 1849, he ranked a dismal fiftieth out of a class of fifty-six in English and at the absolute bottom of his class in French. He graduated thirty-eighth out of forty-three in his class. In the end, he was the lowest-ranking West Pointer ever to rise to the rank of major general. He left only a faint paper trail through the academy, like a moccasined warrior moving across broken stone. He landed in trouble only twice, according to records. He was, in 1849, confined to quarters with other cadets for "offering compositions to instructors that were not their own"; and on September 7 was assigned two hours of guard duty for missing drill.

But he also had a bearing, a maturity, and a self-possession that made him stand out among his classmates. He consistently scored in the upper half in measures of conduct. He was "a farmer's boy, slow to learn, but what he did learn was surely his. He was older, somewhat, than his comrades, and was good-natured, stolid, and was like a big Newfoundland dog among a lot of puppies. He would never permit injustice or bullying of the smaller boys," recalled James A. Greer, a classmate.[2]

That self-possession, maturity, and innate sense of justice would guide Crook through all of the turbulent years to come. Ironically enough, it also made him one of the sharpest-edged tools in the hands of a nation so flushed with a sense of its own manifest destiny that it would perpetrate a terrible injustice in the name of "civilization."

Upon graduation in 1852, newly commissioned Brevet Second Lieutenant George Crook was assigned to Governor's Island in California, where the discovery of gold at Sutter's Mill in 1848 had drawn a rush of adventurers, dreamers, and crooks from all over the world. The inrush of would-be millionaires immediately spawned tragic conflict with the mostly peaceful tribes who occupied the Pacific Coast and interior California. The poorly armed warriors couldn't get out of the way of the hordes of miners fast enough and the prospectors exterminated whole villages. Those not shot or hacked to death soon succumbed to disease. The native population of California, which had survived centuries of occupation by the Spanish, would be nearly wiped out in a generation or two. Sometimes, one of the more warlike tribes would make a stand—and the settlers would call for the army.

Crook was dispatched by steamer to the West Coast, passing up the Nicaragua River in Central America on a harrowing journey with an assorted band of settlers, cutthroats, and frontier characters. They passed through floods, storms, jungles, and assorted hardships and dangers. On his first long journey away from his home, he encountered a vivid foretaste of life on the frontier—and experienced a bout of seasickness. "Although I had my life yet before me and everything was tinted with bright colors," he recalled in his autobiography, "so great was my aging during this sickness that I was indifferent to life, and cared but little whether the vessel went to the bottom or not."

He arrived at length safely in San Francisco, a frantic bustle of wood-frame buildings and streets deep in mud and sand—where day laborers could command a higher salary than a marveling lieutenant. "Everything was so different from what I had been accustomed to that it was hard to realize I was in the United States," wrote the farm boy with officer's stripes. "People had flocked there from all parts of the world; all nationalities were represented. Sentiments and ideas were so liberal and expended that they were almost beyond bounds. Money was so plentiful amongst the citizens that it was but lightly appreciated." Nonetheless, the streets were a sea of mud so viscous that the avenues were sprinkled with boots the owners had abandoned because they could not wrench them loose from the mire.

The frontier army proved a bitter disillusionment to Crook, who would not drink tea, much less alcohol, and remained all of his life restrained in his habits and language. He soon discovered that liquor and gambling plagued the soldiers and their officers. "Almost all officers were almost continuously drunk," recalled Crook in his autobiography. "I never had seen such gambling and carousing before or since." One of his first duties was to serve in an honor guard for a major who had drunk himself to death. The major in charge of the escort said to them all, "Well, fellows, old Miller is dead and he can't drink, so let us all take a drink." Crook confessed, "I was never more horrified in my life."

To his relief, he was soon dispatched from this den of iniquity to a frontline post, the Fourth Infantry under Brevet Lieutenant Colonel R. C. Buchanan in Humboldt Bay in the Pacific Northwest. However, Crook nearly missed his posting as a result of a violent attack of erysipelas—which caused his ankles and body to swell so painfully that he could scarcely hobble and lay a long while in his bed in an agony of pain. The disorder was to plague him intermittently in the next several years, teaching him stoicism and the ability to steel himself against pain—even as Geronimo was learning the same lessons in the mountains of Arizona.

Crook found his new posting in many ways even more disagreeable, and years later poured his disdain for the drunken ego of the officers with whom he served into the pages of his autobiography. Even on the steamer beating through a freezing rainstorm toward Humboldt Bay, he noted the arrogant disregard for the soldiers, who were driven away from the shelter of the overhang near Colonel Buchanan's quarters with curses. The experience had an impact on Crook's own style of command, because he reacted so strongly against the egotistical, undisciplined, and arrogant officers who populated the frontier army. The army of the time was divided along class lines in a way now difficult to appreciate. The officers often came from society's upper class, many of them the younger sons of established families. The ranks were filled with immigrants, the poor, and adventurers mostly seeking transportation to the gold fields—where they would promptly desert. The army's hierarchy rigidly enforced and deepened the class divisions that already existed, and a great gulf in outlook, expectation, and privilege existed between the officers and their men.

"Col. Buchanan's principle was to allow no subordinate to make suggestions unasked," observed Crook, "and he told me, on one occasion, never to take the suggestion of a noncommissioned officer but go ahead and do my own way, even if I knew it was wrong. It was clear he must have followed the principle, judging from the number of mistakes he made. I must say that my first impressions of the army were not favorable. Most of the customs and habits that I witnessed were not calculated to impress one's morals or usefulness. Most of the commanding officers were petty tyrants, styled by some martinets. They lost no opportunity to snub those under their command and prided themselves in saying disagreeable things. Most of them had been in command of small posts so long that their habits and minds had narrowed down to their surroundings. . . . Generally they were the quintessence of selfishness. Everything within their reach was made subservient to their comforts, and should there be more of anything than they wanted, then the rest might take it."

Crook took refuge from the misery and politics of the command in incessant hunting—an avocation that rose to the level of obsession. Just as Geronimo was doing in the wilds of Arizona, Crook dedicated himself to the habits of the animals he hunted with an enduring passion. In the detailed study of nature, he excelled as he could never do when poring over the printed page. He came to the American West at the perfect moment for a hunter, when it still teemed with game. He took to hunting happily around Humboldt Bay, bagging elk, deer, bear, blue grouse, and flocks of ducks whose wings sounded like "distant thunder" when they exploded from the surface of the lakes and waterways.

Here Crook also encountered his first Indians, and the deeply entrenched racism and injustice against which he was to wage a futile struggle for the rest of his life. He viewed the Indians with a combination of racist scorn and sympathy—his deeply programmed assumption of cultural and racial superiority quickly set at war with his equally profound sense of justice and compassion. "There were several small bands living on different parts of the bay," he wrote in his autobiography, "but they were poor, harmless, scorfulertic, and miserable creatures who lived principally on fish. Many of them were deformed, and the most loathsome looking human beings that I have ever seen. . . . One night a lot of citizens assembled and massacred a number of these poor defenseless beings who thought, doubtless, that their very condition would be their safeguard. Some of the local newspapers lauded this, one of the most fiendish acts that has ever disgraced civilization."

He was soon transferred to far northern California to deal with the depredations of the Rogue River Indians, who had turned on the miners and settlers moving into their territory. Crook arrived at Fort Jones by muleback in October, where he was assigned to the Second Infantry command of Brevet Major G. Washington Patten. The smallish Patten, who had lost most of his left hand in the Mexican War, was the most "pompous, irritable, and flighty, and of all men I have ever met the least calculated for the Army," Crook recalled. "He started all sentences with 'he, he, be Jesus Christ.' Nothing short of seeing him and hearing him talk would give an adequate idea of him. He was very funny for a week or ten days, until he commenced repeating, when he became very tiresome."

Crook soon found his sympathies largely with the Indians, although this did not prevent him from hunting them down—a pattern that would dominate the balance of his career. Crook quickly rationalized this contradiction, reasoning that because the destruction of the Indians and their culture was inevitable, it would be a mercy to break their resistance quickly and completely. "Scattered over the country were a few Shasta Indians generally well disposed," he wrote,

> but more frequently forced to take the warpath or sink all self-respect by the outrages of the whites perpetrated upon them. The country was over-run by people from all nations in search of the mighty dollar. Greed was almost unrestrained and from the nature of

our government there was little or no law that these people were bound to respect. . . . It was of no infrequent occurrence for an Indian to be shot down in cold blood, or a squaw to be raped by some brute. Such a thing as a white man being punished for outraging an Indian was unheard of. It was the fable of the wolf and the lamb every time. The consequence was that there was scarcely ever a time when there was not one or more wars with the Indians somewhere on the Pacific Coast. . . . It is hard to believe now the wrongs these Indians had to suffer in those days. I doubt now if there is a single one left to tell their tale. The trouble with the army was that the Indians would confide in us as their friends, and we had to witness this unjust treatment of them without the power to help them. Then when they were pushed beyond endurance and would go on the warpath, we had to fight when our sympathies were with the Indians.[3]

Crook got a further taste of the effect of combining inept, drunken leadership with the undisciplined excesses of the citizen volunteers who often accompanied troops. Hearing word that Indians had killed a party of miners, Crook set out under the command of a Captain Judah with twenty soldiers for the Klamath River. Crook took command of the advanced guard. After hours of marching through the snow, he lost track of Judah's men. The man sent back to find them soon returned in a panic to report they'd been massacred. Crook turned the troops around and sped to the rescue, only to find Judah roaring drunk and his drunken soldiers scattered out for ten miles. Judah spent most of the next day in a delirium. The command eventually located the bodies of the dead prospectors, half-eaten by wolves. A short distance away, they found the Indians, barricaded in a cave. The Indians shot and killed the officer who led a detachment to the top of the bluffs in hopes of shooting down into the cave, whereupon Judah ordered a frontal charge. Judah's second-in-command insisted he would make the foolhardy charge only if Judah put the order in writing, and threatened to prefer charges against Judah if he survived. That convinced Judah to send Crook to get howitzers with which they could shell the cave. Crook returned shortly with a howitzer and a sober officer, who had the intelligence to open negotiations with the Indians. He discovered then that the miners had attacked the Indians, whereupon the soldiers returned to camp. The incident made a strong impression on the young lieutenant, forming his resolve to resort to bullets only when words had completely failed. In the years to come, that resolve would save the lives of countless soldiers under his command, and unnumbered settlers under his protection.

Crook spent the next two years on mostly inconclusive expeditions, chasing down rumors of outbreaks, surveying routes for the railroad through the Cascades, and helping to police the frontier—all the while indulging his passion for hunting. He generally provided all the game for the officers in his mess, bringing back such a bounty that they had meat to sell.

The outbreak of the Rogue River War involving the long-suffering Shasta Indians provoked some of Crook's most daring exploits, demonstrating his nerveless personal courage. He nearly missed the campaign as a result of an agonizing return of rheumatism and erysipelas, which shrank his arm to skin and bones and caused intense pain. He found the drunken post surgeon uninterested in his case, although at one point it seemed he would surely die. Crook prescribed for himself calomel and jalap and a pitcher of cold water poured on his shoulder, which he later decided had done him more good than the morphine the doctor offered. Crook recovered after a month, but it took longer to wean himself from his dependence on morphine. After his recovery in late 1856, he headed alone down the Rogue River to join his command for the campaign that would last through the winter of 1857 against the Indians on the Pit River, who had killed settlers and mauled a cavalry detachment sent out against them.

Crook found himself once again under the command of the despised Captain Judah. The intermittently drunk Judah mounted one "attack" on a swamp where Indians had taken invisible refuge, mounting his men on mules for the charge. "The air was full of soldiers after the command was given to mount, and for the next two days stragglers were still overtaking the command," recalled Crook. In another engagement, Judah scouted some abandoned wickiups in his field glasses—insisting that several crows on a ridge nearby were Indians. "I saw perfectly plainly what it was, but not being asked I ventured no suggestions, as he was in the habit of snubbing persons for volunteering suggestions and there was not the best of terms between us, for I had seen enough of him to realize fully what an unmitigated fraud he was. So he ordered the charge . . . the ground was rough and in places rocky, I could only see what was in front of me, but that was fun enough for one day to see his men tumbling off their mules in the most ludicrous manner . . . Captain Judah had that look of cool impudence which he was such a master of, and I could never make up my mind whether he knew better or not," recalled Crook.

Disgusted, Crook began setting off alone or with one or two soldiers to scout for the Indians—putting the hunter's skills he had perfected to good use. On one occasion while scouting alone, he found tracks that he followed until the trail had become so clear he was galloping. Seeing the Indians running along ahead of him, Crook rode close to one warrior, jumped off his horse to steady his aim, and shot him. Crook then remounted, rode to the wounded warrior, and dispatched him with a pistol shot. "Just then the Indians rose up all about me, and came toward me with frightful yells, letting fly a shower of arrows at me. I had an old muzzle-loading rifle, which was now empty, and one barrel of my pistol had snapped. I thought discretion the better part of valor, so I put spurs to my horse, and ran out of the only opening left, about 100 yards, and a big Indian, seemed to me about ten feet high, was running his best to close this up. He had his hair tucked back of his ears, which gave him a particularly ferocious look. His arrows flew all around me with such a velocity that they did not appear over a couple of inches long. I must have run a couple of miles before I found the command. They being under the bluff had heard nothing. We at once returned to where I had left the Indians, but they had all fled except one old squaw who was lying beside the dead buck I had killed. This was my first Indian."

Later in that same campaign, Crook received his first wound, and once again displayed his striking physical courage. The soldiers came upon a band of Indians camped along a river, and began firing down into the Indians from on top of a steep-sided bluff.

> I saw a buck swimming with his bow and arrows and wolf robe held above his head. I aimed at the edge of the water. At the crack of the rifle he sank, and the robe and weapons floated down the stream. I at once commenced reloading my old muzzle-loader when the guide at the tops of the bluffs yelled, "look out for the arrows!" I looked up and saw the air apparently full of them. Almost simultaneous one hit me in the right hip. When I jerked it out the head remained in my leg, where it remains still. There were a couple of inches of blood on the shaft of the arrow when I pulled it out. The Indians doing the firing were some who had previously swum across, and had screened themselves in the rocks, they set up a yell when I was hit. I at once commenced the ascent through a shower of arrows. The ascent was so steep that I had to pull myself up by catching hold of bunches of grass, rocks, and such things as I could get hold of. In one patch of grass I caught hold of two arrows that had been shot at me. The wonder was that I was not hit oftener. By the time I reached the top, the perspiration stood out on me in large drops, and I was deathly sick.[4]

The wound infected, perhaps because the Indians often poisoned their arrows with a combination of rattlesnake venom and putrefied deer's liver. He deferred treatment for days, afraid he would be sent back to the fort. Crook found fighting as much to his liking as Geronimo did, and his unreflective enthusiasm shines through the description of these desperate fights in his autobiography written decades later. He was wounded on June 10, and was back in the saddle by June 27—once again on the trail of the Indians.

He recounted repeated adventures and clashes with the Indians in the wilds of southern Oregon, fighting often in the tormented landscape created by the volcanic eruptions and lava fields that dominated the area. He seemed to love the battle, but harbored deep doubts about the justice of the effort to exterminate the Indians. He clearly admired those Indians who had the courage to fight and accepted the terms of the battle—kill or be killed. But he also impressed on his troops the importance of capturing rather than killing the women and children, as he hoped to induce the Indians to surrender rather than hunting them down one band at a time. The key lay in convincing the Indians they could safely surrender once he convinced them they could not win. Nonetheless, his soldiers also immediately killed almost any adult males they encountered—a practice that mirrored Apache tactics. He recounted one carefully planned surprise attack on an unsuspecting Indian village in which he detailed one soldier to keep a sentry covered and kill him at the first sound of shooting. Crook then divided his troops into three squads to hit the village from all sides and prevent escape. Through a confusion in orders, the Indian sentry was killed when the attack began although he was trying to surrender. "We met them face to face, so close that we could see the whites of each other's eyes," recalled Crook. "The yelling, screeching, and all taken together made my hair fairly stand on end. We killed a great many, and after the main fight was over, we hunted some reserved ground that we knew had Indians hidden. By deploying as skirmishers, and shooting them as they broke cover, we got them. One or two faced us and made a manly fight, while others attempted to run. There was but one squaw killed."

In another skirmish, the warriors turned to make a brief fight to cover the escape of the women and children. Crook, armed with a single-shot Yaeger rifle firing a heavy minié ball, saw one warrior charging a soldier struggling to reload. Crook spurred his horse forward, hoping to draw the attention of the warrior before he could close on the helpless soldier. His admiration for the courage of the foe, whom he killed with so little expressed regret, comes through. "I dismounted and ran ahead, so that he would not shoot my horse, to within sixty yards of him. He was half bending and half squatting, with his breast toward me, jumping first to one side and then to the other, evidently trying to draw my fire, keeping an arrow pointed at me all this time. He was singing his death song. I took a rest on my knee and, moving my rifle from one side to the other, following his movements. I got a good aim, when I pulled the trigger, and broke his back. In this condition, while lying on the ground, he shot five (bow) shots into the soldier's mule, three of them going through the saddle and three thicknesses of blankets into the mule before I could kill him." Crook then jumped back on his horse, dug in his spurs, and overtook another escaping warrior whom he killed. Although Crook estimated that the camp harbored five hundred Indians, his command suffered no casualties, a measure of the one-sidedness of the struggle in which the Indians' goal was always to escape as quickly as possible. The soldiers seized and destroyed a large cache of food, including great quantities of grasshoppers. Crook understood that the real goal of the campaign was to destroy the stockpiles of food and supplies that the Indians needed to survive the often harsh winters. Throughout his career, Crook displayed an adroit grasp of the economics of this war in which the soldiers drew on an inexhaustible storehouse while the Indians gathered their food as they moved, simultaneously keeping their women and children fed as well. No matter what the outcome of the battles, the Indians could not last more than a winter or two if Crook could keep them from accumulating surpluses in the summer and fall. They must surrender or starve.

In another incident, he was scouting alone when he came upon an Indian camp. Withdrawing cautiously to go get his men, he encountered an Indian woman on the trail, with her baby in a cradle on her back. Silently, he threatened her with his gun, motioned for silence, and directed her to move away from the village. He then took her back to his camp, watching alertly lest she should escape and warn her people. She stopped from time to time to nurse her baby, but gave no sign she intended escape. Collecting his men, Crook returned to the river, only to discover that the Indians had moved their camp to the opposite side. Crook was considering how to cross the river to attack the Indians, when the woman abruptly dove into the water and swam for the other side—leaving her baby on the bank. Although it ruined his attack, Crook admired her courage, her resourcefulness, and her willingness to abandon her baby to save her people. Nonetheless, he hung the baby's cradle in a tree, hid a detachment of soldiers, then marched away with his main force—thus using the baby as bait. The Indians spotted the ambush, but the incident demonstrated the mingling of respect and ruthlessness that distinguished Crook's dealings with the Indians throughout his life. He was at once their sympathetic advocate, and their most determined foe.

Another incident in that campaign demonstrated his adroit use of intelligence from the Indians and his personal daring. He was ordered to take his ninety-man company up the Klamath River by canoe to establish a post on the newly created Klamath Reservation, where two normally hostile tribes had been forced to settle next to each other. Crook's men made their way down the river through assorted adventures, and established a camp amongst the Indians. Crook cultivated relationships with the most friendly of the Indians, and was rewarded with a warning that one of the bands intended to assassinate both Crook and the Indian agent. Sure enough, some Indians named as conspirators soon drifted into camp to ask where Crook slept at night. That night, Crook lay waiting in his bed with a pistol, a bowie knife, a rifle, and a shotgun. Fortunately for the Indians, they didn't attack Crook, but next day attacked the Indian agent. Crook swung into action immediately, killing the leaders and a total of about ten Indians. The remainder of the band fled. They were later allowed to return to their own country in an uncharacteristic display of compassion and good sense on the part of the army.

The incident marked the beginning of Crook's emphasis on using "friendly" Indians against the "hostiles." After being transferred to a company in the Ninth Infantry under the command of Major Bob Garnett, Crook's command was sent out to track down Indians who had killed several prospectors the previous spring. Moving through a country dominated by bogs, rivers, and nests of furious yellow jackets, Crook came upon an Indian standing calmly in their path, staring off into the distance. The warrior soon revealed he was the son of the chief of a band of friendly Indians among whom the Indians Crook sought had taken refuge. The warrior indicated that the band was camped a few miles ahead on an island in the midst of a stream that would be very difficult to approach undetected. Moreover, he indicated that the hos-

tile Indians wanted to ambush them near the village. Crook there-
upon convinced the warrior to bring back the chief, so Crook
could negotiate the surrender of the killers. Otherwise, Crook
warned, the soldiers would have to attack the village and very
likely kill many innocent people. The chief arrived a short time
later and after some conversation agreed to turn over the killers.
He agreed to bring his people to the soldiers' camp to sell them
berries, and then to covertly point out the murderers. The plan
worked perfectly, and Crook's men seized the four men the chief
pointed out. The ringleader of the renegades, a medicine man,
escaped but unaccountably then returned to camp, where the soldiers seized him. "I had them all pinioned, and then told them the
object of my mission and that I intended shooting them before I
left. I wanted them to make any final preparations they wished
and reasonable time would be given them, etc." Crook wrote in
his autobiography. "They all acknowledged their guilt, but made
the excuse that they were forced or persuaded by others, etc.
Except the medicine man, who invoked all kinds of curses against
us. He called his son to him, and gave him what few personal
effects he had with him, and made a speech to him in his own
tongue which we did not understand." Later, Crook learned that
the old warrior had instructed his son to prepare an ambush for
the soldiers and kill as many as they could—something the son
ultimately decided against on the grounds that it was enough
that one person in his family had been killed. "The other four
went through the form of prayers, the burden of which was that
the soldiers had come and caught them, and that they were going
to kill them. . . . The whole business was exceedingly distasteful
to me, and as my Second Lieutenant Turner rather enjoyed that
kind of thing, I detailed him to execute them, which was done
in the following manner. The Indians were set down in a line;
twenty men were detailed to shoot them. Five of their guns were
not loaded, so that no one knew whether his gun was loaded
or not."[5]

This first service against the Indians provided Crook with the
lessons that would make him the most successful Indian fighter
on the frontier. "It can be an easy matter for anyone to see the

salient points of Indian character, namely that they are filthy, odoriferous, treacherous, ungrateful, pitiless, cruel, and lazy. But it is the fewest who ever get beyond this, and see the other side. Above all, you must get his confidence, which means more than I can tell here. There are few people who can get an Indian's confidence to the extent that he will tell you all his secrets, especially those of a sacred character. Until you have these little secrets of the inner Indian which control his baser part, you need not expect to manipulate him to good actions when his baser passions are aroused."

The unrelenting campaign against the Indians of the Northwest had its effect, destroying the resistant bands and confining the rest to small reservations, throwing the country open to settlement and prospectors. Crook spent the fall of 1859 in the Rogue River Valley, mostly hunting and loafing while soldiers built the post. His recollections of that time demonstrate that this first decade of living in the wilderness, hunting game, and matching his wits and courage against the Indians were what he craved, and perhaps accounts for why the stories of these battles of his youth dominate his autobiography emotionally. It also reveals how scarred he was by the army politics, intrigue, and criticism that would mark his later career. "It was the happiest part of my life. I was free from care and responsibility. My rank and position did not interfere with the ambition and excite the jealousies of those others who were in a position to make me feel it. I have learned since that what was commendable in a man as a lieutenant is just the reverse since I have become a general officer. Success in those days was commendated by your superiors, but nowadays it depends on how much your actions interfere with the ambitions and jealousies of your superiors."

But everything was about to change for Crook—and for the nation.

The sectional jealousies that seemed like such a distant rumor on the frontier had torn asunder the fabric of nationhood. The deeply embedded racism of the culture that made both slavery and the Indian wars possible was about to exact its terrible price.

And the Army's West Point–educated officer corps was going to have to choose sides.

The Civil War had started, and fighting Indians suddenly seemed a small matter.

Crook started for the East immediately, the consummate warrior determined to seize this opportunity. His chief concern was whether all the fighting would be over with before he could get there.

Part Three

1861–1871

Taking Command

5

———————————— **1851–1861**

Geronimo
THE UNQUENCHED FLAME

THE TIMES had been hard for the Bedonkohe, who had once
been a powerful people, but now had not enough warriors to
mount a strong raiding party. So they began more and more to
camp alongside the Mimbreno, who were strong on account of the
Power of Mangas Coloradas and the alliances that he had made
with all the other bands. Soon, Geronimo married again—a handsome Bedonkohe girl named Chee-has-kish. It was right that a
warrior should take a wife—and that he should again have children. So in the next few years Chee-has-kish bore him a son they
called Chappo and a daughter they called Dohn-say. He also married another Bedonkohe girl—Nana-Tha-Thtith—although he was
still a young man. In the old times, warriors rarely had more than
one wife. But in times of war, leading men often took another
wife—sometimes even three or four. Often they married the wives
of their brothers, killed in raids. A woman needed a man—needed
the horses, and the food, and the deer meat, and the things he
brought back from a raid. And a warrior had an obligation to provide for the women, and for the children. And even though Geronimo was young, and had no father, and had no mother, everyone
said that he had Power, and that he would rise in respect. Still, not
even a good wife, and new children, could soften Geronimo now.
That part of him had been scourged out. Now, even when he
smoked at his own fire, or watched his own children suckling at

the breast of their mother, he remained beyond the reach of the campfire, pacing like a wolf in the moonlight.

So Geronimo devoted himself to a warrior's calling.

When the next season for raiding came, Geronimo convinced Ah-koch-ne and Ko-deh-ne to go with him to the south on foot with three days' rations and their bows. They went quietly, seeking horses and cattle—not revenge. Geronimo already had a reputation that would make other warriors trust his leadership. He also had a gun ceremony, which his Power had given to him. He always prepared his weapons carefully. He would spit on the palm of his left hand, dip the first finger of his right hand in the saliva, and make a cross on his left foot, thigh, forearm, and cheek—each time calling on Black Thunder, and Blue Thunder, and Yellow Thunder, and White Thunder. He recited a prayer: Black flint is over your body four times. Take your black weapon to the center of the sky. Let his weapons disappear from the earth—then again for Blue flint. Then again for Yellow flint, then again for White flint—four times in the sacred way. Then he rubbed the first finger of his right hand horizontally across his lips four times.[1]

They found a small village, and just at daylight they crept forward to take five horses that seemed carelessly kept. But just as they reached the horses, the Mexicans opened fire. The bullets immediately killed his two companions, who lacked Geronimo's protection from bullets. He immediately began running, although the Mexicans on their horses tried to surround him. Three times that day they closed in around him, and filled the air with bullets. Each time he slipped away, scrambling over rocks where the horses could not follow. Several times, he hid and shot one of his pursuers from hiding. But eventually he ran out of arrows and so had to depend on speed, and cunning, and the protection of his Power. At long last, he eluded his enemies—and so returned home.

He returned in shame. His companions had both died. He brought back no plunder. He had failed. People would talk against him, and the relatives of Ah-koch-ne and Ko-deh-ne would hold their deaths against him. And he knew that now everyone could see that his Power would protect him, but not his companions. This would make it much more difficult to convince warriors to go

Geronimo posed on horseback during negotiations at Canyon de los Embudos in March 1886; this is one in the famous C. S. Fly series. (*Courtesy National Archives*)

back into Mexico with him. Nonetheless, Geronimo said nothing. He had no right to speak. He had no right to defend himself. Words could not undo deeds. But the death of his companions and the criticism of his band changed nothing. He still yearned for revenge. He still slept with death, and ate with death, and planned death.

It took several months of persistent effort before he convinced two other warriors to join him in a raid back down into Mexico— this time along the Sierra Madre, where Juh's band roamed. But once again, Geronimo's Power betrayed him. They were discovered in the darkness as they waited to steal into a village. In the confused shooting, one of the warriors was killed. With the country roused against them, Geronimo and the surviving warrior started home. But on the way, they spied a column of soldiers, heavy with supplies, heading north. They followed the soldiers for a time, until it seemed clear that the soldiers were heading for the camps of The People. Geronimo and his companion hurried ahead to warn the camp, arriving just three hours ahead of the soldiers. The warriors rushed out to prepare an ambush—killing eight soldiers, but losing two warriors and three apprentices in the fight.

Angry that the soldiers had invaded their territory, the war leaders assembled twenty-five warriors to follow the trail of the retreating Mexicans. The warriors got ahead of them, and set up an ambush in a canyon through which the soldiers must pass. But when the hidden warriors opened fire, the soldiers did not panic; instead they dismounted and used their horses to form a breastwork. Geronimo admired the discipline and the courage of the soldiers, which was rare because he had such hatred for these enemies of his heart. He knew that the warriors would soon exhaust their small store of ammunition, and the soldiers would escape. So Geronimo rose up from behind good cover and charged into the guns of the Mexicans. The other warriors, shamed by Geronimo's courage, ran in behind him. The fighting was hand to hand. Geronimo ran in among the Mexicans with his spear, the blood lust full up in him now—Power burned in him with the kindling of battle. Geronimo saw a soldier aiming his gun, but ran straight at him, having no fear now of bullets. Just as they came together, Geronimo's foot slipped in the blood and he fell heavily. The soldier jumped like a cat, bringing his gun down heavily on Geronimo's head. Geronimo awoke some time later, to find that the warriors had killed every soldier. His head was covered in blood, and he felt the pain splitting him open like an ax through rotten wood. His head ached and spun for months afterwards, and he carried the scar of that blow all his life. The warriors struggled back to their camp, but they staged no victory dance. Too many had died—and no one had any more heart that summer for raids. Except Geronimo. He had no quiet in him—but was the stream that hurries down the hill, with no time for pools. Still, no one would go with him now. His luck was no good. It seemed that those who fought alongside him received the bullets Geronimo's Power turned aside.

That winter was hard, as the raids of the previous summer had brought so few horses, and cattle, and supplies necessary for the thin times of the cold dark. The People gathered around their fires and told stories all through the long nights—especially the Coyote stories that the children loved. Once, Geronimo had listened enraptured to those stories, sitting in the fire flicker all through the night and into the dawn without sleeping even, when the other children faltered and nodded. Now, Geronimo told the stories himself, especially since he had Coyote Power.

It made perfect sense that Coyote Power should pick Geronimo, who had two sides—light and dark, victory and loss, strength and weakness. His great victories called forth great losses. Death and life ran through him, each the cause of the other. Was not Coyote just the same? For Coyote opened the bag of darkness to loosen night and all its evil on human beings—but he also stole fire and spread the sparks from his bushy tail as he ran, thus bringing that great blessing to The People. Coyote showed courage and foolishness, and daring and laziness, and strength and greed. Coyote made human beings subject to death, by foolishly making a bet that a stone he threw into the water would not sink—even as Geronimo fought, even when he could not win. All of the foolish things that have afflicted human beings through all time, Coyote did first. And Geronimo loved to tell those stories—weaving a spell of memory and magic through all the long nights. And woe to the child who fell asleep while Geronimo spoke.

The next summer,[2] Geronimo again assembled for a raid some of the young, reckless warriors—hungry for glory, and for horses, and for the eyes of the young women. This time twelve warriors went with him to the south. At first, it seemed that they had luck. Perhaps Geronimo's Power had changed its nature—or perhaps he had merely placated it somehow. They found a pack train east of Casas Grandes and the packers ran away immediately, leaving their laden pack mules. The warriors happily rounded up the mules, and hurried back toward home.

But they had no luck after all.

A few days later, soldiers overtook them. The soldiers struck them by surprise, and in the first volley a bullet glanced off Geronimo's head—just alongside his eye. He fell unconscious as the other warriors abandoned the mules and dashed for cover. The Mexicans, thinking Geronimo dead, chased the other warriors. Geronimo came to himself a few minutes later, and seeing no one around, rose unsteadily and ran for the cover of a cluster of nearby trees. But just at that moment, more soldiers came out of the trees and began firing at him. As Geronimo turned to run, he saw the first group of soldiers coming toward him, riding back toward the shooting. Geronimo ran through all of the bullets, taking only one small wound, and scampered up the side of a steep canyon, where the horses could not follow. He found a hiding place and waited for the soldiers—who conferred among themselves, and then rode away. Geronimo was disappointed that they had not come on after him on foot. He could have killed some of them, among the rocks, off their horses.

The war party returned home empty-handed, having lost even the horses they set out with, and with Geronimo wounded as well.

But the bad luck had not finished with him. One day as Geronimo lay recovering in the camp, shooting suddenly started up. Soldiers surrounded the camp. The warriors scarcely had time to fire a shot—although Geronimo, with one eye still swollen shut, hit one officer with a hurried bowshot. Everyone ran away quickly, but the soldiers captured four women, and many children, and all of their supplies. The soldiers killed many others, including Geronimo's second wife, Nana-Tha-Thtith.[3] Geronimo and about twenty warriors followed the soldiers for a long while as they headed back to the south, but never had a good chance to attack and recover the prisoners or their horses.

Now many spoke against Geronimo. Still, he said nothing. He made no defense. What could he say? But nothing changed in his heart, which smoldered and burned like a log that holds fire, but cannot be consumed. What choice had he? He had made his vow at the grave of his father. He had let his Power bend him back like a bow. He had become death—and it mattered only a little whether he gave it, or received it. His path was fixed. Let others do as they would. He could do only the thing his Power had set down before him.

When the raiding season came again,[4] Geronimo convinced eight ambitious young warriors to go with him into the Sierra Madre. He had learned many trails. He had learned the habit of caution. He had learned how to listen to the warnings of the birds, and read the story of the trail, and attend to the intuitions of his Power. So the war party he led moved unseen through the mountains, and undetected past the towns, and unsuspected to a place along one of the trails the Mexicans used to move supplies from town to town. They waited there a time, not lighting a fire, waiting for luck. It came, finally, in the form of a long train of pack mules with only four drivers and no soldiers. The mule drivers fled as soon as they saw the warriors, abandoning their supplies but saving their lives. The warriors whooped and hollered and accepted the gift of the mules and their supplies. On their way home, they encountered a White Eye, all alone, with a pack train loaded with cheese. He also fled, and the warriors accepted this second gift. They returned two days later, rich now in mules and goods. They immediately gave most of what they had brought back to their friends, and relatives, and clan members—taking special care to supply the needs of women whose husbands had been killed in previous raids.

But scouts came back quickly and said soldiers were coming, following the path of the mules. So the warriors jumped up, eager for the battle, and eager to show that Geronimo and the others with him were not the only ones who could fight. Mangas Coloradas took command of one group of warriors, and gave leadership of the others to Geronimo. Then they all went, and waited for the soldiers—striking them from two directions at once so that they broke and ran—leaving ten men dead but killing one warrior in return. The thirty warriors pursued the cavalry for many miles, driving them far from the village. Then they returned to the women and the children, and to great praise.

Everyone gathered for the great victory dance Geronimo and the warriors finally had earned. They distributed horses, and cattle, and supplies to everyone who took part, and to everyone in need. The women formed a circle around the fire, calling out their wild trilling of applause, while the warriors danced as they acted out the battle. The leaders called out the men by their names, and the singers told what they had done as they danced proudly in the center of all eyes. The dancing went on all night, and all day, for four days. After the warriors danced, the men formed the inside circle, and the women formed the outside circle, and they danced one with the other, the men afterward giving gifts to their partners. Many marriages started here, with the downcast eyes, and the upturned smiles as the circles of the men and of the women rotated around the fire, one within the other, all through the night. Everyone called out for their favorite singers, who each had his own song for the social dancing, repeated again and again, with a booming, and a trilling, and a hundred individualized variations each savored, and commented upon, and called for.

> I've been wandering around
> Wandering around;
> When I got home,
> Everyone had moved.[5]

Thus called the singer, so that everyone laughed, and maybe a girl who had been waiting for the return of a certain warrior would look up and blush, and look away again quickly. Geronimo danced, and he sang, and he reveled in all of it. But in truth, he had not gone into Mexico for this glory, nor had he killed the soldiers who had followed them for the songs, or the praise, or even to protect The People. He had a need now for it, simple as blood.

So he waited impatiently through another long winter, little comforted by the things he had provided to his family and his

People. He set off as soon as he could in the spring with three men, going far down into Mexico. Now his Power moved strong with him. So even though they had not one gun between them, the four warriors decided that they should attack the small town of Cassanas—near Casas Grandes. So they crept into town at midday, when the Mexicans were all inside at their lunch, and at their naps, and there in the middle of town they began to scream, and shout, and rip the air with their war cries. They fired at everyone who emerged onto the narrow, dusty street so that the terrified people of Cassanas fled as fast as they could run in every direction. The warriors laughed, and yelled insults after them, and looked about in amazement—for the Mexicans had left to the four warriors the whole town. The warriors hurried to round up all of the horses and mules they could, then loaded onto the mules everything that seemed of value. They went through each of the houses, and found many curious things. Some of them they understood. But many they could not understand at all—or imagine what use the Mexicans made of them.

The warriors returned safely home from the raid, protected by Geronimo's Power. It seemed perhaps that his Power had been merely testing him—giving him bad luck at first to see if Geronimo would remain faithful, but rewarding him now. Geronimo talked to his Power every morning, to find out what he should do. Then he would talk to his warriors, telling them what would happen. He would say, you should go here, you should go there.[6] He did not talk much about his Power, and that was good, because Power does not like to be talked about. It comes to you in private. It will come to you and say, I can't find a better man than you. I like your ways. There are many men here, but I can't find a better one. You are the very person for me. I want to give you something to live by through this world, because you will meet many difficulties.[7] And sometimes a person might say back, I am a poor person, and there are many other people here good enough for that. Let me alone, I don't want your ceremony. But that is dangerous, too, because the Power might resent that, and make trouble. Power makes itself known by a word, or it may assume the shape of something—like a bird. Power usually lives in a certain place, and so a person can go to that place, and pray. But the Power lives in everything—so that the rocks can hear you, and remember you, so that the trees may miss you, or think of you when you have gone someplace else. Power speaks to those who listen, because everything has the life force, and everything wants to be heard—to be remembered. Some say that the earth talks to them, and they get their ceremony from that. Some say the wind has life, or the mountain, or the rocks, or a cliff. Sometimes Power makes a certain muscle twitch. Sometimes it is only a feeling. Sometimes it is a bird, or a badger, or a gopher—which speaks to you. But Power is dangerous, too—and may turn on you, or become disappointed in you, or become angry that you have given away its secrets. So Geronimo did not talk about his Power. He merely did his ceremonies, and fasted, and prayed. Then he used what he learned in that way to move unseen among his enemies—and to come safely home through the great forest of his enemies in ways that other men, without Power, would not dare to do.

But you can never know whether Power is with you, or whether it is only using you. One other war shaman, who was respected and had great Power in war, told about the time that he argued with his Power. One time before a fight, the war shaman was singing, praying so that no one would receive a wound. He did it right in front of them, as they were sitting around the fire because he never kept things secret from them. But in the middle of the ceremony, his Power said to him, Tomorrow I'm going to take two of your very best men during battle. It called their names out to him, his two best warriors. The shaman turned to the men and said right away, You two men are going to be killed tomorrow. That is what my Power says. Then he kept right on with the ceremony, although he was now angry with his Power. But his Power said to him, This must be done. I have helped you and have done everything you asked for up to this time. Now you must do what I tell you. But the shaman answered back, speaking out loud now so that everyone could hear him, These men and their families, I love every one of them. I want to see them as long as I live. I will not let you have any of them. I will not agree with you. I must tell you right now. But his Power answered back, It must be done. The shaman replied, very angry, It's not going to be done. Still, his Power insisted. So the shaman said, If you think it must be done, take me. Then you can do whatever you want after that. Take me first. If that's the kind of thing you want me to do, take your ceremony back right now. I don't want it. I want to do only good things with it. When I have to pay you men, I will not put up with it any more. His Power had to stop then and think about that, knowing it would lose the ceremonies, and the prayers. So the Power answered, If you don't want anything to happen, don't go into battle tomorrow.[8]

Geronimo only listened to such stories. He did not talk about his own Power or what they said, one to the other, in the darkness. But others looking at him, covertly so that they would not challenge him, wondered whether he would fight in that way for the lives of his men, against his Power.

But whatever others might say, Geronimo went ahead. And so in those years,[9] Geronimo grew in experience, and in Power. He remained always ready to join a war party, and forever moved among the warriors to find some willing to join his expeditions.

He led twenty warriors back down into Sonora, and attacked several settlements, gaining horses and supplies. On that raid, they seized a pack train loaded with potent Mexican mescal. The delighted warriors immediately pitched camp and drank the heady mescal as quickly as they could.[10] The camp degenerated quickly into chaos, although Geronimo made a futile effort to quell the fights that quickly broke out. Scattered fights progressed into a drunken brawl, which left two men dangerously wounded. Geronimo vainly pleaded with several of the more responsible warriors to stand as sentries around the camp, lest the Mexicans sent out to recover the pack train attack them while the rest of the warriors were in a stupor. But no one would stand watch. So Geronimo waited helplessly, until the warriors had drunk themselves into a stupor. Then he poured out the remaining mescal, treated the wounded warriors, and nervously stood guard through the interminable night, expecting shots to erupt out of the darkness at any moment.[11]

Another time, he went with four warriors deep into Mexico—so far that he glimpsed the greatest lake that he had ever imagined, stretching all the way to the horizon.[12] The warriors, who went all through the midst of the Mexicans on foot, returned with sixty cattle, inspiring much feasting and praise.

Once he went with Mangas Coloradas deep into Mexico with thirty warriors, moving as far south as Santa Cruz in Sonora, collecting a whole herd of horses and killing perhaps fifty Mexicans—which helped to sate even Geronimo's great appetite for death. On a raid for horses and supplies, warriors usually tried to avoid killing anyone. But when they were moving deep in the territory of their enemies, they could not afford to leave alive anyone who saw them. If they killed a farmer in an isolated valley, it might take days or weeks for anyone to know. But if they let such a man live after he had seen them, the alarm would spread quickly through the countryside and ruin the raid. Sometimes, if a man in a remote place surrendered immediately, and made no trouble, and promised to tell no one—they let him live. But usually they killed anyone who saw them.

Once they killed several Mexican cowboys and stole a herd of cattle. But as they were returning home, they encountered a detachment of Mexican soldiers, who began firing with their rifles while still safely out of range of the warrior's bows. The warriors fled into the cover of some nearby trees, where they abandoned their own worn-out ponies and scrambled up the rocky slopes of a nearby mountain where the soldier's horses could not follow them. They returned home without any booty, and without even the horses on which they'd ridden so confidently out of camp. The taunts of the other warriors galled Geronimo—who had for a long time basked in success and glory of the victory dances. So he set out immediately with six warriors and went on foot to hated Arispe, returning with enough horses and cattle to silence the criticisms.

Even the setbacks Geronimo sometimes suffered now seemed only a challenge to him. One day soldiers attacked the camp and put everyone to flight and so captured all of the horses they needed to get through the winter. The soldiers rode quickly away, too quickly for the warriors to regroup and follow them on foot. But Geronimo took twenty warriors, and followed the trail back down into Sonora, where he took the horses back from the Mexicans and killed two cowboys. Nine cowboys, well armed, set out after the raiders. But Geronimo sent the main group of warriors on ahead with all of the horses, and then went back with three warriors. Geronimo waited until the cowboys were asleep, and then slipped into camp and took all of their horses. The warriors rode away, laughing, and retelling the story of the raid, knowing that the victory dance upon their return would be good.

Geronimo grew so much in respect among the fighting men, that he soon married She-gha,[13] who was a relative of Cochise. Geronimo then went to live with Cochise's Chokonen, the most powerful of the Chiricahua. Geronimo also married a third wife, a Bedonkohe woman named Shtsha-she. Thus everyone could see that Geronimo had become a leading warrior—with enough wealth from raiding to support three wives. He was known and respected among the Mimbreno, and had raided often with Mangas Coloradas. And now he was also family to Cochise, who was the other great chief of The People. Geronimo had shown his Power in war, so that he was sought after for raiding parties—although he did not in other ways act as a leader of The People. Everyone could see that his Power was limited to war, because that was all that his heart could hold.

But even as Geronimo grew in Power and experience in his usually successful forays into the south, the world darkened for The People.

The White Eyes had returned, and the shadow they cast was deep and long as sunset. The most farseeing leaders of The People saw the threat. For as long as anyone could remember, The People had gone every summer to the south to fight the Mexicans, and returned every winter to the safety of their homeland. Sometimes the Mexicans followed, and sometimes they surprised the camps of The People. But not often. Usually the scouts that guarded the camps and watched the back trails of the raiding parties saw the soldiers coming up out of Mexico long before they could strike. True enough, the Mexicans had pushed The People back—forcing them into the mountains, making them move their camps, and guard their trails—but the Mexicans could not inflict a fatal wound. Geronimo thought of the Mexicans as cattle, enemies put into the world to be killed, and to test the mettle of the warriors, and to provide The People with the supplies to stage ceremonies and get through the thin times of winter.

But the White Eyes presented a different problem. They came toward the last, best hiding places of The People. At first, Mangas Coloradas and Cochise and other leaders thought perhaps the White Eyes would become allies of The People against the Mexicans. Many said that the White Eyes and the Mexicans fought a great war, which the White Eyes had won. But The People saw little enough evidence of that, except for the increasing number of White Eyes that came into their territory from the east. At first, these were only trappers, to whom The People had little objection. But then there came another band of White Eyes, who dug in the earth. The People had only contempt for these crazy people, who profaned the body of the earth, ripping it open and leaving the ugly scars. The White Eyes had the gold sickness—and would do anything for this worthless metal, which was too soft even for making bullets. They took terrible chances. They killed anyone they encountered, even one another. Many came with the first of the White Eye soldiers who had camped near the Mimbreno. Many Diggers, men who dug in the ground, stayed even after the soldiers left. At first, Mangas Coloradas commanded that the warriors should leave the crazy White Eyes alone, because he did not want to make new enemies. He would not let his warriors molest the stagecoaches that often passed now through his territory, nor even the settlers who came and lived along the rivers.[14] But more and more came, frightening the game, fouling the water, and frightening the children. Mangas Coloradas had considered how he might convince the White Eyes to leave, without killing them. After a great deal of thinking, he settled on a plan and went into their camps to tell them about a different place where they could find much more gold. But one time when he went alone as a friend into their camp at Pinos Altos, they seized him, and tied him up, and lashed him with their whips, as though he were a dog.[15] Mangas Coloradas's son cut him down in the darkness, and when his wounds had healed, Mangas Coloradas called upon Cochise for help in driving the White Eyes out of his lands. Geronimo joined a war party that set out to cut off the White Eyes in Pinos Altos from their supplies. They surprised a wagon train, and surrounded it. Mangas Coloradas insisted that they let escape a wagon carrying women and children, but he killed the sixteen men defending the wagon train and seized nine hundred cattle and four hundred sheep. For months that followed, the warriors stole livestock, and killed any miners they found away from Pinos Altos. Once, they even attacked Pinos Altos. The White Eyes began to leave, and soon all work at the mines came to a halt.

But just when it seemed that The People had taught the White Eyes a lesson, the White Eyes again showed their treachery.

Cochise had long maintained a stern peace with the White Eyes in his territory, which stretched from the invulnerable hiding place of the Dragoon Mountains to the bewildering spires and canyons of the Chiricahua Mountains.[16] He let the White Eyes set up a stopping place for the horses that pulled the wagons coming through the Chiricahua territory every week in the middle of Apache Pass, which provided the only reliable watering place for a full day's ride. Cochise even let his warriors bring wood to the horse station, and would not let any warrior harm any White Eye.

One day in the Season of the Ghost Dance,[17] some soldiers came to Apache Pass. Cochise sent a message to his friend who worked at the horse station who sent word that the soldiers were friendly, and only wanted to meet Cochise, who had been so good a friend to the White Eyes. So Cochise went to meet with the *nantan* of the soldiers—a man too young, who talked too loud. When Cochise, and his brother, and his son, and other relatives, had gone into the tent of the *nantan*, the man rudely demanded that Cochise give back a half-breed boy who had been taken from the home of a local rancher. Cochise said that he had not taken the boy, but that maybe he could find out who had done so. But the *nantan* ordered his soldiers to seize Cochise, and his relatives, and make them prisoners. Cochise pulled out his knife, and cut open the tent, and ran through the middle of the soldiers so quickly that they could not hit him, although many fired their guns. However, the others in the tent were not so quick and so the soldiers seized them all—after wounding the brother of Cochise.[18]

Cochise could see that the *nantan* was a man without honor. So he sent his warriors out to find prisoners to trade for his brother, and his son, and his wife. Cochise went quickly to the horse station, and took prisoner three of the White Eyes there, even the man who had been friendly with Cochise. The soldiers came just as the warriors were ready to leave, and in the fighting the soldiers shot one of the White Eye prisoners. Then the warriors found a wagon train, and captured two more White Eye prisoners—killing the eight Mexicans they found with the wagon train.

Cochise tried for several days to convince the foolish *nantan* to exchange prisoners, but the *nantan* would not listen—insisting Cochise return the kidnapped boy he did not have. Seeing the soldiers would not return their prisoners, Cochise killed his own prisoners, and mutilated their bodies with his lance so that the soldiers would see the consequences of lies and treachery. Then the warriors left, knowing that more soldiers would come on quickly. The soldiers killed the prisoners they had seized by treachery and left their bodies hanging for the vultures and the crows in Apache Pass until the skin had fallen away, leaving only the bones hanging in the trees.[19]

Cochise then made war on the White Eyes. He killed every farmer and cowboy that he could find. He attacked the stagecoaches, so that they stopped coming. He followed the soldiers, and killed them when he could. He made so great a war on them that even the soldiers quailed, and left their forts—burning them down to ashes. Geronimo rode happily with the war parties, seeing now that the White Eyes whom he had admired for a time were just as treacherous as the Mexicans, whom he hated with his whole heart.[20]

6

———————————— 1861–1871

Crook

THE POLITICS OF DEATH

CROOK ARRIVED in the East after an arduous journey to find that it appeared this war would take far longer than anyone thought. The Union had already suffered a disastrous defeat at the first battle of Bull Run on July 21, 1861, in which horrified picnickers who had turned out for a grand show had watched the virtual disintegration of the inexperienced Union army.

Crook set about immediately obtaining a command in one of the regiments being raised in Ohio, his native state, knowing that his experience would win him a much higher rank in one of the newly formed volunteer regiments. He was appointed a captain in the Fourteenth Ohio Infantry, but continued to finagle for a better post. At one point, he met with President Lincoln, whom he described as "the most ungainly man I had ever seen, particularly his hands and feet." Crook lobbied the governor of Ohio, and eventually took a leave of absence from the regular army and accepted a commission as a colonel in the Thirty-sixth Ohio Regiment of Infantry.

He found a gaggle of Ohio farm boys who had been taken from their plows and subjected to the harsh discipline of the army and were already teetering on the brink of mutiny. "The regular army officer in charge of them was very severe, and they were in a state of near-mutiny," he recalled. They were mostly barefooted and dressed in rags and tatters, with the cold weather of September

General George Crook wore his uniform for this studio photo by famed Civil War photographer Mathew Brady. In fact, Crook rarely wore his uniform in the field and had a reputation as a modest, informal man who usually looked more like a disheveled volunteer than a commanding general. (*Courtesy National Archives*)

setting in. However, Crook observed, "I must say I never saw a more willing set of men in my life." He called them in, like a band of reservation Indians, and convinced them of the value of drill and discipline to prepare them for the coming ordeal. He set to work training the men with a will. "Never in all my life did I work so hard, mentally and physically, as I did through that winter . . . about a third were down with typhoid fever at any one time."

Crook's first task was to restore some semblance of order in the Ohio countryside where his troops were based. The Summersville area had always been prey to robbers and counterfeiters, but the onset of the war had greatly increased the lawlessness. Groups of bushwhackers haunted the hilly, brushy country—robbing stages, wagons, and travelers. Most of the robbers were local toughs, many in sympathy with the South, determined to take advantage of the chaos of the war. Crook organized as if for an Indian campaign, learning the terrain in detail, and establishing a network of spies and informants throughout the countryside. His soldiers began rounding up the bushwackers and turning them over to headquarters. However, the arrested men generally returned a short time later, "fat, saucy, with good clothes." Crook decided that the officers at headquarters were either corrupt or inattentive, and so resolved to stop sending them prisoners. Crook observed that the bushwackers began meeting with accidents after their capture—falling off logs and breaking their necks, or being killed by the "accidental" discharge of a firearm. His handling of the lawless element fit perfectly with the tactics he'd learned among the Indians, and apparently excited no interest on the part of his superiors. In short order, the region enjoyed a greater degree of peace and quiet than had reigned before the war.

Meantime, the larger war was not going well for the Union. Expectations of an easy victory had faded quickly with Confederate success at Bull Run and the flat-footed inertia of the Union commanders. The Union enjoyed overwhelming material advantages, with a population of 22 million pitted against a Southern population of 9 million, including 3.5 million slaves. The Union's military potential totaled some 4 million men, compared to just 1.1 million whites of military age in the South. Perhaps more importantly, Northern factories could produce some five thousand rifles a day to the South's three hundred. The Union imposed a largely successful blockade, which prevented the South from selling its cotton to Europe to buy the munitions it so desperately needed. However, the superior generalship and strategy of the South and Lincoln's long, frustrating search for a general who could effectively carry the fight to the enemy kept the war going long after the North's economic advantages should have proved decisive.

George B. McClellan, appointed to command the Army of the Potomac after the disastrous battle of Bull Run, set to training his assembled army of 150,000. He planned to march on Richmond, although Lincoln fretted that this move would leave Washington vulnerable to capture by the more mobile Confederates. McClellan launched the Peninsular campaign on March 17, 1862, setting out ponderously for Richmond. The 11,000 Confederates at Yorktown managed to imitate a larger force, convincing McClellan the enemy's strength equaled his own. McClellan dug in to await reinforcements—despite Lincoln's desperate urging to attack. The Confederates' General Stonewall Jackson forestalled the dispatch of reinforcements for the inert McClellan with a brilliant offensive through the Shenandoah Valley. After hesitating for months, McClellan finally took Yorktown and moved on toward Richmond.

The Union did score victories in the West. First, General Ulysses S. Grant defeated the Confederates at the bloody battle of Shiloh on the Tennessee River. The 40,000-man Union force withstood a Confederate attack on April 6, 1862, then counterattacked, reinforced by 20,000 fresh troops. The North suffered 13,000 casualties and the South 10,000, but the Confederates retreated and the Union claimed the victory. Later that month, a Union fleet captured New Orleans, constricting the South's ability to import the war material it would need for a long struggle. Union forces also captured Memphis, on June 6, 1862.

Crook moved slowly into the larger war in the East with the formation of a provisional brigade under his command in the spring of 1862, which included the Second West Virginia Cavalry and the Thirty-sixth and Forty-fourth regiments of Ohio infantry. Crook's force fought a short, pitched battle on August 13 at Lewisburg, Virginia, on the Greenbrier River, during which Crook's well-drilled but still green troops withstood a Confederate assault and counterattacked, breaking the Confederate line. At one point in the battle, Crook crouched behind a board fence being pelted by enemy musket balls. "The enemies' bullets striking against it sounded like hail, and I instinctively held my neck to one side so as to prevent the hail from going down my neck. It was in this enclosure I was struck on the foot by a spent ball, which gave me no particular trouble until the battle was over, when my foot became very painful."

The small battle provided Crook with his first victory in what was to prove a long and frustrating conflict for him. The Confederates lost 60 killed and 175 captured, while Crook's command lost 7 killed, 5 captured, and 44 wounded.[1]

Meanwhile, McClellan's army had stumbled from bad to worse. Moving slowly toward Richmond, McClellan found himself beset by the smaller but much more mobile and aggressive Confederate forces. Confederate cavalry commander J. E. B. Stuart unnerved McClellan by galloping completely around the Union army in a bewildering three-day raid. Two weeks later, in June and July, Confederate general Robert E. Lee harried the larger Union army with a series of attacks known as the Seven Days' battles. The Confederates scored no decisive victories, but so confounded McClellan that he withdrew to the James River to await reinforcements under the command of General John Pope. However, Lee seized the opportunity to attack before Pope's command could unite with McClellan. Pope rashly attacked a well-defended Confederate position and his force was mauled at the second battle of Bull Run on August 30, with roughly ten thousand casualties on each side. The Union then abandoned the initiative, and retreated to Washington.

Crook's command was attached to the Army of the Potomac, initially to serve as bodyguard for McClellan's headquarters. Crook got a glimpse of the confusion and inertia that prevailed at headquarters, which set in motion his steady disillusionment with the Union leadership. After this glimpse of the politics of death, Crook was shifted to command of a brigade composed of the Eleventh, Twenty-eighth, and Thirty-sixth Ohio regiments in the Army of the Potomac.

Seizing the initiative from the bamboozled McClellan, Lee counterattacked into Maryland with 50,000 men—hoping that a big victory would convince European governments to recognize the Confederacy. Ever daring, Lee actually divided his force, sending General Stonewall Jackson with 25,000 men to capture the Union arsenal at Harpers Ferry while he continued to outmaneuver McClellan's slowly pursuing army. McClellan then received a huge stroke of good fortune, when one of his men looking through an abandoned Confederate camp found a copy of Lee's orders wrapped around three cigars. The discovery that Lee had split his forces finally prodded McClellan to move toward the attack on September 15. McClellan moved slowly into place, convinced that the 18,000 Confederates facing him on a three-mile ridge east of Sharpsburg, Maryland, outnumbered his 95,000 men drawn up along Antietam Creek. By the time McClellan actually attacked on September 17, Jackson had joined Lee on the ridge and the chance for a decisive Northern victory had slipped away. The result was one of the bloodiest battles of the Civil War. It also proved one of the most frustrating battles of Crook's career, reinforcing his growing contempt for the Union leadership, which seemed at the same time so timid and so reckless with men's lives.

The battle opened with General Joseph Hooker's brave but foolish charge up the road into the teeth of the Confederate guns, which quickly killed 224 of the 334 men Hooker sent forward. The battle raged back and forth over a sunken cornfield throughout the day, the Union commanders still refusing to accept the Civil War's repeatedly administered lesson that modern rifles and artillery had shifted the advantage in combat decisively to the defense—a lesson the Apaches had quickly learned and never forgot. The attacking Union forces surged back and forth over the sunken cornfield on the Confederate left fifteen times, leaving 8,000 dead and wounded. The battle then shifted to a sunken country road in Lee's center that served as a perfect rifle pit for the Southern infantry. After suffering appalling casualties, the Union soldiers broke through to the road, shooting down its length and piling up Confederate bodies. McClellan might have broken the Confederate line by following up with an all-out attack on the center, but decided it wouldn't be prudent. Action then shifted to the Confederate right flank, where General Ambrose

Burnside hurled his 12,000 men against 400 Confederates defending a stone bridge. The Confederates held off the attack on the bridge for three hours, fighting off four attacks.

In this engagement, Crook, attached to Burnside's corps, demonstrated his shrewd sense of tactics and terrain in the face of confusion and indifference on the part of his superiors. Crook's brigade did not participate in the frontal assault on the bridge, but when that attack failed he received orders to take "the bridge." Crook confronted the staff officer who brought the orders, demanding to know which bridge he was supposed to take. The staff officer could only shrug. "I made some remarks not complimentary to such a way of doing business, but he went off, caring not a cent. Probably he had done the correct thing," recalled Crook. "The consequence was that I had to get a good many men killed in acquiring information which should have been supplied to me from division headquarters." Only later did he learn that his brigade had been assigned a task an entire division had failed to accomplish. "Such imbecility and incompetency was simply criminal, a great deal of which lasted until the close of the war," railed Crook in his autobiography. "It was galling to have to serve under such people. But many of them, by maneuvering in politics and elsewhere, are looked upon by certain people throughout the lands as some of our military luminaries."

Crook sent out skirmishers to scout the terrain, and immediately saw that a frontal assault on the bridge would be foolhardy. He therefore moved down the creek until he found a crossing, then flanked the thinly manned Confederate positions on the bluffs overlooking the bridge.

Crook's brigade was then attached to the Philadelphia Corn Exchange Brigade that had been ordered to make a charge on the Confederate left. Crook reconnoitered the terrain, and discovered that the planned charge would take the men into the barrels of an artillery battery defending the road to Sharpsburg. Crook made his report to General O. B. Willcox, who looked at the batteries through field glasses and said he could see no men manning the guns, "which so disgusted me that I left him and went off," recalled Crook.

The doomed attack proceeded despite Crook's suggestion that Union forces attempt to flank the battery. "The moment we raised the crest of the hill and were in full view, we were met with such a hail of musketry bullets, with several batteries dealing death and destruction in our ranks, that it would seem nothing could survive it. . . . After reaching the crest of the hill we had to pass over a quiet stretch of ground before we commenced descending into the hollow laying between the ridge occupied by the enemy and ourselves. The enemy not only had a direct, but a cross fire on us. It was in going down this slope that Col. Clark, commanding the 36th (Ohio Infantry) was killed by a round shot that came from our left. It struck him sideways, just above the hips, tearing him almost in twain," Crook wrote in his autobiography. Almost all of the Corn Exchange Brigade were dead by the time they reached the bottom of the hollow, where Crook's brigade took refuge behind a stone wall. Willcox ordered them forward, but the officer whose division included Crook's brigade refused to advance without written orders—pointing out that his decimated unit was the only force between the Confederates and the Union's supply train and field hospital. To Crook's great relief, Willcox decided not to put the order in writing. "My few orphans would not have lasted 10 minutes had we once gone on their side of the fence," Crook remembered. With darkness, Crook's men retreated to a safe distance. Huge numbers of dying men littered the battleground between the two exhausted forces. "It was heartrending to hear the wails of the wounded and dying men in our front all night. Our men alleviated all this suffering they could, but we had to keep ourselves intact for fear of an attack," Crook recalled.

Crook performed well that day, but the terrible toll and the wretched leadership had made a deep impression on him. The battle represented the bloodiest single day of the war. The Union lost 2,018 dead and 10,293 wounded, while Lee suffered 10,318 dead and wounded—a quarter of his army. The Union claimed the victory, having halted Lee's advance into the North. Lincoln took the pretext of this muted victory to issue the Emancipation Proclamation on September 22, a move he had postponed as long as possible for fear of alienating the border states. But McClellan's hesitation once again squandered the fruits of victory. He could have moved into the battle the next day with fresh troops, when he would have outnumbered Lee's mangled force by a three-to-one margin. But Lee retreated, and McClellan waited nineteen days before moving slowly in pursuit. Exasperated, Lincoln removed McClellan from command on November 5.

Meanwhile, Crook's brigade was detached from the lumbering Army of the Potomac to reoccupy the Kanawha Valley in West Virginia. He was sent to reinforce Major General Williams Rosecrans's Army of the Cumberland in Tennessee, which had been depleted by the battle of Stones River, fought from December 31 to January 2, 1863. The Union forces had advanced south from Nashville and collided with the Confederates commanded by General Braxton Bragg, who had invaded Kentucky to draw the Northerners out of the crucial border state of Tennessee. Each side suffered about nine thousand casualties in the long, confusing battle.

Crook's brigade joined the Army of the Cumberland in Nashville in mid January of 1863, where his forces were augmented by several unruly Kentucky regiments and ordered to occupy Carthage. Crook found the new soldiers almost uncontrollable, noting in disgust that many set to looting churches. They were "perfectly lawless and with little or no discipline. Because of my effort to discipline them, they accused me of disloyalty." Fortunately, General Rosecrans backed him—but Crook spent months trying to control his own troops. On July 1, 1863, he was transferred to the command of a cavalry division.

Crook's horse soldiers spent the summer making constant reconnaissance and raids in the area of the Tennessee River, acquiring fresh reasons to distrust his commanders and bemoan the leadership of the Union armies.

Rosecrans's 55,000-man army pursued Bragg's Confederates through the summer and fall of 1863, prompting the Confederates to abandon the strategically vital Tennessee River town of Chattanooga. As headlong as McClellan had been cautious, Rosecrans chased a retreating Confederate force reinforced by James Longstreet's corps to a strength of 70,000 men. When Bragg turned on him at Chickamauga, just south of the Georgia-Tennessee line, the Union right flank crumpled and nearly collapsed. However, the Union left under General George H. Thomas, the "rock" of Chickamauga, held and prevented a disaster. General Philip Sheridan, Crook's West Point classmate, also distinguished himself in the fighting—rising to a prominence which would soon fully eclipse Crook. Sheridan's and Crook's careers were to become intertwined in the years to come. The two-day battle cost 4,000 lives and more than 16,000 Northern and 8,000 Southern casualties.

Crook's units fought dismounted on the right flank, after the collapse of the Union lines, and then helped cover the Union retreat to Chattanooga. Once again, his autobiography reflected disagreements with his superiors that still rankled decades later. He was at one point ordered forward to keep the advancing Confederates from crossing Chickamauga Creek. Crook protested orders to bring his artillery battery along, maintaining the slow-moving artillery would hinder his cavalry. But General John G. Mitchell brushed aside Crook's protests and sent him forward. Crook groped forward, trying to find the creek. He ordered his artillery to open up on a suspicious thicket, only to see a swarm of Confederates charge his position. Crook suffered one hundred casualties in the next fifteen minutes, mostly in an effort to protect the artillery. At one point in the furious fighting, Crook was entirely surrounded by Confederates and nearly captured before he managed to spur his horse back to his own men. Later, he listened as his commanding officer distorted and twisted the report of the day's fighting to his own advantage in reporting to General Rosecrans. Crook concluded, "It was humiliating to see persons wearing uniforms of general officers be so contemptible."

The disordered Union forces fell back on Chattanooga, and were probably saved from total defeat only by the exhaustion and caution of the Confederate forces. Confederate General Nathan Bedford Forrest was so enraged at Bragg's failure to remain on the attack that he sought an independent command and Bragg dismissed three staff officers for failure to obey his orders. Crook supported the idea that the Confederates could have scored a decisive victory had they pressed the attack, noting that the Union army degenerated into a "rabble." He wrote, "We had made no preparations for a reverse, no defenses were prepared, and our position without them was a weak one."

Crook was then transferred to the river bank opposite Chattanooga and detailed to guard all the fords for fifty miles with a force of fifteen hundred cavalrymen arrayed against an opposing Confederate cavalry force of about six thousand. Crook protested the impossibility of the task, but scattered his troops in small detachments as best he could, hoping they could gallop back to bring help if the Confederates showed up. Shortly, several Confederate officers under a white flag showed up and demanded Crook's surrender. He stalled them in conversation for some time, carefully pumping them for information about the disposition of the Confederate troops—in much the same manner he would make talk a major weapon in his armory in his confrontations with the Apache and the Sioux in the years to come. He used the warning offered by the surrender demand to concentrate his forces, and move his headquarters out of harm's way.

By the time the Confederates did move to besiege Chattanooga on November 23, it was too late to dislodge the now entrenched Union troops. General Ulysses S. Grant, the hero of Vicksburg earlier that summer, had assumed command of all of the armies of the West and now hurried to Chattanooga, bringing General William T. Sherman's army from Vicksburg and two corps under General Joseph Hooker. Grant and Crook shared many characteristics: they were both rumpled, unimpressive-looking men who eschewed ceremony but who operated from a core of quiet, unshakable determination. They were both relatively remote and uncommunicative, but dogged, persistent, and relentless in seeking and exploiting the weaknesses of their enemies. Grant replaced Rosecrans with General Thomas and directed preparation of the Union defense. The Confederates set up a strong position on Missionary Ridge south of the city, with guns on the 2,000-foot summit of Lookout Mountain. Typically audacious, Grant resolved to drive them off. Sherman's attack on Bragg's right flank stalled, but Hooker's attack battered the Confederates on Lookout Mountain. Meanwhile, Thomas's charge up Missionary Ridge in the Union center, in which Sheridan played a leading role, broke the Confederate center and hurled the Southerners into retreat. The North suffered 5,500 casualties to the Confederate's 2,500, but the battle forced the Southerners to retreat from most of Tennessee, a vital upper south state.

Crook's command participated in the battle, and then played a lead role in the ensuing pursuit of the retreating Confederates. One incident in that running series of engagements demonstrated that Crook was not above the confusion and mistakes he criticized so harshly in many of his superiors. It also demonstrated a problem in his communications with both superiors and subordinates that would surface from time to time throughout his career. Gruff, taciturn, unbending, and stern, Crook remained a remote figure—easy to respect but hard to like. His terse style, utter self-reliance, preference for independent action, unflinching self-confidence, and poorly concealed contempt for less resolute and disciplined officers spawned communications problems throughout his career. In one engagement, Crook was pursuing the retreating enemy—breaking up the protection of their rear guard with several risky but successful cavalry charges. He nearly trapped the fleeing Confederate force, but it slipped through his fingers when another Union brigade under his command failed to link up. When Crook's anticipated linkup fell through, the larger Confederate force turned on him. Crook could not retreat because his horses were so played out that he would have been cut to pieces. Instead, he ordered his men to dismount within two hundred yards of the enemy and to fight from the ground with their .56 caliber, seven-shot repeating carbines—which gave them far greater firepower than a like number of infantry. Crook's men held their position under a storm of fire in which Crook noted "every few minutes someone near me would be torn to atoms." Supported by his battery of artillery, Crook's smaller force broke up the charge and then boldly resumed its pursuit of the now routed enemy. But after the battle Crook turned on the commander of the brigade that had missed its rendezvous, insisting that Robert H. G. Mintry had failed to follow his orders. The dispute provoked a court-martial, during which Crook realized he had forgotten to send the disputed order. Mintry was acquitted.

Grant's victories in the West prompted Lincoln in early 1864 to give Grant command of all the Union forces. Lincoln had been searching desperately for a commander who could use the North's enormous material advantages to crush the Southern resistance. After Antietam, he had replaced McClellan with General Ambrose E. Burnside, who rashly attacked Lee's entrenched positions at Fredericksburg in December 1862 and suffered a bloody setback, including 12,000 casualties. Burnside asked to be relieved of command of the 120,000-man Army of the Potomac, which was twice the size of Lee's army. General Joseph Hooker assumed command. He split his forces and tried to flank Lee's positions near Fredericksburg on May 4, 1863, but lost his nerve in mid maneuver and settled into defensive positions. Lee then pulled out of Fredericksburg and struck the Federals near Chancellorsville, nearly routing the Union army. The North suffered 11,000 casualties, but Lee lost 10,000 men plus the irreplaceable General Stonewall Jackson. The defeat led to Hooker's resignation, which prompted Lincoln to replace him with General George G. Meade. Lee now shifted back onto the offensive with an invasion of the Shenandoah Valley and Pennsylvania. The two armies collided at the battle of Gettysburg in July of 1863, where Lee paid a terrible price for shifting to a tactic of frontal assault. The bloody repulse of Lee's offensive forced the South onto the defensive for the balance of the war and inflicted 22,500 Northern casualties and more than 28,000 Southern. But to Lincoln's disgust, Meade failed to follow up his victory at Gettysburg and allowed Lee to escape safely to Virginia. All that history of confusion and indecision prompted Lincoln to finally seize on Grant's dogged persistence, solid strategy, and willingness to fight and appoint him overall commander in 1864.

Grant moved quickly to coordinate the efforts of the various Northern armies. The Army of the Potomac under General Meade would close with Lee in Virginia in a bid to capture the Southern capital in Richmond. An army under General Sherman would advance into Georgia from Chattanooga to seize Atlanta. A third planned offensive striking up the Red River to capture Shreveport was blunted, and played little role in the rest of the war.

Grant's promotion proved good for Crook's career, and Grant remained a supporter and admirer of Crook through the rest of his career—several times in later years rescuing him from the political difficulties spawned by Crook's unconventional tactics and blunt, sometimes disdainful dealings with his superiors and critics. Crook was transferred back to the East and ordered to provide cavalry support for an effort to disrupt the operations of the Virginia & Tennessee Railroad, which played an important role in supplying Lee's armies.

Meanwhile, Grant and the Army of the Potomac headed south for Richmond. On May 5 and 6 of 1864, Grant's 115,000 men collided with Lee's 75,000-man army in a desolate area of northern Virginia nicknamed the Wilderness. The two-day battle in the dense thickets inflicted heavy casualties as the two sides fought to an appalling draw, although Lee could not readily replace the men and arms he lost in the struggle.

News of Grant's bloodying in the Wilderness prompted Crook to fall back from his advance into Virginia lest he be cut off with his cavalry command in Southern territory. Reinforced, Crook advanced again into the Shenandoah Valley—the granary of the Confederacy—under the command of General David Hunter, winning a sharp engagement with a hastily assembled Confederate force at Lynchburg that included cadets from a local military academy. Hunter ordered the burning of the military academy over Crook's protests, then ordered a retreat when Confederate reinforcements arrived. Crook's cavalry covered the retreat—fighting a sharp battle to delay the Confederates, only to discover that the main column had squandered a half-day head start when some artillery pieces bogged down on a muddy road. The lead elements of the column abandoned the artillery in the middle of the road, and the second half of the force settled down to wait for someone to clear the road. Crook fought desperately to buy the escaping Federals more time. "This was one of the hardest nights I ever put in. I had no confidence in those in front. I was so worn out that it was only with the greatest exertions I could keep awake. The men were dodging out of ranks so that they could hide away and go to sleep. I stayed in the rear so as to look out for these things. I knew that the enemy's cavalry would be along early in the morning and gobble up stragglers. But even knowledge of that fact had no terrors for the poor, worn-out wretches. I had to be very cross and make myself exceedingly disagreeable, but that all failed to prevent many from falling out."[2] The Lynchburg campaign, from May 26 to June 30, proved an exhausting ordeal, although the Union forces suffered relatively few casualties. In this it resembled the wars of endurance with the Indians that lay in Crook's future more than the dreadful carnage of frontal assault played out elsewhere. Future president Rutherford B. Hayes, a colonel in the Twenty-ninth Ohio in Crook's command, in his diary noted: "While we suffered a great deal from want of food and sleep, we have lost a very few men, and are generally in the best of health. . . . General Crook has won the love and confidence of all. General Hunter is not so fortunate."[3]

The command rested for a time at Harpers Ferry before Crook's cavalry was dispatched to intercept the retreat of a Confederate force that had briefly threatened Washington. Crook was again dismayed by the failings of his commanders—at one point openly criticizing another general for lack of physical courage. In another instance, Crook's commanding general ordered him across the Shenandoah River to probe the enemy strength. Crook found the enemy in great numbers and sought permission to re-cross the river and rejoin the main Union force. Instead, he was ordered to remain and promised reinforcements. But as the strength of the enemy forces became clear, the reinforcements were withheld—leaving Crook to make it back across the river as best he could. Many of the units that had been recently added to Crook's command disintegrated and fled under the pressure. Crook lost 65 men killed, 301 wounded, and 56 missing by the time he made the crossing.[4] "I lost some valuable men here, murdered by incompetency or worse," Crook wrote, "while I suffered in the estimation of my men as having made a useless sacrifice."

Meanwhile, Grant had resumed his plunge into Virginia, determined not to turn back despite his heavy losses in the Wilderness. Grant grappled inconclusively with Lee again at Spotsylvania Court House, then forced Lee to turn and fight again at Cold Harbor, throwing his men at Lee's line in a brutal frontal assault which cost him 6,000 men in a single hour and forced him to reconsider his tactic of head-on assault. Grant had lost 55,000 men in a month of fighting, and feared that Lee would simply fall back to the strong defenses of Richmond. Grant therefore changed strategy, crossed the James River, and marched south toward Petersburg, the rail center south of Richmond. But a small Confederate force stood him off until Lee arrived, and Grant accepted the necessity of a protracted siege. Lee managed to slip away before the city fell in April 1865, foiling Grant's attempt to destroy his army. However, the ruinous attrition Grant had inflicted had fatally weakened Lee's forces.

In the meantime, on July 18, Crook had been promoted to brevet major general of volunteers and placed in command of the newly raised Army of West Virginia, commonly dubbed Crook's Corps. He was assigned to the Army of the Shenandoah under the command of General Sheridan. Once again, Crook's sense of righteous propriety and blunt candor spurred conflicts with other officers—and even with Sheridan. He could not stoop to the sort of military politics that so fascinated officers like George Armstrong Custer, who also made his reputation in the Civil War as a cavalry commander. Successful generals usually combined courage and battlefield tactics with adroit political maneuvering to ensure their accomplishments were recognized and promotions assured. Crook was never good at this political maneuver, believing with biting asperity that advancement in the army should flow from deeds— not politics. Throughout his career, his nature prevented any graceful surrender to the political realities of command.

Nonetheless, Crook continued to perform with distinction in the field. For instance, in one engagement he improvised on Sheridan's orders to lead his six-thousand-man force in a frontal attack on a Confederate position by sweeping around the flank of a whole Confederate division. The attack routed the Confederate force, and Crook swept up a thousand prisoners. However, other cavalry units came along behind Crook and gained credit for the capture. Crook protested to Sheridan, who promised to give Crook credit for both the capture and the flanking attack. However, Sheridan took credit himself for the maneuver—provoking a bitter complaint from Crook. Hayes observed in a letter to his uncle after the war: "At Fisher's Hill the turning of the rebel left was planned and executed by Crook against the opinions of the other Corps generals . . . General Sheridan is a whole-souled, brave man and believes in Crook, his old class and roommate at West Point. Intellectually he is not Crook's equal, so that, as I said, General Crook is the brains of the army."[5]

On another occasion, at Massanutten Mountain, Crook's command drove the Confederates out of strong positions. Crook drove his men to pursue the Confederates, although some lingered in the cover of trees, unwilling to move out into the open ground. Crook gathered up an armload of rocks, and began pelting the soldiers skulking in the underbrush—and "made it so uncomfortable for this rear that they tarried no longer." Crook's troops took up an advanced position, but didn't have enough men to picket the approaches. Sheridan promised to dispatch pickets to prevent a surprise attack; however, the pickets were never posted and a dawn Confederate attack took Crook by surprise and cost him most of his artillery. Sheridan arrived and helped Crook rally his troops for a counterattack on the smaller Confederate force, driving the enemy back. General Sheridan later took prominent credit for the success, while Crook nurtured his resentment for Sheridan's failure to send the promised pickets. Crook wrote in his diary on December 26, 1889, after visiting the battlefield: "It renders Gen. Sheridan's claims and his subsequent actions in allowing the general public to remain under the impressions regarding his part in these battles when he knew they were fiction all the more contemptible. The adulation heaped on him by a grateful nation for his supposed genius turned his head, which, added to his natural disposition, caused him to bloat his little carcass with debauchery and dissipation, which carried him off prematurely."

Crook returned to West Virginia with his command in 1864 to once again clear the country of bandits. It seemed a small duty after the massive battles in which he'd fought, but it was to produce one of the most remarkable and embarrassing incidents of Crook's career—his capture by Confederate guerrillas.

This posting also influenced the rest of Crook's life by introducing him to his future wife, a Southern girl he met during one of the rounds of social events the officers usually held when stationed in a place where such diversions were possible. A newspaper account years later claimed that she had met the rumpled, reticent general by nursing him back to health while he was recovering from a serious wound. But since he was wounded only once in the Civil War, and that several years earlier, the story seems more like the romantic invention of a reporter than fact. On the other hand, Crook might have been convalescing from some illness, or the aftereffects of one of the wounds he had already collected. He doesn't mention the subject in his autobiography. The newspaper account described Mary Daily as a "spirited southern girl, who refused to be gracious to the Yankee officer, although she liked him."

But the developing relationship between the general who specialized in killing Confederates and the woman who sympathized with the South might have played a still mysterious role in his subsequent capture by Confederate irregulars, one of whom was Mary Daily's brother. Bands of Confederate irregulars had been operating behind Union lines throughout the war, especially in the border states. These groups often acted more like outlaws than like soldiers, robbing and murdering more often than they inflicted militarily significant damage. Sheridan at one point decided to respond with irregulars of his own, and set up squads dressed in Confederate or civilian clothing who were supposed to hunt down the raiders. On the evening of February 19, 1864, a Confederate guerrilla band known as McNeill's Rangers crossed the Potomac River just upriver from Cumberland with seventy men. They knew that Crook stayed at the Revere Hotel in Cumberland, and they had conceived the daring plan of slipping into the Union-held town and capturing him. The raiders approached cavalry pickets at 2 A.M. several miles outside of Cumberland, dressed in Federal uniforms. They captured the pickets and forced them to reveal the password. They did the same to a second group of pickets they encountered at the outskirts of town. Crook, in his autobiography, suggests that the pickets were confused because Sheridan's bands of irregulars dressed in Confederate uniforms were operating in the area. However, another officer's account indicates the raiders were dressed in Union uniforms and simply overpowered the pickets.

The raiders then broke into several groups. One group cut the telegraph lines leading out of town. A second group headed for the house of another Union general, and six or eight headed to the Revere Hotel, where Crook was sleeping peacefully. They quietly captured the two soldiers on guard at the door, slipped down the hallway to Crook's room, and roused him. A Union officer sleeping across the hall heard the muffled sounds of the raiders leaving with their high-ranking prisoner, but the raiders had a good head start before he could determine that Crook was missing. Patrols set out in pursuit, but the raiders escaped with the two Union generals in tow.

The Confederates offered to exchange Crook for Confederate prisoners. Secretary of War Edwin Stanton initially opposed the exchange, angered by some typically blunt and impolitic remarks that Crook had made previously. But General Grant insisted on the exchange, unwilling to lose a hard-fighting general in his own mold.

Crook's return occasioned another embarrassment, which illustrated the confusion and jealousy that prevailed in the Union ranks and Crook's noteworthy lack of tact. During Crook's imprisonment, Lincoln had appointed General Winfield S. Hancock to Crook's position in command of the Army of West Virginia. When Crook returned, Grant directed him to resume his command. However, when Crook showed up and began issuing orders, the indignant Hancock ordered him arrested and confined. However, Crook was never actually arrested and Grant smoothed things out by giving Crook a new cavalry command in the Army of the Potomac. Lincoln sent Hancock a copy of the orders Grant had issued to Crook, saying that it had all been a mix-up.

The ironic postscript to the incident was that on August 21, 1865, Crook married Mary Daily, whose brother had assisted in his capture. They were to remain placidly married for the rest of Crook's life, although he scarcely mentions her in his autobiography. In fact, they spent most of their time apart, since he spent most of his career in rugged, frontier posts. They had no children, and she lived mostly at Crook Crest, a family estate in Oakland, Maryland—which he visited only occasionally.

Crook reported to the Army of the Potomac, only to find that General Sheridan had edged him out for the overall cavalry campaign. Instead, Crook received command of three brigades of cavalry. He also played a role in the closing campaign against Lee. Crook's cavalry units saw continuous action in that final Union pursuit of Lee's army. In one bloody cavalry battle at Dinwiddie Court House on March 31, 1865, Crook lost a third of his effective force in a single engagement. Crook's units clashed again with Lee at Petersburg, Sayler's Creek, Farmville, and finally Appomattox. Crook noted that many of his men were now mounted on mules, and recalled one engagement during which the number of riderless mules returning to his lines convinced him his men had been devastated. To his relief, he discovered that most of them had simply jumped off the backs of their mounts when the headstrong mules took off running straight toward the enemy lines and refused to stop. One rider remained on his mule, which jumped the Confederate breastwork with his astonished rider still upright. The resourceful man immediately demanded the surrender of the Confederates, and took advantage of their astonishment to spur the mule on and escape through the middle of the Confederate position.

At Appomattox, Crook also had an encounter with a man who would cast a dark shadow across his career in the years to come—George Armstrong Custer. Both Crook's and Custer's commands closed with a Confederate position. Custer moved his division sharply forward to attack, sending three hundred cavalrymen charging at the position with swords drawn and the band playing. Solid frontal fire from the Confederates quickly broke up the charge. Scouting the weak points in the Confederate position, Crook sent a detachment to the Confederate rear. This forced the forty defenders to hoist a white flag. Custer then charged forward and accepted the surrender. "Custer's division rushed up the hill and turned in more prisoners and battle flags than any of the cavalry, and probably had less to do with the surrender," observed Crook.

Crook was in for Lee's final surrender as well. His cavalry units had been clinging to the flanks and rear of Lee's retreating forces, fighting one sharp engagement after another—hoping to slow Lee enough for the Union infantry to catch up. Once the infantry arrived, Lee surrendered to the inevitable.

Crook's view of that terrible conflict remained stolid, seemingly unemotional, and tinged with bitterness. He had commanded troops throughout the conflict, performing efficiently, sometimes brilliantly, and always courageously under fire. But the politics, chaos, needless carnage, and stupidity that swirled throughout the conflict had increasingly embittered him. He clung to his fierce code of personal conduct and fumed when generals who swore, drank, and preened rose to greater prominence and responsibility than he because of their superior political skills. He seemed better suited to the frontier, far from the reach of the meddlesome placeholders and uniformed politicians who actually ran the army. When the war ended, the army collapsed in size to about twenty-five thousand. Generals who had taken leave from the regular army and acquired lofty volunteer ranks scrambled to land a much lower rank in the regular army. Crook mustered out on January 22, 1866, and received an appointment as lieutenant colonel of the Twenty-third Regiment of Infantry in July of 1866. He noted with some bitterness that two of his subordinate officers received higher ranks in their return to the regulars.

"I regret to say that I learned too late that it was not what a person did, but it was what he got credit of doing that gave him a reputation and at the close of the war gave him position," Crook concluded in his autobiography.[6]

ALTHOUGH LESSER COMMANDERS retained higher rank after the war than Crook, the army still had need for his services—especially since the army returned almost immediately to Crook's strongest suit—killing Indians. Crook joined his new regiment on December 11, 1866, relieved to be back on the frontier—but appalled at the conditions. The army had largely abandoned the West during the Civil War. In almost every area, Indians reclaimed control of areas from which they'd been driven. Moreover, the territories soon filled up with deserters, former rebels, outlaws, and opportunists seeking to take advantage of the chaos. The officers and men who had been left on post in the West were often among the dregs of the army. Crook noted on his arrival that "the feeling against many of the officers was very bitter. They were accused of all manner of things. There was much dissipation amongst a good many officers, and there seemed to be a general apathy amongst them and indifference to the proper discharge of duty." Goaded by the lawlessness and the indifference of the army, a band of vigilantes formed in Boise, Idaho, and promptly hung sixty suspected outlaws. Remarkably enough, the legislature itself proved so unruly that at one point the governor called in troops to "keep them in bounds."

Crook spent the next two years restoring order and pursuing the Paiute Indian bands that had taken to raiding settlements and stealing cattle. He also indulged his passion for hunting, with sometimes dangerous results. On one pursuit of raiding Indians he came across bighorn sheep tracks. Sending his horse back with the soldiers, he scaled a one-thousand-foot bluff following the sheep sign. Abruptly, a dense fog set in, followed by rain and freezing sleet. Groping back toward camp, he tumbled down a twenty-foot embankment. After taking shelter at the base of the bluff, Crook was nearly buried in a cave-in. Caught without matches, fire, or anything to burn, he wandered through the storm, trying to keep from freezing. He finally sat down on a sagebrush and thrust his hands into his shirt to keep his fingers from freezing, and waited philosophically for the storm to abate. The sleet stopped at about 3 A.M., and in the light of the rising moon he could look down on the camp—his wilderness instincts having guided him aright.

The campaign consisted of the familiar pattern of exhausting expeditions climaxed by surprise attacks on Indian rancheros during which the soldiers killed as many as possible before the Indians could escape into the underbrush. The fighting contrasted sharply with the wholesale death that dominated the Civil War battles. But Crook returned to Indian fighting still convinced that he was doing the work of civilization, a representative of the morally and materially superior culture. He viewed the Indians as human beings, but as savages doomed to either extinction or assimilation. He continued to display the self-possession, determination, and fair-minded ruthlessness that had always distinguished his attitudes toward warfare. On one occasion when his detachment launched a surprise attack on an Indian ranchero, Crook's horse bolted straight toward the Indian camp, running so far ahead of Crook's men that he soon found bullets whistling past him from both the front and the rear. Abandoning his efforts to control the terrified horse, he jumped off and ran back toward his own men. "I found some of the Indians coming toward me. Particularly one fellow, stopped, surrounded by soldiers, singing his death song, and letting slip his arrows at his enemies. He must have been shot through and through half a dozen times before he fell." In that battle, only two warriors escaped. Crook's men killed sixty Indians and captured twenty-seven, with the loss of only one soldier. In another engagement, Crook's men attacked Indians hidden in a collapsed crater in a lava field. The battle pitted sixty-nine soldiers plus fifteen Indian scouts against about a hundred Paiute and Pit River Indians. The soldiers lost seven killed and ten wounded in assaulting the crater, only to discover that the Indians had withdrawn into a virtually unattackable network of caves and collapsed lava tubes under the crater. The soldiers spent the day dodging sniper fire from the invisible Indians, who shot upward out of the caves at any soldier that showed himself against the sky. Lacking dynamite, the soldiers could do little against them and the Paiutes slipped away in the darkness, taking their wounded and dead with them.

After breaking the resistance of the Paiutes and convincing the survivors to return to reservations, Crook was shifted for a time to San Francisco, where he was put on a board charged with determining which men should be retained as the army continued the rapid reduction in its ranks.

He was then offered command of the Department of Arizona, where the postwar rush of settlers found that the Apache Indians had made large areas of the territory virtually uninhabitable during the war. Crook refused the command. Arizona had a dreadful reputation and a terrible climate. Besides, Crook said he was "tired" of Indian work, although his most arduous service in the seemingly interminable Indian wars lay yet ahead of him. Moreover, he knew that several officers of higher rank should have been considered first for the position—one of the most prominent and active military commands in the country. Arizona governor A. P. K. Safford, on a visit to San Francisco, interviewed Crook and again pressed him to take the job. Once again, Crook declined. Nonetheless, Safford devoted his considerable political skills to winning Crook's appointment, although both the secretary of war and William T. Sherman, who was now general in chief, opposed the appointment on the grounds that Crook was only a lieutenant colonel, and should not be preferred over higher-ranking officers. In the end, Safford won Crook's attachment to "temporary" duty in Arizona in June of 1871. Crook complied without enthusiasm, knowing the difficulty of the task ahead, and the resentments his appointment would inspire among the superior officers he'd leap-frogged for the command.

He could not know then that he was about to face the great enemy of his life, and that his service in this bloody, confusing, morally wrenching drive to destroy an ancient warrior culture would dominate the rest of his life and determine his place in history.

7

—————————————— **1861–1871**

Geronimo

THE AMERICANS RETURN

FOR A TIME after Cochise began his war on the whites, things had gone very well for The People. They killed anyone they found in their land, so that the whites would understand what it was to make enemies of The People. At first, the soldiers came out after them. But they moved slowly, and could not find a trail, and the warriors simply faded away from in front of them. Sometimes they would attack when they had all the advantage. Sometimes a man to show his courage would creep into the soldier camp at night and come away with some horses. But mostly the warriors went where the soldiers were not, and drove the whites out of their land.

Soon the soldiers grew discouraged. They gathered up their things, and rode out of their forts—abandoning the struggle. The warriors all rejoiced. The People held victory dances and decided that the white soldiers were not so strong as they thought. The White Eyes had given up even easier than the Mexicans, although they had better guns and more of everything.

But after a time, the far-ranging scouts Cochise sent out to watch the trails of the White Eyes reported many soldiers coming along from the west. So Cochise sent for Mangas Coloradas, and they gathered the largest force of warriors that anyone had seen in many long seasons of raiding—more even than had gone down to Arispe in the battle of Geronimo's naming. Cochise and Mangas

Coloradas lay their plans carefully, knowing that the soldiers would come on slowly with many thirsty horses. One group of soldiers had gone several days' march ahead of the main force, so Cochise planned to kill these men first. He hid his warriors on the rocky slopes above the water hole in Apache Pass, knowing the soldiers would come to that place careless and eager after a long day without water. Cochise resolved to fight the soldiers near the place where the White Eyes had started the war in the first place, by taking him prisoner under a flag of truce. The warriors built breastworks of stone on the slope above the water, and waited there for the enemy—hoping the soldiers would be easy to kill.[1]

But some of the young warriors who tried to take mules from the pack train spoiled the ambush, and the warriors on the hillside only hit a few of the soldiers before the White Eyes fell back under good cover. Then the soldiers brought up something new. They had wagons, which had long black tubes on them. They turned these wagons around, and fired them at the warriors hidden on the hillside. The wagons made great explosions, which broke apart even the rocks, and made a terrible noise. The warriors took it as long as they could, but at last Cochise and Mangas Coloradas saw they could do nothing against the wagons and so called the warriors to retreat to where the guns could not hit them.

But worse awaited them, just ahead. Mangas Coloradas saw some soldiers ride away, out of the canyon. They were running back to warn the others, and to bring on so many more soldiers that the warriors would have no hope at all. So Mangas Coloradas took several warriors and chased after those soldiers, shooting from horseback until he brought down one of their horses. The warriors then circled around the soldier who took cover behind the body of his horse, riding to draw his fire so he would run out of ammunition. But the soldier had a new kind of gun that could shoot a long time without reloading, and as the warriors pressed closer the soldier shot Mangas Coloradas in the chest, knocking him from his horse.

The war leaders knew they had been beaten. They could not fight a large group of soldiers, with their wagons that shot fire, and their long-shooting rifles that did not need reloading. They took Mangas Coloradas to one of the healers in Mexico—warning the Mexican healer that they would destroy his village if he did not save the chief. Mangas Coloradas lived, but he was not the same afterward. He said the warriors could not defeat the soldiers, even if they were all gathered together.[2] Soon the country was filling up with soldiers. They built a fort near the water in Apache Pass. And they began hunting down The People everywhere, especially the Mescaleros, and the Mimbreno, and the others who did not live in easily defended places like the Dragoons, and the Sierra Madre.[3]

Mangas Coloradas brooded for months after he recovered from his wound, trying to find some solution to the riddle of the White Eyes. The more he thought about it, the more he saw that The People would all be destroyed if they were caught between the Mexicans and the Americans. Geronimo watched him carefully, seeing that the wound had weakened him. The matter seemed much simpler to Geronimo. They could not trust the White Eyes, any more than they could trust the Mexicans. The White Eyes had no honor. They had no Spirit. They held nothing sacred. They were like mud people, made to look like human beings but with nothing inside. Only greed. They wanted gold, and horses, and cattle, and everything that belonged to anyone else. That was the only thing on which you could depend. The People had no true choice. They could give in to the White Eyes, and live where they were told, and eat the scraps the White Eyes left for them, and give up everything that Child of Waters had set for them—everything that made them men. Or they could go on fighting. Certainly, they could be clever and make peace when it favored them, or use the White Eyes against the Mexicans. They could refrain from raiding near home, so that they would not stir up the White Eyes. But they must still, in the end, fight. What choice had they? Were they not warriors? Every man dies. It is only the manner of dying that varies.

Then Mangas Coloradas called together the leaders, including Geronimo and Victorio and Loco and the others, and said he had heard the White Eyes around Pinos Altos wanted to make peace. Geronimo warned him not to put himself in the hands of the

White Eyes. They could not be trusted. So also said Victorio, who along with old Nana had become the leading man among the Chihenne. Victorio was a tall, intent, quiet man with eyes that could pierce you like an awl, and a graceful, beautiful face edged by hard lines, and the resolution of stone. He had great Power in war, and could lead a war party through a thicket of enemies without harm. He fought often with his sister, Lozen, who was small, quiet, and proud—tough and supple as leather. She had a great Power to see the enemy, and so could keep a war party safe from harm. Even Loco agreed that in seeking peace Mangas Coloradas should not put himself in the hands of his enemies. Loco was a tough old warrior, who had once killed a grizzly bear with his knife, bearing the scars on his face, and a drooping blinded eye, as proof of that encounter, and of his Power. He had earned his name one day when he ran through a fury of bullets to bring a wounded warrior safely away, and the Mexicans had all cried out in surprise and admiration that he was a "Loco Apache."

But Mangas Coloradas would not listen. He had the idea of peace with the Whites Eyes now stuck in his head, like a dream of foretelling recalled upon wakening. The People divided, about half wanting to go with Mangas Coloradas to make peace with the White Eyes, who had promised to give them rations so long as they lived peacefully on the land left to them. Mangas Coloradas seemed so happy in the going, saying that he had found White Eyes who would be kind to The People. But the rest resolved to wait and see whether they could trust the White Eyes. The ones who stayed back nonetheless gave Mangas Coloradas's group most of their good guns. Of course, Geronimo was right. The White Eyes seized Mangas Coloradas and turned him over to the soldiers, who taunted him and tormented him. They heated their bayonets in the fire and stuck the heated blades into Mangas Coloradas's feet until he rose up, and said that he was not a child, that they should not play with him. So they killed him. Then they cut off his head, and boiled it in a great pot, so that Mangas Coloradas must go forever through The Happy Place without his head, because he had been foolish enough to trust the White Eyes. The soldiers went to where Mangas Coloradas's family was waiting for him, and killed every one they could catch. The soldiers decorated their bridles with the scalps of Mangas Coloradas's wife and children, and wore the buckskins that they stripped from the dead bodies.[4]

The Mimbreno, who had been once so powerful, divided then. Many followed Loco, who was gruff, and hard, and brave—but anxious to find some accommodation so The People could survive. Many others followed Victorio and his sister Lozen and Nana, who resolved that they should live in Ojo Caliente as peacefully as possible. A few others followed Geronimo, mostly the remains of the Bedonkohe.[5]

Geronimo led his group into the mountains around Apache Pass, where they had fought the great battle with the soldiers that had changed everything. They hid in the mountains for a time, expecting an attack at any moment. But they had no supplies, and only a few weapons. So they killed four cowboys who were tending a herd of cattle, but before they could even butcher the cattle, soldiers came out from the fort to chase them. The soldiers came on them quickly in the morning, and it seemed that they must surely all be killed or captured. But Geronimo ran in among the soldiers, shooting and dodging, until he had thrown his spear, and used up his few arrows. The warriors then retreated to some rocks and fought the soldiers all day—using clubs and stones in the end to hold the soldiers off. This gave the women and the children time to scatter and head for the rendezvous point some fifty miles away. When night came, the warriors slipped away. The soldiers killed only one warrior, but captured six of the women and children.

So Geronimo moved about constantly, forever at war. He seemed the very spirit of war, moving from band to band, constantly seeking warriors who would go with him on raids—down into Mexico if possible, where he could kill Mexicans. He took his small band sometimes to live with Victorio and Loco and their people, who remained near Warm Springs, hoping the White Eyes would let them live in peace there.[6] More often he stayed with Cochise and his people, who continued to fight the White Eyes, although the warriors of Cochise seemed like the leaves clinging to the branches in the season of Earth is Reddish Brown.[7] Both family obligations and the chance to make war against the White Eyes bound Geronimo to Cochise, who remained the rock of The People's hope. Cochise killed any White Eyes he found in his territory, but he could not keep the soldiers from returning and setting up their forts—one in Apache Pass and one in Tucson. After that, the soldiers came quickly whenever a raiding party struck. Of course, this meant the warriors must kill anyone who saw them, so no one would run back to the soldiers and bring pursuit. But Cochise had also made friends with one White Eye, Thomas Jeffords. Cochise admired the courage of this man, and trusted his word. The People despised a liar. Any warrior who lied could not carry messages, could not speak before council, could not bear witness in any dispute, and must endure the scorn of the other warriors. But the Mexicans lied all the time, and so did the White Eyes.[8]

Geronimo also sometimes raided with Juh, the friend of his youth and his brother-in-law. Juh now led the Nednai, the most wild of all The People, who lived in the spectacular jumble of the Sierra Madre. Many warriors who had been cast out of other tribes made their way to the Sierra Madre, and joined with Juh's Nednai. Sometimes Juh would come with a band of warriors up to visit his friends and kinsmen living with Cochise. One time he left Ishton, who was pregnant, with Geronimo—so that Juh could go back down into Mexico and get more horses and cattle.

When her time came, she had trouble. So Geronimo hurried to her side, because he had already gained a reputation as a healer. Usually, he used his Power on war injuries. He could dig a bullet out with a knife, and then conduct prayers, and ceremonies, so that the warrior would survive. He also had Coyote Power, and his first ceremony showed him that Ishton had stepped on a coyote track, and that was why she was having trouble.[9] He began the ceremony on the evening of the first day, sitting with Ishton on the west side of the fire, facing east, while others sat in a circle in the back of the shelter—leaving the space to the east open. Geronimo took out of a basket an eagle feather, and an abalone shell, and a bag of pollen carefully wrapped up in a bundle. He rolled a cigarette, and puffed to the directions, first to the east. Then he threw the cigarette away, and rubbed Ishton with pollen, praying to the four directions as he did this. She lay in great pain, but made no outcry. Then Geronimo started to sing many different songs about Coyote. As he sang, he beat on a drum with a curved stick. Geronimo's songs explained that Coyote was a tricky fellow, hard to see and find. He had given these characteristics to Geronimo so that he could make himself invisible, and even turn into a doorway. At the end of each song, Geronimo called, sounding exactly like a Coyote. He sang until the evening star had risen halfway between the horizon and the zenith. This he did for four nights, each night just the same.[10] On the fifth day, just at sunrise, as he lifted up his eyes to the east, he heard the voice that had spoken to him before, when he had waited in his despair alongside Alope's body. Now his Power said to him, The child will be born and your sister will live; and you will never be killed with weapons, but live to an old age.[11]

And it was just as the voice said. The child was born, and they named him Daklugie, which means "Forces His Way Through."

So Geronimo knew his Power stood behind him, and that he was not just a warrior. Such Power is given for the protection of The People, and not for one man. And he also knew he was right to fight the Mexicans, and the White Eyes, and all of the enemies of The People, and that no one of his enemies could ever kill him. This imposed on him a responsibility. Geronimo must lead in war, knowing that he could not be killed, so that others might use his courage as the strong poles that support the wickiup. He did not know then what price Power might demand.

And he did not know that everything was about to change and that he was soon to encounter the great enemy of his life.

Part Four

1871–1883

A Fight to the Death

8

Crook

The Coming of the Fox

CROOK TOOK CHARGE with his customary energy and efficiency upon his arrival in Arizona in the sweltering summer of 1871. He had already decided that he could not hope to run down the Apache using only soldiers. His long experience on the frontier had demonstrated that he needed gifted trackers with a deep knowledge of the country. Governor Safford recommended that Crook enlist Mexican trackers, so Crook promptly hired fifty Mexican scouts on his arrival in Tucson and set out for Fort Bowie, located in Apache Pass, where Cochise and Mangas Coloradas had made their futile attack on the Union soldiers nearly a decade before.

Crook discovered that mismanagement and the near-absence of the army for the past five years had aroused Indian bands against the whites all across the territory. Cochise had waged his bitter, decade-long war against the whites with dogged ruthlessness—driving settlers out of most of southwest Arizona. Tucson remained a stronghold, as did scattered mining towns like Tombstone. But the Apache held sway over a huge area, striking seemingly at will and then disappearing into their mountain retreats. Meanwhile, the Tonto Apache and the Yavapai were waging war on the settlements at Prescott, the Verde Valley, and the wild, mountainous Tonto Basin. Like the Chiricahua, the Tonto Apache had initially greeted the whites with wary acceptance, but resisted when whites seized the best land, drove off the game, and murdered many Indians. The White Mountain Apache, settled on a reservation that included most of their original home territory around Fort Apache, had remained relatively quiet.

Two incidents shortly before Crook's arrival had brought the war with the Apache to national attention. One was the death of Lieutenant Howard Bass Cushing, a well-known Civil War hero and Indian fighter who had dedicated himself to tracking down and killing Cochise—only to be ambushed and killed himself by Juh in a canyon near Tucson.

The second issue that captured the nation's attention was the massacre of some 150 Apache women and children nominally under army protection near Camp Grant. The incident embodied one of the most tragic and poignant incidents in the long, bloody conflict. The post was commanded by Lieutenant Royal Whitman, an abolitionist New Englander with a stern conscience who was inclined to view the Apache as human beings. The Aravaipa Apache, under their renowned war chief Eskiminzin, had been hunted and harassed to the brink of starvation. When Whitman received several old women of the band with kindness and courtesy, the entire band soon surrendered to him and pleaded for permission to settle near Aravaipa Canyon. Whitman allowed them to camp near the post, and began a frustrating effort to create a reservation for Eskiminzin's band. But as he waited, Tucson settlers blamed some of Eskiminzin's band for several raids and murders near Tucson. The Tucson vigilantes raised a mixed force of whites, Tohono O'odham Indians, and Mexicans. They attacked Eskiminzin's camp at dawn on a day when most of the warriors were off hunting. The attackers hacked and clubbed to death between 86 and 150 people, mostly women and children. They took many of the younger children back to Tucson. The horrified Whitman raced to the scene of the massacre, too late to do anything but bury the dead and tend the survivors. When Eskiminzin and the warriors returned, Whitman managed to convince them not to retaliate for the massacre. The incident engendered national sympathy for the Apache, particularly among former abolitionists. Whitman pushed for a trial of the men who had led the slaughter, but a Tucson jury promptly acquitted the vigilantes and extended its thanks for the massacre. Whitman's principled stand on behalf of the Indians earned him the hatred of many settlers, who were convinced that only extermination would solve the Apache problem. Whitman was subjected to a series of courts-martial on apparently trumped-up charges, including drinking and behavior unbecoming in an officer. As Crook's frontier experience had demonstrated, even if true, such behavior rarely resulted in courts-martial.

Crook set out quickly from Tucson with his Mexican guides and five companies of cavalry, but saw few Indians. He attempted to set a trap for one band of warriors at a spring, but the Indians spotted the soldiers and escaped. Crook's command attacked one Apache camp on a mountain peak, but the Indians simply melted away, scrambling down a cliff face and escaping safely. Upon reaching Fort Apache in the White Mountains, Crook fired the Mexican scouts. He turned then to the peaceful White Mountain Apaches, determined to use Indian scouts whenever possible. The use of Apache scouts would prove the keystone to his success—and the goad to years of scathing criticism in the territorial press.

At Fort Apache Crook also encountered the eloquent, insightful, courageous Captain John G. Bourke, who was to become Crook's aide all through the Apache and Sioux conflicts as well as Crook's most effective advocate against the judgment of history. Bourke, who won the Congressional Medal of Honor as a private in the Civil War by taking charge of his detachment in the midst of a bloody charge after all the officers were killed, kept an absorbing and voluminous diary throughout his service in the West. Trim, athletic, with a bushy mustache and a charming manner, Bourke was a gifted storyteller and a decent, conscientious, compassionate officer. Repeatedly in his career he displayed stirring physical courage, a ready wit, and a deep concern for both his men and the Indians they hunted to extinction. He exemplified the best of the officer corps—an educated, intellectual, fair-minded man devoted to his duty and his men. He learned to speak several native languages, and wrote several well-regarded anthropological works on the Apache and the Sioux. He also wrote numerous magazine articles and books that became priceless, primary sources for generations of historians. He became an articulate and outspoken admirer of Crook, and a scathing critic of Washington's policy toward the Indians. More than any other single person, Bourke set the pattern for how Crook and the Apache wars have been viewed.

Bourke also served as a tenacious defender of Crook's controversial decision to rely heavily on Apache scouts. Bourke noted that the Apache had perfected the tactic of hit-and-run warfare, striking only when they had all the advantages, and vanishing whenever troops were concentrated against them. So the pursuit would "degenerate into a will-o'-the-wisp chase. The Apache could find food on every hillside, and the water holes, springs, and flowing streams far up on in the mountains were perfectly well known to them . . . Caucasian troops, of whatever nationality, would wander about, half crazed with thirst, and maddened by the heat of the day or chilled by the cold winds of night in the mountains, and unable to tell which plants were of value as food." Bourke appreciated the warrior's strategy and rules for warfare. "The Apache was in no sense a coward. He knew his business and played his cards to suit himself. He never lost a shot, and never lost a warrior in a fight where a brisk run across the nearest ridge would save his life and exhaust the heavily clad soldiers who endeavored to catch him. . . . They knew how to disguise themselves so thoroughly that one might almost step upon a warrior thus occupied before he could detect his presence. Stripped naked, with head and shoulders wrapped up in a bundle of yucca shoots or sacaton grass, and with body rubbed over with the clay or sand along which it wriggled as sinuously and as venomously as the rattler itself, the Apache would and did approach to within ear-shot of the whites, and even entered the enclosures of the military camps as at Grand and Crittenden, where we on several occasions discovered his foot-prints alongside the water jars."[1]

Bourke viewed Crook as the perfect opponent for the Apache. "All the baggage he had would not make as much compass as a Remington typewriter. The only thing with him which would in any sense be classed as superfluous was a shotgun, but without this or a rifle he never traveled anywhere. He came, as I say, without the slightest pomp or parade. His whole idea of life was to do each duty well, and to let his work speak for itself. . . . From each officer he soon extracted all he knew about the country, the lines of travel, the trails across the various mountains, the fords where they were required for the streams, the nature of the soil, especially its products such as grasses, character of the climate, the condition of the pack mules, and all pertaining to them, and every other item of interest a commander could possibly want to have determined. But in reply not one word, not one glance, not one hint, as to what he was going to do or what he would like to do."

Before Bourke's admiring gaze, Crook's gruff distance seemed a positive virtue. "This was the point in Crook's character which made the strongest impression upon everyone coming in contact with him—his ability to learn all that his informant had to supply, without yielding in return the slightest suggestion of his own purposes. He refused himself to no one, no matter how humble, but was possessed of a certain dignity which repressed any approach to undue familiarity. He was singularly averse to the least semblance of notoriety, and was as retiring as a girl. He never consulted with any one; made his own plans after the most studious deliberation, and kept them to himself with a taciturnity which at times must have been exasperating to his subordinates. Although taciturn, reticent, and secretive, moroseness formed no part of his nature, which was genial and sunny. He took delight in conversation, especially wherein he did not have to join if indisposed."

Bourke noted that Crook dispensed with military formalities and led by personal example.

No officer could claim that he was ever ordered to do a duty when the Department Commander was present which the latter would not in person lead. No officer of the same rank, at least in our service, issued so few orders. According to his creed, officers did not need to be devilled with orders and instructions and memoranda; all they required was to obtain insight into what was desired of them, and there was no better way to inculcate this than by personal example. Therefore, whenever there was a trouble of any magnitude under Crook's jurisdiction, he started at once to the point nearest the skirmish line, and stayed there so long as the danger existed; but he did it all so quietly, and with so little parade, that half the time no one would suspect that there was any hostility threatened until after the whole matter had blown over or been stamped out, and the General back at his headquarters. . . . In personal appearance General Crook was manly and strong; he was a little over six feet in height, straight as a lance, broad and square-shouldered, full-chested, and with an elasticity and sineweness of limb which betrayed the latent muscular power gained by years of constant exercise in the hills and mountains of the remoter West.[2]

Bourke noted that Crook often struck out from the column, following tracks, or hunting.

He used to take great, and, in my opinion, reprehensible risks in his encounters with grizzlies and brown bears, many of whose pelts decorated his quarters. His sense became highly educated; his keen, blue-grey eyes would detect in a second and at a wonderful distance the slightest movement across the horizon; the slightest sound aroused his curiosity, the faintest odor awakened his suspicions . . . There never was an officer in our military service so completely in accord with all the ideas, views, and opinions of the savage whom he had to fight or control as was General Crook. In time of campaign this knowledge placed him, as it were, in the secret councils of the enemy; in time of peace it enabled him all the more completely to appreciate the doubts and misgivings of the Indians at the outset of a new life, and to devise plans by which they could all the more readily be brought to see civilization as something which they all could embrace without danger of extinction.

And yet, Bourke also felt the need to insist that Crook remained a civilized man, and therefore morally entitled to wage a ruthless war of extermination against the Indians. "Crook never ceased to be a gentleman. Much as he might live among savages, he never lost the right to claim for himself the best that civilization and enlightenment had to bestow."[3]

Crook found the White Mountain Apache willing to scout against other Apache bands. At this distance in time, perhaps the readiness of the Apache to serve the army against fellow Apache seems strange. But most warriors identified only with their band, and the links between even different bands of the same group were weak. Different groups like the White Mountain and the

Chiricahua often clashed before the whites arrived and were often enmeshed in long-running blood feuds. Moreover, most Apache wanted to live peacefully and fully understood the army's overwhelming advantage in numbers and armament. Many disagreed vehemently with the warriors who continued to fight and blamed them for the death and devastation inflicted on the whole band. The warriors who did enlist as scouts generally fought alongside relatives and clan members and under the leadership of their own chiefs. For men settled on the reservation, scouting for the army provided one way to pursue the traditional, high-status trade of a warrior.

But Crook's motivations for employing scouts—from a closely related band if possible—went deeper than their abilities as trackers, fighters, and experts on the terrain. Crook knew the failure of scattered bands to see their common interests, the lack of central leadership or authority, and the deep existing divisions all crippled the Apache in their struggle against the army. He attempted to exploit and deepen those divisions whenever possible.

As Crook later explained to Charles Lummis, a reporter for the *Los Angeles Times*, "To polish a diamond there is nothing like its own dust . . . It's the same with these fellows. Nothing breaks them up like turning their own people against them. They don't fear the white soldiers, whom they easily surpass in the peculiar style of warfare which they force on us, but put upon their trail an enemy of their own blood, an enemy as tireless, as foxy, and as stealthy and familiar with the country as themselves, and it breaks them all up." More important, the use of scouts turned one band against another. "It is not merely a question of catching them better with Indians, but of a broader and more enduring aim—their disintegration. I first began using them (Apache scouts) in 1872, and have used them ever since. Nothing has ever been accomplished without their help. Have they acted in good faith? We have every assurance that they have. They followed the hostiles' trails like bloodhounds. No one else can follow a trail as they can, and no one else can stand so much fatigue. My scouts will start at the bottom of a steep mountain, fifteen hundred feet high, and go up on a trot clear to the top without stopping. There isn't a white man alive who could run fifty yards up the same pitch without stopping to catch his wind. I have been climbing the mountains of Colorado, New Mexico and Arizona for the last seven years, but I can't keep sight of these fellows once they start."[4]

Crook met quietly with the leaders of the White Mountain Apache, listening attentively, responding directly, and insisting that an officer write down everything. "He told the circle of listening Indians that he had not come to make war but to avoid it if possible," wrote Bourke. "Peace was the best condition in which to live, and he hoped those around him would see that peace was not only preferable, but essential. The white people were crowding in all over the Western country, and soon it would be impossible for any one to live upon game; it would be driven away or killed off. Far better for every one to make up his mind to plant and raise horses, cows, and sheep, and make his living in that way; his animals would thrive and increase while he slept." Crook also took care to turn the peacefully inclined warriors against those who remained resistant.

> So long as the Apache behaved himself he should receive the fullest protection from the troops, and no white man would be allowed to do him harm; but so long as any fragment of the tribe kept out on the war-path, it would be impossible to afford all the protection to the well disposed that they were entitled to receive, as bad men could say that it was not easy to discriminate between those who were good and those who were bad. He had no desire to punish any man or woman for any acts of the past. He would blot them all out and begin over again. It was no use to try to explain how the war with the whites had begun. All that he cared to say was that it must end, and end at once. If every one came in without necessitating a resort to bloodshed he should be very glad; but if any refused, then he should expect the good men to aid him in running down the bad ones. That was the way white people did. He hoped the Apaches would see that it was their duties to do the same.[5]

After enrolling a detachment of White Mountain Apache scouts, Crook set off again for Fort Whipple, near Prescott. The soldiers moved along the Mogollon Rim, a great uplift that separates the forested north from the low deserts to the south. Throughout the journey, which eventually stretched to seven hundred miles, Crook made a close study of the pack mules and the conditions. He knew only exquisitely organized and equipped pack trains could enable soldiers and scouts to remain in the field long enough to wear down the hostiles. "We learned to know a great deal about packers, pack-mules and packing," noted Bourke, "which to my great surprise I found to be a science and such a science as a great soldier as General Crook had not thought it beneath his genius to study it . . . and make them as nearly perfect as they have ever been or can be in our army's history."[6] In fact, Crook paid such attention to the selection and training of the mules, their saddles, their care, and the character and training of the packers that his mules, with their custom-fitted packsaddles, could carry 320 pounds each, compared to the army standard of 175 pounds.

One afternoon as Crook and Bourke rode in the lead, several arrows whistled suddenly past their heads, burying themselves so deeply in a tree just behind them that the soldiers later could not pull them out. Looking about, the officers saw about fifteen Tonto Apache warriors leaving at a dead run. The soldiers spurred their horses, and managed to cut off two of the warriors, forcing them to take shelter behind several boulders. "There they stood; almost entirely concealed behind great boulders on the very edge of the precipice, their bows drawn to a semi-circle, eyes gleaming with a snaky black fire, long unkempt hair flowing down over their shoulders, bodies almost completely naked, faces streaked with the juice of the baked mescal and the blood of the deer or antelope—a most repulsive picture and yet one in which there was not the slightest suggestion of cowardice," Bourke wrote. "They seemed to know their doom, but not to fear it in the slightest degree." Seeing the soldiers closing on them, the warriors

fired their arrows more in bravado than in hopes of inflicting injury, as our men were all well covered by the trees, and then over the precipice they went, as we supposed, to certain death and destruction. We were all so horrified at the sight, that for a moment or more it did not occur to anyone to look over the crest, but when we did it

was seen that the two savages were rapidly following down the mer-
est thread of a trail outlined in the vertical face of the basalt, and
jumping from rock to rock like mountain sheep. General Crook
drew bead, aimed quickly and fired; the arm of one of the fugitives
hung limp by his side, and the red stream gushing out showed that
he had been badly hurt; but he did not relax his speed a particle,
but kept with his comrade in a headlong dash down the precipice
and escaped into the scrub-oak on the lower flanks although the
evening air resounded with the noise of carbines reverberating from
peak to peak. It was so hard to believe that any human beings could
escape down such a terrible place and for that reason no one could
do his best shooting.[7]

Crook's composure, endurance, and knowledge on that exhausting march impressed Bourke. "He was the most untiring and
indefatigable man I ever met. No matter what happened in the
camp, or on the march, he knew it; he was always awake and on
his feet the moment the cook of the pack train was aroused to prepare the morning meal, which was frequently as early as two
o'clock, and remained on his feet during the remainder of the day.
I am unable to explain exactly how he did it, but he knew the
name of every plant, animal, and mineral passed near the trail, as
well as the uses to which the natives put them, each and all; like-
wise the habits of the birds, reptiles, and animals, and the course
and general character of all the streams, little or big. The Indians
evinced an awe for him the first moment of their meeting; they
did not seem to understand how it was that a white man could so
quickly absorb all that they had to teach."

After assorted hardships, but only a few inconclusive brushes
with the Indians, Crook arrived at Fort Whipple, where the indignant citizens presented him with a list of four hundred settlers
and prospectors killed by the Indians in the past several years.
Crook found another unwelcome dispatch awaiting for him there
as well—notice that his old commander, now President Ulysses S.
Grant, had dispatched a peace commissioner, Vincent Colyer, to
try to settle the Indians on reservations that Colyer had broad
authority to create. News of the Camp Grant massacre had stirred
national interest in the plight of the Apache, and key religious

under arrest, awaiting trial." Collusion with the Tucson Ring was one of Crook's favorite charges, but no factual basis for that charge against Whitman exists in the historical record. In fact, Whitman struggled to settle the Apaches peacefully on a reservation, which was seemingly counter to the interests of the Tucson Ring, the very existence of which as an organized conspiracy some historians have since questioned. Crook arrived on the post and was immediately offended to see General Howard and Whitman strolling up and down the parade ground engaged in animated and friendly conversation. Crook took this as evidence that Howard was taking Whitman's side, and working to turn his own officers against him. However, Howard and Whitman were actually related by marriage. Crook observed, "There was more or less feeling against me amongst the officers at this post. One of the first things General Howard did after his arrival was to parade up and down the garrison, arm in arm, with Whitman. . . . Howard seemed anxious to have persons under my command espouse his views as contrary to mine."

There followed a conference between Howard and the Apache leaders, which Crook also took pains to ridicule in his autobiography. "A more saucy, impudent lot of cut throats I had never seen before. Many of them were armed with lances and guns. They would walk through our camp in that defiant, impudent manner, as much as to say 'I would like to kill you just for the fun of it, just to see you kick.' . . . Howard said that he had commanded 30,000 men in the war, and that if the Indians did not behave themselves he would exterminate them. . . . Esiminmi-yan looked at General Howard in a half quizzical, half contemptuous and defiant manner, as much as to say, 'go to hell!' When it came Skimmy's time to talk, he evaded all the points at issue, but told General Howard that he, Skimmy, had heard all his life of a man who was so pure that the Great Spirit had kept him on an island in order that he could not witness the frailties of mortals, and that he was satisfied that Howard was that man. He said he wanted his children."[8]

Eskiminzin also pleaded with Howard to return to the band the children who had been taken from their camp at the time of the massacre. Most of the kidnapped children had been given to settlers in Tucson, some of whom had been invited to attend the conference. Howard eventually promised Eskiminzin that the government would return their children to them, which outraged the settlers present and spurred a heated shouting match between Howard and the U.S. district attorney from Tucson.

A short time later, Crook and Howard had a bitterly worded confrontation. Crook warned Howard that "many of these people have lost their friends, relatives, and property by these Indians. They carry their lives constantly in their hands, not knowing what moment is to be their last. These people have suffered too much to have any false ideas of sentiment. Besides, you have come here under the garb of religion and have been prostituting my command by holding out inducements of Eastern stations if certain officers do so and so." Crook reported with some satisfaction that the confrontation so upset Howard that he prayed until 3 A.M.

However, Howard did win the confidence and esteem of the Indians. After leaving Camp Grant, Howard largely settled matters with the Warm Springs Apache. He then set out for the Dragoon Mountains to make peace with Cochise, guided by two warriors from Cochise's band and by Thomas Jeffords, the white man whose unflinching courage and honesty had helped him forge a strong friendship with Cochise. Howard talked with Cochise for several days before agreeing to establish a reservation that included the Dragoon and Chiricahua Mountains with Jeffords as the Indian agent. Howard then returned to Washington, believing that he'd laid the foundations for a lasting peace.

Crook, however, had little confidence in the agreement. He was particularly irritated by the settlement with Cochise and his Chiricahua, steady in his belief that they would never settle for peace until they were decisively humbled militarily.

Crook complained that he was never even given a copy of the treaty Howard signed with Cochise. "The Indians understood that they could raid as much as they pleased in Mexico provided they let us alone. . . . This treaty stopped all operations against them by me. It had a bad effect on my Indians, as they thought I was afraid of Cochise, because I left him unmolested. They said there was no justice or sense in not subjugating him, as he was the worst in the whole business."[9]

Crook now resumed preparations for an offensive against the Tonto Apache, determined not to be thwarted again. "I had made up my mind to disobey any order I might receive looking to an interference of the plan which I had adopted, feeling sure if I was successful my disobedience of orders would be forgiven," he wrote in his autobiography, a remarkable admission that captured his resolve, certainty, and disdain for politics, placeholders, and anyone who disagreed with his unflinching assessments. "I felt sure of success, for all the time I had been prevented from operating against these Indians I had been hard at work organizing, and getting a good knowledge of my scouts, which I saw was to be my main dependence. Also, I had been stopped twice from assuming the offensive, and felt if I was stopped again, I would lose my head anyway."

Besides, the Tonto Apache had given him the perfect pretext. A band of raiders had attacked a stagecoach outside of Wickenburg and slaughtered most of the passengers—including a well-known writer. Crook then learned through his network of spies among the Indians that several warriors who had ambushed the stagecoach planned to assassinate him the next time he came to the Date Creek Reservation outside of Wickenburg, where some one thousand Indians had been settled. Crook's informants warned him that the would-be assassins would come to his headquarters, ask to talk, roll a smoke, and then kill him with the first puff on the cigarette. Crook resolved to set a trap for the assassins, just as he had years ago when he lay in the darkness with his guns about him in the wilds of Oregon. Crook hurried to Date Creek, arriving without military escort, but with a force of packers—each heavily armed. Crook strolled about the grounds, while the packers moved about inconspicuously, waiting for the arrival of the renegades who had been named by Crook's informants. Once the suspects arrived, they asked to sit down and have a talk just as Crook had been warned. "The talk was very agreeable," recalled Bourke, "and not an unpleasant word had been uttered on either side, when all of a sudden the Indian in the center asked for a little tobacco, and, when it was handed to him, began rolling a cigarette; before the first puff of smoke had rolled away from his lips one of the warriors alongside of him leveled his carbine full at General Crook and fired. Lieutenant Ross was waiting for the movement, and struck the arm of the murderer so that the bullet was deflected upwards, and the life of the General was saved. The scrimmage became a perfect Kilkenny fight in another second or two, and every man made for the man nearest to him." One soldier grabbed the Indian who had fired the shot, first subduing him and then smashing his head against a stone. Many of the Indians escaped, and Crook quickly mounted a pursuit. A cavalry unit guided by friendly scouts located the escapees and their families a short time later, killing forty Indians in the ensuing battle.

That fight signaled the start of Crook's twice deferred offensive. In November of 1872, Crook began operations against the Tonto Apache and Yavapai, who had continued to raid in the Verde Valley and the surrounding area. He divided his command into independent units, each composed of a detachment of forty mostly White Mountain Apache scouts and a company of soldiers. Crook was disappointed he could not move against Cochise and "iron all the wrinkles out of his band," but the Chiricahua had settled peacefully on the reservation under Jeffords's supervision.

Crook directed the offensive against the Tonto Apache and the Yavapai that ranged through a great swath of central and eastern Arizona. Much of the fighting was centered on the Tonto Basin, a rugged contortion of deep canyons, cliffs, volcanic landforms, and steep, arid mountains. The Yavapai were actually related to the Yuman tribes along the Colorado River and often clashed with the Tonto Apache, but they were lumped together for the campaign, although Crook made every attempt to use one group against the other. The primary chiefs were Cha-lipun, whose name meant "buckskin colored hat," and Delchay, whose name meant "red ant," although Crook in his autobiography mistranslated it as "the liar." Crook ordered his officers to make full use of scouts to pursue any band not on the reservation. His instructions were to give the Indians every opportunity to surrender, avoid killing women and children, and induce any prisoners to enlist as scouts. They were never to leave a trail, following on foot if necessary, noted Bourke.

Crook moved from fort to fort, coordinating the movements of three independent commands, making sure they had plenty of supplies and well-organized pack trains whenever they returned to one of the forts for resupply. He also took every advantage of the time to hunt in the rugged wilds of the Tonto Basin—wandering out among the rocks in search of game when almost every other man in his command had flopped down to recover from a fourteen-hour march. "It was this insensibility to fatigue, coupled with a contempt for danger, or rather a skill in evading all traps that might be set for him, which won for Crook the admiration of all who served with him; there was no private soldier, no packer, no teamster, who could down the 'ole man' in any work, or outlast him on a march or climb over the rugged peaks of Arizona; they knew that, and they also knew that in the hour of danger Crook could be found on the skirmish line, and not the telegraph office," wrote Bourke in *On the Border with Crook*.[10]

Crook sketched some of the hardships in his annual report for 1873: "The officers and men worked day and night and with our Indian allies and would crawl upon their hands and knees for long distances over terrible canyons and precipices where the slightest mishap would have resulted in instant death, in order that when daylight came they might attack their enemy and secure the advantage of surprise."

The campaign was an exhausting war of attrition in which the pack trains and the Indian guides proved decisive. Two major battles finally broke the back of the Indian resistance. The first came on December 2, 1872, in a remote, inaccessible canyon along the Salt River. An Apache scout named Nantaje offered to lead the soldiers to a cave at the base of a cliff that served as a fortress for one large band of Yavapai. The soldiers and scouts made their way up the rugged canyon, and fell upon the Indians at dawn—killing six warriors at the first volley. The officers called on the trapped warriors to surrender, but they merely jeered, slapping their buttocks in the universal Apache gesture of contempt. The warriors

Captain John Bourke left compelling first-person accounts
of the Apache wars and served as General Crook's chief
defender in the historical record. He studied both Sioux and
Apache culture and wrote several valuable anthropological
works. (*Courtesy Arizona Historical Society, Tucson*)

arched arrows up over the boulders behind which the soldiers had
taken cover, but the arrows did little damage. The soldiers then
begin bouncing bullets off the sloping ceiling of the cave with
deadly effect.

A strange, haunting sound floated out of the cave. "It was a
weird chant, half wail and half exultation–the frenzy of despair

and the wild cry for revenge," wrote Bourke. "Now the petulant, querulous treble of the squaws kept time with the shuffling feet, and again the deeper growl of the savage bull-dogs, who represented manhood in that cave, was flung back from the cold, pitiless brown of the cliffs."[11]

"Look out," cried the Apache scouts, "there goes their death chant, they're going to charge."

Sure enough, a moment later twenty warriors rushed from the cave, "superb-looking fellows all of them," noted Bourke. They charged the double line of soldiers, providing cover for warriors trying to slip around the end of the soldiers' line. However, the soldiers' fire drove the warriors back into the cave.

One warrior did slip through the first line of soldiers. He rose to jeer at his enemies, thinking himself beyond their line. "His chant was never finished; it was at once his song of glory and his death song," wrote Bourke. "Twenty carbines were gleaming in the sunlight. The Apache looked into the eyes of his enemies, and in not one did he see the slightest sign of mercy; he tried to say something, what it was we never could tell. 'No! No! Solados!' in broken Spanish, was all we could make out before the resounding volley had released another soul from its earthly casket. He was really a handsome warrior; tall, well-proportioned, finely muscled, and with a bold, manly countenance. . . . I have never seen a man more thoroughly shot to pieces than was this one."[12]

The Apaches in the cave resumed their death chant "with vigor and boldness."

The soldiers resumed bouncing bullets off the roof of the cave.

Suddenly, a four-year-old boy ran to the mouth of the cave "and stood, thumb in mouth, looking in speechless wonder and indignation at the belching barrels," wrote Bourke.

> Almost immediately, a bullet glanced off his skull, knocking him to the ground. Nantaje rushed forward and dragged the boy to safety amidst the cheers of the soldiers who stopped firing momentarily—then resumed with redoubled intensity.
>
> It was exactly like fighting with wild animals in a trap: The Apaches had made up their minds to die if relief did not reach them.

At this point, another company of soldiers arrived at the top of the four-hundred-foot cliff. They fashioned harnesses of suspenders so that two soldiers could lean out over the edge and fire down into the boulders protecting the front of the cave. When they used up their ammunition, they hurled their revolvers in their excitement. "This kind of ammunition was rather too costly, but it suggested a novel method of annihilating the enemy," observed Bourke.

The soldiers rolled boulders off the cliff, which landed with shattering effect at the entrance to the cave. "The noise was frightful; the destruction sickening," since most of the Apaches were crouched behind boulders at the front of the cave to avoid the bullets bouncing off the roof of the cave, recalled Bourke. "No human voice could be heard in such a cyclone of wrath."

Soon, all signs of life in the cave ceased. Soldiers advanced to find a ghastly scene of slaughter. "There were men, and women dead or writhing in the agonies of death, and with them several babies, killed by our glancing bullets, or by the storm of rocks and stones that had descended above," Bourke reported. The soldiers found seventy-six dead and thirty-five survivors, half of whom later died. The one surviving warrior had six wounds, and did not live long. They left the bodies where they lay, retreating with their prisoners, lest another band of Apaches ambush them on the trail out of the canyon.

The next major battle of the campaign came after raiders struck scattered settlements around Wickenburg, stealing horses and killing three settlers. Their victims included a well-known Indian fighter who once proudly nailed the scalp of a Yavapai chief to the door of the *Prescott Miner* newspaper, and two local miners. The raiders tied two of the men to cactus and filled them full of arrows. They bound another man hand and foot and then shot arrows into him as he rolled back and forth in his agony— until his body bristled with 150 arrows. Crook ordered several detachments to scour the surrounding countryside, and one command brought back a woman prisoner whom they "intimidated" into revealing the location of her band.

The troopers and scouts approached Turret Mountain in the darkness, feet wrapped with rags to muffle any possible sound. At the top of the hill they crouched at the base of a natural stone wall to await the dawn. "Just at dawn our people fired a volley into (the Indians') camp and charged with a yell," wrote Crook.[13] "So secure did the hostiles feel in this almost impregnable position that they lost all presence of mind, even running past their holes in the rocks. Some of them jumped off the precipice and were mashed into a shapeless mass. All of the men were killed; most of the women and children were taken prisoner."[14] The attack virtually wiped out the renegade band, killing between thirty-three and forty-seven Indians, without the loss of a single soldier. Surviving accounts offer widely divergent statistics.[15]

Several thousand[16] Yavapai and Tonto Apache surrendered piecemeal in the next few months, lamenting that they could not fight both the army and the scouts. Cha-lipun came in with three hundred of his followers. Wrote Burke:

Cha-lipun said that he had come in, as the representative of all the Apaches, to say that they wanted to surrender because General Crook had "too many cartridges of copper." They had never been afraid of the Americans alone, but now that their own people were fighting them they did not know what to do; they could not go to sleep at night, because they feared to be surrounded before daybreak; they could not hunt—the noise of their guns would attract the troops; they could not cook mescal or anything else, because the flame and smoke would draw down the soldiers, they could not live in the valleys—there were too many soldiers; they had retreated to the mountain tops, thinking to hide in the snow until the soldiers went home, but the scouts found them and the soldiers followed them.

Crook took Cha-lipun by the hand and told him that if he would promise to live at peace and stop killing people, he would be the best friend he ever had. Not one of the Apaches had been killed except through his own folly; they had refused to listen to the messengers sent out asking them to come in; and consequently there had been nothing else to do but to go out and kill them until they changed their minds. It was of no use to talk about who had begun this war; there were bad men among all peoples; there were bad Mexicans, as there were bad Americans, and bad Apaches; our duty was to end wars and establish peace and not to talk about what was past and gone. The Apache must make his peace not for a day or a week, but for all time; not with the Americans alone, but with the Mexicans as well; and not alone with the Americans and Mexicans, but with all the other Indian tribes. They must not take upon themselves the redress of grievances, but report to the military officer upon their reservation who would see that their wrongs were righted. . . . So long as any bad Indians remained out in the mountains, the reservation Indians should wear tags attached to the neck. . . . They should not cut off the noses of their wives when they became jealous of them. They should not be told anything that was not exactly true. They should be fully protected in all respects while on the reservation.[17]

Delchay was among the last to surrender. But like Geronimo, Delchay remained wary and suspicious and prone to bolting from the reservation. He had once been shot, and in another incident his brother had been murdered, by soldiers while on the reservation—so he remained deeply suspicious. Major George Randall reported that during one of his surrenders, "Delchay commenced crying and said he would do anything he would be ordered to do. He wanted to save his people, as they were starving. He had nothing to ask for but his life. He would accept any terms. He said he had 125 warriors last fall, and if anybody had told him he couldn't whip the world he would have laughed at them, but now he had only twenty left. He said they used to have no difficulty eluding the troops, but now the very rocks had gotten soft, they couldn't put their foot anywhere without leaving an impression we could follow, that they could get no sleep at nights, for should a coyote or a fox start a rock rolling during the night, they would get up, and dig out, thinking it was we who were after them."[18]

The Tonto and Yavapai settled uneasily on the reservation, accepting Crook's promise that he would protect them if they became peaceful farmers and hunt them without mercy if they left. A rumor that the soldiers were about to slaughter them several months later prompted many to flee, including both Cha-lipun and Delchay. Crook hurried back to the Camp Verde Reservation and sent out word he wanted to meet with the leaders. They then returned, promising that if Crook would forgive them they would never leave the reservation again.

Delchay, however, could not master his suspicions and his yearning for the freedom of the warpath and left again with about forty followers. Other bands that had bolted from the San Carlos Reservation at about the same time reconsidered when they learned Crook had again come to the reservation. They returned to the reservation, but to their consternation Crook refused to accept their surrender. "I told them I would not hurt them as they had thrown themselves on my mercy, but I would drive them back into the mountains and kill them all," Crook wrote. "They had lied to me once and I didn't know what they were lying to me now. They begged to be allowed to remain, making all kinds of promises for the future. I finally compromised by letting them stay provided they would bring in the heads of certain of the chiefs who were ringleaders, which they agreed to do. A couple of mornings afterwards they brought in seven heads of the proscribed. The same edict was sent out to the Tontos, which was also responded to with alacrity. Delchay[19] had two heads." Crook was sitting in a chair on the porch of his headquarters when the Indians approached with a large sack, and then dumped six or eight heads on the planking at his feet. "Being satisfied that both parties were in earnest in their beliefs, and the bringing in of an extra head was not amiss, I paid both parties," wrote Crook in his autobiography.

Initially, the Tonto and Yavapai bands fared well. Crook settled them near Camp Verde alongside the Verde River and put the Indians to work providing hay and firewood for the fort, and planting crops. The Indians labored, using fire-hardened sticks and wicker baskets, to dig a five-mile-long, four-foot-deep, three-foot-wide irrigation ditch. They also made a waterwheel out of packing boxes. But the labor paid off, with successively larger crops in two growing seasons. In 1873, they raised five hundred thousand pounds of corn, thirty thousand pounds of beans, and had become largely self-sufficient. The bands' herds also began to grow.

The now cooperative Tonto and Yavapai provided an early test of Crook's solution to the Indian problem—economic self-sufficiency. He insisted that the army buy forage for its horses from the Indians rather than from white contractors, and the Apache were soon cutting tons of grass, bundling it, and delivering it to the fort. When he observed that the Apache scouts in his units spent their pay almost immediately on drinking and gambling—as did most of the soldiers—he went to the chiefs to convince them that the cash wages of the scouts were an invaluable resource. "He explained that money could be made to grow just as an acorn would grow into an oak; that by spending it foolishly, the Apaches treated it just as they did the acorn which they trod underfoot; but by investing the money in California horses and sheep, they could be gaining more money all the time they slept, and by the time their children had attained maturity the hills would be dotted with herds of horses and flocks of sheep. Then they would be rich like the white man; then they could travel about and see the world; then they would not be dependent upon the Great Father for supplies, but would have for themselves and their families all the food they could eat, and would have much to sell," wrote Bourke, who recorded many of Crook's conversations with the chiefs.

However, Crook was about to learn once again the harsh economics of greed. Throughout Crook's career, both military and civilian authorities supported him when he was killing Indians, but disregarded his recommendations that would have made the pacified Indians self-sufficient. In the spring of 1874, Crook was ordered to move the increasingly prosperous Tonto and Yavapai bands from the reservation along the Verde River to the sweltering, disease-prone San Carlos Reservation. Crook once again blamed the Tucson Ring for this betrayal of the promises he had made in good faith and clear conscience to induce the surrender of the Indians.

Crook observed, "Their removal was one of those cruel things that greed has so often inflicted on the Indians. When the Indian appeals to his arms, his only redress, the whole country cries out against the Indian. As soon as the Indians became settled on the different reservations, gave up the warpath, and became harmless, the Indian agents who had sought cover before, now came out as brave as sheep, and took charge of the agencies, and commenced their game of plundering. . . . The American Indian commands respect for his rights only so long as he inspires terror with his rifle."[20]

Bourke maintained that the contractors who profited from the graft that surrounded the management of the reservations did not want the Indians to become self-supporting. Bourke noted that contractors would often deliver sacks of sugar weighted with boulders, scales that effectively doubled the weight of cattle delivered, and goods so shoddy as to be useless. But even when an honest agent was assigned, he could not resist the system. "The influences against it are too strong; once let the Indian be made self-supporting, and what will become of the gentle contractor?" wrote Bourke. "Just as soon as a few of the more progressive people [Indians] begin to accumulate a trifle of property, to raise sheep, to cultivate patches of soil and raise scanty crops, the agent sends in the usual glowing report of the occurrence, and to the mind of the average man and woman in the East it looks as if all the tribe were on the highway to prosperity, and the next thing that Congress does is to curtail the appropriations. Next we hear of disaffection, the tribe is reported as 'surly and threatening,' and we are told that the Indians are 'killing their cattle.' But whether they go to war or quietly starve on the reservation effect no change in the system; all supplies are bought of a contractor as before, and the red man is no better off, or scarcely any better off, after twenty years of peace than he was when he surrendered."[21]

As Bourke explained it,

General Crook believed that the American Indian was a human being, gifted with the same God-like apprehension as the white man, and like him inspired by noble impulses, ambition for progress and advancement, but subject to the same infirmities, beset with the same or even greater temptations, struggling under the disadvantages of an inherited ignorance, which had the double effect of making him doubt his own powers in the struggle for the new life and suspicious of the truthfulness and honesty of the advocates for all innovations. The American savage has grown up as a member of a tribe, or rather of a clan within a tribe; all his actions have been made to conform to the opinions of his fellows as enunciated in the clan councils or in those of the tribe. By the Crook method of dealing with the savage he was, at the outset, de-tribalized without knowing it; he was individualized and made the better able to re-enter into the civilization of the Caucasian, which is an individualized civilization. . . . General Crook believed that the Indian should be made self-supporting, not by preaching at him the merits of labor and the grandeur of toiling in the sun, but by making him see that every drop of honest sweat meant a penny in his pocket. . . . The American Indian, born free as an eagle, would not tolerate restraint, would not brook injustice; therefore, the restraint imposed must be manifestly for his benefit, and the government to which he was subjected must be eminently one of kindness, mercy, and absolute justice, without necessarily degenerating into weakness.[22]

Crook protested the relocation of the Tonto Apache and the Yavapai, but then complied with his orders. In February of 1875, the government ordered a small detachment under a Lieutenant Eaton to escort some 1,426 Indians from Camp Verde across 180 miles of snow-covered peaks, icy, rushing rivers, and hard terrain to the San Carlos Reservation, a bleak, malaria-ridden lowland selected as the ideally worthless place to concentrate the defeated Apache bands. Eaton, his sympathies all with the Indians, called it "about as ugly a job as was ever laid on the shoulders of a subaltern in the days of our service in old Arizona."[23]

The government insisted that the procession of mostly women and children march over the mountains instead of along a wagon road. One man carried his disabled wife on his back the whole way. Most of the cavalrymen gave up their horses so children could ride. The soldiers did their best to keep the Tontos and the Yavapais separated, since Crook had often used one band as scouts against the other—sowing a harvest of deep hatred. At one point, a ball game between children of the rival bands led to an outbreak of fighting in which five Indians were killed before the soldiers could break it up. All told, nearly one hundred Indians died or slipped away on the journey. "Ten days have passed since we left the Agency," wrote Dr. William Corbusier at one point, "ten days of untold and unnecessary suffering and privation—ten days which have left their scars on whites and Indians alike, never to be healed."

Crook's policy of divide and conquer had produced victory, and reaped its bitter fruit for the Apache. It also earned him a promotion to brigadier general on October 29, 1873—the news carried on the just-completed telegraph line from Yuma to Prescott. With the promotion came word that he would be transferred to the High Plains, where the Sioux threatened to unleash a sweeping war.

Crook had done more to break the resistance of the Apache in four years than anyone in perhaps three hundred years. All of the bands were settled more or less peacefully on reservations. The Tonto and Yavapai had been completely reduced, and would in the future fight only as scouts for the army. The loyalty and cooperation of the White Mountain Apache and Coyotero had been secured, and they would remain loyal to the army. Only two groups remained problematical. The unbowed Chiricahua under Cochise lived peacefully on their reservation under Jeffords's protection and advice. Cochise used his great prestige and powers of persuasion to maintain peace on the American side of the border, but raiding parties continued to journey down into Mexico. Meanwhile, the Chihenne, or Warm Springs, Apache under the leadership of Victorio, Loco, and Nana remained peacefully settled near their homeland, although perched on the edge of conflict as a result of the persistent rumors that the soldiers might close down their reservation and move them to San Carlos.

But to Crook these seemed only distant threats.

And he had barely heard of Geronimo, who would eventually come to overshadow his whole career.

Besides, another great enemy lay just ahead. George Crook was about to meet Crazy Horse and fight the most controversial, frustrating, and bitterly debated battle of his long career.

9

Geronimo

MAKING PEACE
WITH THE WHITE EYES

SOMETIMES EVEN Geronimo grew weary of fighting. At least, he exhausted the willingness of his warriors to live always in hiding—rising in the middle of the night and seizing their weapons at the smallest sound. Besides, raiding had grown difficult. The Mexicans seemed to grow every year more numerous. Worse yet, The People had no good place to spend the winter—because the White Eye soldiers kept them constantly on the move in their war with Cochise. Geronimo's small band spent a peaceful year living with Victorio and his people, who waited an answer from the White Eyes about whether they could keep Ojo Caliente. They molested no one. They did not even go into Mexico, but lived in perfect peace. Victorio's people kept the peace with the White Eyes, and went every so often to get rations—since they could not feed the children if they had to remain in such a small space without raiding the whites or the Mexicans. They could no longer even support themselves by hunting, since the White Eyes had killed or scared off so much of the game. Still, Geronimo lived quietly for that year, gradually accumulating supplies so he could go about freely once more. When they decided to leave, Victorio's people gave them a celebration—with everyone dancing, and singing, and the girls laughing and looking away, and the boys stepping out proudly.

Geronimo loved the dances, and the ceremonies that remembered White Painted Woman, and Child of Waters. For that time, he could almost believe the world would remain always as it had been—and forget about the shadow that lay across The People.

Geronimo went then to live again with Cochise and his people once he had replenished his supplies. He thought he might convince some of the Chokonen warriors to go raiding in Mexico, so he could get more horses and cattle. But he found Cochise discouraged and downhearted. Once Cochise could raise as many warriors as Mangas Coloradas in his strongest times, but Cochise's force had dwindled because he had been fighting all the time now for ten seasons of the Ghost Dance—so that the names of most of the warriors who had been with him in the old days were no longer spoken.

Cochise camped mostly in the Dragoon Mountains, where the rocks had always been his friends, and had long sheltered him from his enemies. They were resting in camp one day when the scouts came back to say that Ponce, who was a son of Mangas Coloradas, and Chee, the nephew of Cochise, were approaching the camp along with Thomas Jeffords and several White Eyes. For a long time, Cochise had suffered no White Eye to come into the Dragoons and leave again alive—except for Jeffords. But the scouts had talked to Ponce, and had learned that one of the White Eyes he brought was a great *nantan*, who had come to make a peace with Cochise.

So Cochise rode to meet the *nantan*, taking with him his sons Naiche and Taza, and also Geronimo and other leading men. The *nantan* was called General Howard, and he seemed not at all like other White Eyes. He had only one arm, and Geronimo thought he must have great Power to survive such a wound. Oftentimes General Howard would start off the talking by falling down on his knees, as though he were ill—talking in a loud voice with his eyes closed. This frightened some warriors, who thought the *nantan* was witching them. But General Howard said he was praying to the Great Spirit to bring peace between the White Eyes and The People. This seemed good to Geronimo. Did not The People pray before undertaking any hard thing? Geronimo had always

NA-CHISE, -- Son of Cochise,
a celebrated warrior.
1 8 8 2

Naiche was the son of Cochise and the last chief of the free
Chiricahua. Shown here with his rifle and a blanket, Naiche
never enjoyed the authority of his father. Although he fought
to the end of the Apache wars as the leader of the last Chiricahua band, Geronimo, who was a war shaman but not a chief,
has overshadowed him in historical accounts. (*Courtesy Arizona
Historical Society, Tucson*)

thought the White Eyes were an empty people, who had never
known any prayers, and held nothing sacred—not even the earth,
or the animals they killed, or the food they ate. But perhaps they
had once known prayers, which only a few remembered—like this
one-armed *nantan* who talked to the warriors like one man to

another, with respect. General Howard played with the children with affection, and behaved like a man of honor, and not like a White Eye at all. Ponce said that when they were coming to see Cochise, some White Eyes had tried to kill the warriors but General Howard had ridden right in the middle to protect his friends. Ponce said General Howard was like Jeffords—a true man.

Cochise listened to all of this, and watched General Howard in his careful way—for Cochise understood men, and how to measure them, and when he could trust them. Then Cochise met with *Nantan* Howard and spoke in this way: You Americans began the fight and now Americans and Mexicans kill The People on sight. I have retaliated with all my might. I have killed ten white men for every Indian slain, but now I would make peace.[1]

So Cochise and General Howard talked each day for eleven days, while they waited for the leaders of the scattered Chiricahua to come and decide whether they should stop fighting. Each band had to make its own decision, although Cochise's words had great weight in the council. General Howard first said Cochise would have to go and settle near the Mescalero, along with the Mimbreno and Chihenne. But Cochise would not agree to do that. The water was not good. There were too many White Eyes. It was too far from the rocks that knew his name, and which had been his good friends all of his life. Cochise said he would make peace, because he had not enough warriors left to continue making war. But he would not leave his mountains, and he would not let any White Eye have charge over his people except for Jeffords—who was the only white he could trust. Besides, the place General Howard wanted them to go was too far away from Mexico, and Cochise knew his warriors would not leave the cattle and the horses of the White Eyes alone if they could not still go down into Mexico to get what they needed. Cochise and General Howard went back and forth about this, until General Howard saw how much these mountains meant to Cochise, and saw that otherwise Cochise would go on fighting—even if he had no hope of winning. So General Howard agreed to these things. And when the other chiefs came in, they met in council and talked a long time about the peace, until they all came to agree with Cochise, who spoke with grave eloquence in council and with such force of his character that he convinced them all, even Geronimo.

Still, Geronimo wondered whether the White Eyes would once again prove treacherous. When they had made the peace, General Howard sent for the soldiers to come to the Dragoons so that everything should be set out. Geronimo took care to ride on the back of Howard's horse, with his arms around the *nantan's* waist. As they rode toward the soldiers, Cochise spread out his warriors, ready at any instant to fight. Geronimo trembled with anticipation as he rode behind the *nantan*.[2] But the soldiers made no hostile move, and Howard kept his word to Cochise.

Howard set Jeffords in charge over a reservation for the Chiricahua that embraced the Chiricahua and the Dragoon Mountains, and stretched out all the way to the border with Mexico. Jeffords let the bands live any place they chose on the reservation, and did not make them live only near the soldiers. Jeffords made sure that they had the rations Howard had promised, and also let them move about as they pleased to hunt. Geronimo lived near Cochise's band, but also continued to go down into Mexico and returned with horses, and cattle, and with the good memories of the Mexicans he killed there, as he had promised at the grave of his father, as he owed to his Power. In return, Cochise kept his word and prevented any of the warriors from touching anything that belonged to the White Eyes.[3]

Of course, Geronimo took note that the White Eyes did not keep all of their promises, once *Nantan* Howard went away leaving lesser men in charge. Howard had promised that Victorio's people could stay at Warm Springs, but the other White Eyes continued to refuse them permission to stay there. Even though the soldiers would not give them rations, Victorio would not let his warriors take anything from the White Eyes so long as he thought that maybe he could convince the soldiers to let him stay at Ojo Caliente. So sometimes Chihenne and Mimbreno warriors would leave their families on the Chiricahua Reservation, where they would be safe, when they went down into Mexico to get the supplies they needed.[4]

So Geronimo waited, and raided the hated Mexicans, and enjoyed the time of peace, although he did not believe it would last.

Then Cochise died. Some said he had been witched, so Naiche went and found the one many said had done the witching. Naiche would have burned the witch and maybe saved his father, but the soldiers came along and saved the witch. So Cochise died, in great pain, never complaining. Word that Cochise had died spread quickly, the women keening in sorrow for the things that now had passed away for all time, and the warriors gathered in little groups, wondering what would become of The People without Cochise.[5]

Many were afraid the war would begin again and the White Eyes would break their word and take back the reservation General Howard had given to Cochise. Some who had relatives with the White Mountain people said the White Eyes had already done that, making many different bands live at San Carlos, which was a bad place, barren as a fire pit burned down to coals and ash. The Tonto, and the Yavapai, and the White Mountain and the Coyotero had all been made to live in the same place together with their enemies, under the eye of the soldiers. Lots of people said that the Creator left San Carlos just as he found it, so that The People would appreciate how well He had fixed up every other place. Many of The People worried that the soldiers would come and make them live in a place like that also.[6]

Most of the Chiricahua followed the son of Cochise, Taza, who had Power. Cochise had trained Taza for leadership, seeing that he had Power, and a fierce heart. Naiche, the other son of Cochise, had no Power, so he followed his brother in all things. Still, he was a respected warrior. His face was fine as ice crystals, his voice soft and melodious, and his eyes kind and lively. He was slow to anger and quick to forgive. Naiche loved gambling, and charming the women, and he did not mind at all that the responsibility of leadership fell on Taza. Naiche was a brave man and a good fighter, with a gift for making men and women both like him. He laughed easily, but sometimes had a hard time making a decision, and a hard time making an enemy. Cochise had called each of his sons to him before he died, and made them promise to keep the peace with the White Eyes—because he saw that the Chiricahua had no hope if the war started again.

But Taza was not Cochise. He was a fierce man, strong, and proud, and mindful of a slight. He had his father's strength, and some of his Power, but he had not his father's gift in holding the hearts of men in his hands. His father had schooled him for leadership, but he was yet too young, and the times were yet too difficult. All the other chiefs feared and respected Cochise, so when he said that they should keep the peace with the White Eyes no one could question his courage or wisdom. But the same words sounded more like weakness from Taza, who had not himself earned the deference of the warriors. Soon, the other chiefs who had been kept in the pouch of Cochise's Power begin to make trouble. Sklinya and his brother Poinsenay said they had listened to Cochise, but that they would not follow Taza. Geronimo and Juh also spoke against Taza, arguing that the White Eyes could not be trusted and that they would eventually take from the Chiricahua the lands they had promised, and lock them up on a small reservation—maybe San Carlos. It would be better to go down into Mexico and live in the Sierra Madre, said Geronimo, so they could remain men, and warriors, and so that The People would not become the camp dogs of the White Eyes. They had only the same choice that had doomed Mangas Coloradas, and would be destroyed if they trusted the crooked words of the White Eyes. The words followed one another like warriors, until everyone was in the fight. And because words have power, they made wounds. Fighting soon broke out, so that Sklinya and Poinsenay and a dozen other warriors broke away and made a new camp. Jeffords saw the trouble, and warned the traders who made their money from selling weapons and whiskey to The People to stay away from Poinsenay and the other young warriors gathered around him. But one of the keepers at the horse station for the stagecoach sold Poinsenay and his warriors a great deal of whiskey. The foolish man then grew frightened and refused to give them any more. So Poinsenay and Skinya killed the station keeper and two other white men, and ran to hide in the Dragoons.[7]

Soon the San Carlos agent John Clum came with fifty-four warriors—White Mountain men who kept the peace for Clum on the reservation there. Clum was a young man, so vain, and proud, and self-important that the Chiricahua called him Turkey Gobbler. But the White Mountain warriors liked him, and they said he was the best *nantan* they had ever had. Turkey Gobbler let the chiefs run things and did not call the soldiers onto the reservation. He met with Taza and Naiche, and explained that the government would punish them all if they did not find Poinsenay. So Naiche and Taza and some of their warriors went with Turkey Gobbler and the White Mountain men and in the fight that followed Naiche killed Skinya, and Taza wounded Poinsenay, and they killed six of the Poinsenay's warriors.[8]

That was a hard thing—for one Chiricahua to kill another at the direction of a White Eye. But worse was yet to come. The next day, Turkey Gobbler convinced Taza that the Chiricahua must leave the land Howard had promised to Cochise and come to live at San Carlos, where they would be safe from the soldiers, and from the White Eyes who hated all of The People and would kill them wherever they went. A few days later,[9] Taza and Naiche, who were bound by their promise to their father to keep the peace, met with Geronimo and Juh and other leaders so Turkey Gobbler could convince them also to go to San Carlos.

Geronimo listened carefully to everything Taza said. He listened also to Turkey Gobbler. He could see immediately that Taza had his hands tied by the promise to his father and that Naiche must follow along in the moccasin prints of his brother. But he saw also that Turkey Gobbler was just another White Eye, full of his own importance, and in love with the sound of his own voice. The White Mountain warriors all said he was a good man, and could be trusted. But Geronimo had heard that promise often enough before. He was not fooled. So he nodded his head, and listened carefully, and looked for his opening, as a man in a knife fight reads the pattern in the movements of his opponent. He looked at Juh, who looked back at him. Then they said they would go to San Carlos with Taza, Naiche, and the others, but that their people were scattered across the reservation, and they must gather

San Carlos Indian agent John Clum (center, standing) is photographed surrounded by several Apache leaders and scouts. The scouts called him "Boss
with the High Forehead," but the Chiricahua called him "Turkey Gobbler."
He is the only man to ever actually capture Geronimo. (*Courtesy Arizona Historical
Society, Tucson*)

them up so everyone could go to San Carlos together. They asked
for twenty days, but Turkey Gobbler said they could have only four.

That night, Juh and Geronimo camped together. Then they
killed all of their dogs so they would not bark, and stole away in
the darkness with their bands. Others had warned Turkey Gobbler
not to trust Juh or Geronimo, and he sent the scouts to their camp
during the night, but the camp was already empty when the scouts
arrived. Juh went back down to the Sierra Madre with his warriors,

while Geronimo went toward Ojo Caliente, where Victorio's people still waited for a decision from the Great White Father about the reservation *Nantan* Howard had promised them.

The next day, Turkey Gobbler took 325 Chiricahua to San Carlos, which included only 60 warriors. Most of the warriors, perhaps 135, had slipped away with Geronimo, or with Juh, or with other war chiefs. Still, Turkey Gobbler strutted and bragged. After that, Turkey Gobbler blamed every bad thing that happened on Geronimo, who had made him look foolish.

The warriors who left the reservation, some with Geronimo and some with other leaders, now killed many White Eyes to obtain the horses, and cattle, and guns they knew they would need when the soldiers came after them.[10] They did not hesitate in this, for the White Eyes had broken their word and now the warriors must survive. They had never agreed to give up their land, so they thought any White Eyes who now came on the land that had been theirs deserved no mercy. Moreover, the obligation of revenge was already great between the warriors and the White Eyes, so they had the right to kill anyone they encountered. Besides, no raiding party could afford to let anyone see them and then run to the soldiers, who were riding everywhere.

Meanwhile, Taza and Naiche and the others paid the normal cost for trusting the White Eyes, even as Mangas Coloradas had done. Turkey Gobbler took Taza and other of the leaders to see the Great White Father. But when they were there, Turkey Gobbler poisoned Taza and buried him there, far away from the places that knew him.[11]

Geronimo's band of some forty warriors moved around, taking what they needed, and avoiding the soldiers. After a while, they wanted to see some other people, and rest, so they went to visit Victorio's people at Ojo Caliente, because he had always been friendly to them. But they found that many people there were not happy to see them. They had heard that the government had closed the Chiricahua Reservation, and sent everyone to live at San Carlos, which was a bad place. The Chihenne still waited to hear from the Great White Father whether they could stay at Ojo Caliente, and many feared they would be made to go to San Carlos as well. Many said Victorio should not let Geronimo stay, because he was like the raven who always brings trouble and lives always on death. But Victorio turned his ears away from that talk, saying the Chiricahua had always been brothers to the Chihenne, often helping them in troubled times. Victorio would not turn away the Chiricahua now.

After a time, Geronimo heard that Clum had come to the Ojo Caliente agency with a few White Mountain men to have a talk.[12] Geronimo took his warriors and even his women and children to see Turkey Gobbler, who had only a few men and who was not a warrior, but only a young man full of ignorance. Geronimo and Ponce and five other warriors went up to the agency building to talk to Clum, who sat with six or seven scouts. Clum sat in his chair, very arrogant, and immediately began talking in a rough way, saying Geronimo had stolen cattle, and killed people, and must now come with him to San Carlos.

Geronimo looked at Turkey Gobbler as though he was already dead. Then Geronimo said, We are not going to San Carlos with you. And unless you are very careful, you and your police will not go back to San Carlos either. Your bodies will stay here at Ojo Caliente and make food for the coyotes.

At that moment, the doors to a building behind the warriors burst open, and eighty scouts with their rifles ran out from them and stopped, pointing their guns at Geronimo and the small group of warriors standing with them.

Everyone stood perfectly still, while Geronimo balanced the moment in his mind, his eyes darting from Turkey Gobbler, to the scouts, and back again. He knew he could kill Turkey Gobbler. He knew he could run through all of the bullets, because his Power would take the powder from the guns of each man who aimed at him. But he knew also that the scouts would kill most of his men and the women and the children he had so foolishly brought to this meeting. He silently berated himself, seeing that his overconfidence had delivered him into the hands of his enemies.

Suddenly, a woman jumped on the back of one of the White Eyes who led the scouts, grabbing at his gun, and screaming. The White Eye threw her off his back, and raised his gun up again.

In that moment, Geronimo's thumb moved to the trigger of his gun, but Turkey Gobbler called out for them to drop their guns. Geronimo stood, frozen, not knowing what he should do and not willing to condemn most of his men to death by the simple tightening of his finger on the trigger. Then Turkey Gobbler stepped forward into the space that separated him, and pulled the gun out of Geronimo's hands.[13] The other warriors lay down their guns, at the signal from Geronimo. They all sat then on the porch to talk, while the scouts kept them under their guns. Once again, Turkey Gobbler insulted Geronimo—cutting him with his words, shaming him, goading him. Finally, Geronimo could bear his insolence no more, and rose to his feet, his hand going to the handle of his knife. But this time one of the scouts beside Turkey Gobbler stepped forward, and took the knife from under Geronimo's hand. Geronimo let him take it, not entirely understanding why he did so. All right, he grunted, relaxing now that he had no choice. Perhaps his Power had made him give up his weapons and not fight. Perhaps his Power knew that there would be a better time than in the open, with all of his people standing helpless before the guns of the treacherous scouts. In any case, it was done. He could only wait and see what the White Eyes would do with him.

Turkey Gobbler now seemed so proud of himself that Geronimo longed to cut open his long, soft throat. Instead, Geronimo rose and followed Turkey Gobbler toward the blacksmith shop. Geronimo stood, wordless, watching the blacksmith pump the bellows on the fire. He let nothing show on his face, but he thought of Mangas Coloradas, who had been tortured by the heated bayonets of the soldiers before they killed him. Geronimo drew further back into himself, determined to die well. Often enough he had killed Mexicans, and sometimes White Eyes. He could call them up in his mind, with a twist of contempt. Sometimes Mangas Coloradas had tied prisoners up by their feet over a fire, and watched while they twisted, and screamed, and pleaded for death until their heads burst open. The People understood pain, and a warrior was schooled all of his life to ignore it so it would purify him and burn away weakness. A warrior knew also how to use pain to so completely break the spirit of an enemy that his Chindi would not dare to linger and harm the one who had killed him. A warrior also used pain to inspire fear so The People might remain safe in a world filled with enemies. So Geronimo stood motionless, disdaining fear, and waiting for the touch of the glowing metal.

But Turkey Gobbler did not torture him, at least not in a way that was quick, and final, and clear. Instead, he put chains on the legs of each warrior. Then he led them to the corral and put them there with the scouts as guards. Then Turkey Gobbler ordered all the other people to line up for a counting. Nulah, who had fought for years alongside Geronimo, refused to line up. He said he would not be counted until Turkey Gobbler took the chains off Geronimo. Turkey Gobbler ordered that Nulah also be chained and put in the corral with Geronimo, but Nulah pulled free and sat down again. Turkey Gobbler reached down to pull him to his feet, and when Nulah pulled out his knife Turkey Gobbler hit him on the head with his rifle, then put him in the corral with the others. Geronimo watched this silently, helpless now because he had given away his weapons, and had let Turkey Gobbler put the chains on him. He thought that he was already a dead man, and resolved to give Turkey Gobbler no satisfaction, not even the smallest expression on his face. But his heart hardened, stretched tight across his growing hatred for the White Eyes.

Unaccountably, Turkey Gobbler did not kill him. Instead, he put the eight[14] leaders who were in chains in a wagon and took them to San Carlos, along with the 110 people who had been in their group. Turkey Gobbler made Victorio and Loco and all their people also go to San Carlos, although they had kept the peace for all the long while they had waited to see if the Great White Father would honor the promise that General Howard had made. The scouts, and the disarmed warriors, and the soldiers all traveled together, but kept each to themselves. One night the scouts and the soldiers started gambling, and then they started fighting and the soldiers ran in among the Chihenne and Chiricahua for protection from the scouts, who were mostly White Mountain people. Geronimo watched it all happen, with his fierce, hooded eyes, wondering why Usen had given the White Eyes such Power. During the journey, some people began to weaken, and then lay down helplessly with the spotted sickness the White Eyes brought with them into the camps of The People—better weapons for them than even the limitless bullets of their far-shooting guns. This, too, Geronimo watched, riding in the wagons—waiting for the voice that would tell him what he must do.

When they arrived at San Carlos, Turkey Gobbler put Geronimo and the others in a small room with bars on the windows, and the chains still on their feet. He left them there, where they could see only a small piece of the sky. Days passed, and then weeks, and then months, until Geronimo thought that perhaps this was the torture the White Eyes had devised; to leave him forever in a small place locked away from the stars, and the moon, and the wind, and the rocks that remembered him, and the mountains that thought of him, and the people who loved him. Turkey Gobbler would simply leave him here, to rot into the ground like a tree that has fallen—denied not only a warrior's death, but any kind of death at all.

Then one day the soldiers came and opened the door, and let him go free.[15] Geronimo thought maybe the White Eyes had a trial, and decided to let him go. But he was never sure. He merely shrugged, and went to find his family. Who could make sense of the White Eyes? He understood the Mexicans; they were cattle created to supply the needs of The People. But the White Eyes remained a puzzle. Some seemed to be honorable men, whose word could be trusted. They made promises, and gave rations, and took prisoners and let them go again. You could not ever be sure how things would turn out when dealing with White Eyes. Sometimes they fought each other most of all. And yet, in the end, they always turned away from their promises, and turned on The People. They were like a wounded bear, powerful and unpredictable. And they were without spirit or reverence, disdaining the nature of things, and yet never paying for their arrogance and irreverence. Perhaps they had some great Power against which even Usen was baffled. He considered this problem in his long time with the chains on his feet. Now that he had gone free, he resolved to solve it, knowing the survival of The People depended on the answer.

Geronimo went to camp with the Chiricahua, in the middle of great trouble. The People had always roamed free—living for a little time in this place, or that place. Now they found themselves in a few camps, close by one another, in such numbers that they could not hunt, counted and watched over by the soldiers. They had barely enough to eat. Worse yet, the sicknesses of the White Eyes ran back and forth through them—like a wolf among sheep in a pen. It seemed strange, that the sickness that killed The People so quickly did not kill the White Eyes. Maybe they had better medicine, or maybe it was some poison that they put in the rations they gave to The People. Certainly, Geronimo had heard stories of times that the White Eyes had put poison in food they gave to The People in the name of friendship. There seemed nothing the White Eyes would not do. Some people even said that they ate human flesh, putting it in cans with pictures of people on them.[16] In the old times, sickness rarely found the camps of The People, and the medicine men could chase it out when it came. If someone did die, his relatives burned all his things and moved away from the Chindi and the sickness. But that had all changed now, on the killing ground of the reservation. They could not leave, but must remain as their numbers dwindled in the hot, fetid bottomlands, maddened by the mosquitoes and the crying of the babies. Geronimo watched it all happening, and saw that sickness now killed more children than the bullets of the soldiers' guns had ever done.

Moreover, the bands fought among themselves, the old cycle of offense and revenge running back and forth like a coyote in a pen. Many of the bands confined together at San Carlos had often been enemies. The Chiricahua had often fought the Tonto, and sometimes the White Mountain. Now they fought like camp dogs for the scraps of the White Eyes. The families of men who had died in long-ago battles found themselves living now close by the enemies who had done it and so took the revenge due them. But even the bands that had long been friends had trouble. The Chiricahua and the Chihenne had always been friendly, but now they began to have problems—a fight, a drunken shooting, a horse gone missing.

Nonetheless, Geronimo resolved to remain on the reservation. At least the children and the women had something to eat here. At least they were not always running, and hiding, and fighting. Perhaps things would settle down. Perhaps the White Eyes would give them the full rations they had promised. The White Eyes had too much Power for The People to keep on fighting. Besides, the voice that had always guided him had fallen curiously silent, so that he did not know what he should do. So Geronimo waited and watched.

Then, in the season of Reddish Earth, Poinsenay and his men, who had been raiding in Mexico, came onto the reservation. They swaggered and bragged and urged the young warriors festering on the reservation to go with them back into Mexico. Juh also sent warriors to the reservation to seek recruits. He lived now in the Sierra Madre, in the old haunts from which the Mexicans had never been able to dislodge him.

When Poinsenay left again, he took many of the horses from Victorio's herd. This spun rumors all across the reservation, a dust devil of confusion. Victorio had been watching his people die in the hated lowlands of San Carlos for a year, longing only for Ojo Caliente. At last he could stand it no more and left just after Poinsenay, taking 323 of his Mimbreno and Chihenne followers with him. Victorio fought several battles with the soldiers, and killed any White Eyes to obtain guns, and horses, and supplies for his fleeing people, most of whom were women and children. Lozen, his sister, guided him—using her Power to warn her brother when the soldiers approached. They traveled quickly, reaching the mountains near their homeland and hiding there, sending messages to the soldiers asking to return to Ojo Caliente, where the waters of the hot springs remembered them, and where their ancestors lay buried in secret places on the sacred mountains. Old Nana left also, taking a few family groups and some warriors to the Mescalero Reservation in New Mexico. Only about 143 of Victorio's people stayed behind, knowing that the soldiers would hunt them down if they left.

Geronimo and Naiche and most of the other Chiricahua did not leave. The Indian agent even went to Geronimo and put him

in charge of the Chihenne and Mimbreno people who had not
gone with Victorio. Naiche, who still remembered his promise to
his father, promised to tell the agent if any other bands planned to
leave. But Geronimo made other plans in secret. He hoped that
things would get better now that Victorio had left, now that Poinsenay had gone. But he did not think so. The Chiricahua did not
have the guns, or the horses, or the supplies to leave now, so he
knew he must bide his time. He would wait, and convince the
agent to trust him, and see what happened to the Chihenne. So he
quietly urged the warriors to collect guns and ammunitions, and
he cached supplies, and he sent messengers to Juh. He gathered
up information from his friends and his relatives, sorting through
the rumors that the soldiers planned to round up the leaders remaining on the reservation, and chain them together, and kill them.

And he drank. Some leaders like Victorio did not drink much,
and did not let their men drink when the enemy was near. But
Geronimo liked to drink. Perhaps it was because he had so much
darkness gathered up inside of him, a wound that would not heal.
He sometimes yearned for the oblivion of drinking, when it did
not matter that Alope was dead, and The People were penned like
cattle, and the way ahead seemed so hopeless. So he drank when
he could, great, roaring, dangerous drunks when anyone with
good sense would avoid him altogether. He had often enough seen
the disasters that stalked warriors who got drunk and then turned
on one another, or committed some murder that would invite the
inevitable retaliation, or when they lay helpless while the treacherous Mexicans moved among them. But he could not always stop
himself when the great pots of tizwin had been brewed or when
the whiskey sellers moved among them. And it was always the
same. At first, the drinking chased off the darkness, so that he had
no worries and could defeat any enemy. But in the end the darkness returned, thicker and deeper than it had been before.

One day when Geronimo had gotten drunk, he got to thinking
about how living on the reservation had rotted the heart of the
people—like a log full of termites. He remembered the days of his
youth, when he had plunged in and out of the ice-covered stream,
and run to the top of the hill every morning with the mouthful of

unswallowed water, and let the ash burn his skin without flinching, and dodged the stones thrown by the other boys. He remembered how he had directed the training of the novices, making each of them strong and resilient as a bow of ash. It was not like that now for the young people on the reservation. They waited in their camps for their rations, with their weak legs, and their small chests. Thinking in this way, Geronimo's eyes fell upon his nephew, who was the son of Nana and Geronimo's sister. Who can say what anger or loathing moved through Geronimo's drink-dimmed mind as he looked at the boy? Perhaps he was shamed because Nana had left while he remained on the reservation of the White Eyes. Perhaps he was shamed because he saw what The People had become. Or perhaps he was only drunk and so the darkness he held always inside himself spilled out, like water through the crack in an olla. No matter. He used powerful words, like blows. The boy had no defense against them—not when they came from Geronimo, who was loved, and hated, and feared, and respected. What boy could dodge stones hurled by such a hand? And perhaps the boy shared the darkness, and the shame, and the helpless, lost yearning for the times he would never know—when The People were proud, and free, and the bane of all their enemies. So the boy took the heavy blow of Geronimo's words and then went alone and killed himself.[17]

When Geronimo returned to himself, he was horrified at what he had done—killing his nephew with his words. He saw now that everything he had feared had come to pass and that the reservation was only a longer, slower death than a bullet. So in the season of Many Leaves[18] Geronimo took his wife Chee-has-kish with her two children Chappo and Dohn-say, and She-gha, his second wife,[19] and set out with Ponce and a few others to join Juh. They attacked a wagon train and killed the drivers to obtain supplies, and they fought a little bit with the soldiers who chased them, but they all got away safely.

Geronimo returned then to the life he loved best, living in the Sierra Madre with Juh, and killing Mexicans. Juh had remade the peace with Janos, and so they went into Sonora, or into the United States, and took cattle, and horses, and other things that they could sell in Janos for ammunition, and guns, and whiskey. They lived in the old way, rising each morning to pray to the dawn, making the masks for the crown dancers, hunting in the dark canyons, and holding the elaborate four-day coming-of-age ceremonies for the girls when they each briefly became White Painted Woman. They roasted the heart of the agave, they brewed *tizwin*, they gathered raspberries and strawberries and sumac and grapes and chokeberries, they collected the cactus fruit and the saguaro fruit, they cooked the stalks of the yucca, and hunted deer, and cougars, whose skin they prized for bow quivers. They played the moccasin game with each side gambling, and shouting, and laughing in their attempts to guess where their opponents had hidden the bone, just as the birds had done when they played against the night creatures and so brought light into the world.

Geronimo, who was a strong singer and knew already many songs others had forgotten, was sometimes called on to prepare things for the dances and to prepare the Crown Dancers, who would imitate the mountain spirits who watched over The People.[20] He would prepare each dancer carefully, singing as he did so in the old way.

> Thus speaks earth's thunder:
> Because of it there is good about you,
> Because of it your body is well:
> Thus speaks earth's thunder.
>
> In the middle of the Holy Mountain,
> In the middle of its body, stands a hut,
> Brush-built, for the Black Mountain Spirit.
> White Lightning flashes in these moccasins;
> White Lightning streaks in angular path;
> I am the lightning flashing and streaking!
> This headdress lives; the noise of its pendants
> Sounds and is heard!
> My song shall encircle these dancers!

He knew also songs for the short step, and the free step, and the high step, so he could orchestrate the movements of the dancers all through a long night of singing. The dancers would dance stiff, and rigid, with small precise steps when he sang the short step songs. They would improvise steps of their own design when he sang the free step songs. And when Geronimo sang the high step songs the dancers would twirl, and leap, and dash about with such wild abandon that the watchers would shout, and laugh, and cry out for that High Step song, until the singer and the dancers all were exhausted, and proud. The songs made great bursts of melody, suddenly hushed, suddenly resumed—swelling so that they would bear up the heart of any who heard, as the form-less air makes the eagle rise. In the camps of the Nednai, many already knew Geronimo's songs, and many others learned them quickly, so that many joined in with his firm, strong, graceful voice on the choruses.

He sang also the tobacco songs, when the men would gather to roll the wild tobacco in oak leaves, to sit and talk and remem-ber how it was for Child of Waters when the world was young.

> The time for smoking has come.
> With the sun's tobacco let all be made pleasant.
> From here on let good constantly follow,
> From now on let many old men and old women rejoice;
> Let them come back to many ceremonies like this;
> Let all the girls be happy;
> Let them know many ceremonies like this;
> Let all rejoice;
> Let all the boys rejoice;
> Let them attend many ceremonies like this.

And he sang even the sly, funny songs at the social dances, which made everyone laugh, and which made the girls dancing in the inner circle smile and look at the ground, and made all of the boys dancing in the outer circle laugh with their eyes flashing, hoping to intercept the arrow of a glance on the shield of their pride. The girls waited for the gift the boy must give for the danc-ing, wondering whether it would be a valuable gift showing great regard, or a small gift showing only polite compliance with cus-tom. So Geronimo would sing in his warm voice:[21]

Young woman, you are thinking of something;
Young woman, you are thinking of something.
You are thinking of what you are going to get:
That man of whom you are thinking is worthless.

And he sang the love songs for the third and fourth night of the social dances that followed the White Painted Woman Ceremony, just as other singers had done in the impossibly long ago time when he and Alope had exchanged their furtive glances, and danced opposite each other in the circle, and he had struggled to find some gift worthy of her.

I see that girl again,
Then I become like this;
I see my own sweetheart again,
Then I become like this.

Maiden, you talk kindly to me,
You, I shall surely remember it,
I shall surely remember you alone,
Your words are so kind,
You, I shall surely remember it.

He thought of Alope as he sang the songs, as he watched the young lovers circling, and he knew they were each as he had been: thinking no one suspected what they did in the darkness and no one had ever felt as they felt. As he thought of Alope, he remembered his oath, and felt the old deep yearning for revenge, for danger, for the death of his enemy. So he returned wholeheartedly to the warrior's life with Juh, now a great warrior who was stocky, and powerful, and careful as a bear. He had a broad, flat face—hard and durable as the great slabs of stone on which mountains rested. Juh's warriors followed his directions with fear and respect. They would even fight at night, if he asked it, or make an organized and coordinated assault on a group of soldiers. Only a few war leaders had such Power to command the fiercely independent warriors of The People.[22] And although Juh was himself a respected singer, he often stammered when he spoke, even in council. Because of this, he avoided speaking much—relying on the force of his will and on his reputation as a war leader to bind the warriors to his purpose rather than on the eloquence that had served Cochise and Mangas Coloradas. Sometimes Geronimo spoke for Juh in the councils, because they were of like mind and always the first to talk for fighting and the last to talk for peace. Geronimo himself was not a great speaker, with a voice that could stretch out words like the feathers at the tip of an eagle's wing. But his Power and his intensity and his singleness of purpose moved listeners to him—especially if they were eager young warriors already yearning for a reason to fight.

Juh and Geronimo with their warriors went sometimes to the United States, although Victorio had stirred up the soldiers like a boy throwing stones at a hornet's nest. Victorio had at first surrendered to the soldiers, pleading that they let the Chihenne keep Ojo Caliente. The soldiers had gone back and forth, first letting them stay and then saying they must go back to San Carlos, and then saying that they could go live with the Mescalero. But then soldiers had come to take Victorio to hang him as a lesson to everyone else. But Victorio heard that they were coming, and fled with his people, knowing he would have no peace save death.[23] Juh and Geronimo moved carefully through the area, taking advantage of the turmoil Victorio had caused, knowing Victorio would get the blame for anything they did.[24]

But after a time, Geronimo began to miss his relatives, who remained with most of the Chiricahua at San Carlos. Besides, Juh did not have enough warriors to last a long time. The Mexicans had grown stronger, and sent soldiers to hunt them even in the Sierra Madre. And the Americans had more soldiers than could be counted—riding ceaselessly back and forth looking for Victorio. Geronimo knew The People's ammunition could not last forever, nor could their luck. So his mind turned back to the reservation, and the people he had left there. Geronimo and Juh sent out a runner to the soldiers, saying that they would talk about coming back in if the soldiers sent someone whom they trusted to negotiate. The soldiers sent Archie McIntosh, a white scout who had always treated The People fairly, and Jeffords, who had become a quiet farmer in Tucson after the death of his great friend Cochise. Juh and Geronimo said they had not been with Victorio and had not done any harm, and then went back to San Carlos.

They camped at the reservation and found things were quiet there now, since the soldiers were all off chasing Victorio. They learned that some of the Chiricahua, angry that the Chihenne had taken their horses in leaving, had become scouts for the soldiers who were hunting Victorio. Chihuahua, a fierce, eloquent, clever man who had become one of the leading men of the Chiricahua, enlisted as a scout with his warriors, thinking they could get their horses back, and earn the goodwill of the soldiers. Victorio grew bitter when he learned that some of the Chiricahua had turned against him, even though he had always been a friend to the Chiricahua. So he sent his son, Washington, with some of their warriors to attack the Chiricahua camps on the reservation to teach them a lesson. Washington attacked Juh's camp, perhaps because he was angry Juh and Geronimo had come in, but perhaps because he had made a mistake.

The agent came quickly to Juh and Geronimo, and asked them to help fight Victorio. But Geronimo hesitated. He remembered when Victorio's people had sheltered him. So he didn't want to ride against them, although he now needed to convince the soldiers that he would live peacefully at San Carlos. So he did not answer, only waited.

While he waited, Victorio finally used up his luck. He went down into Mexico to get away from the American soldiers, who pursued him even there. But after Victorio had used up all his ammunition, and run a long ways down into Mexico, a Mexican army trapped him. Victorio and his warriors fought all night, with bows, and stones, and knives, so that some of the women and children could escape. Then Victorio killed himself with his own knife as the soldiers closed in. The Mexicans took all their scalps, sold the women and children as slaves, and staged a great parade to show off their trophies.[25]

Geronimo settled once more into life on the reservation, still struggling for a solution to the great riddle of the White Eyes. He felt like Coyote—brave and foolish and forever caught in his own traps. Victorio's fate sobered him. It was not death that made him hesitate. He still believed in what his Power had told him and had no fear of the soldiers' bullets. He did not seek death, but he did not fear it. He was ready to sing his death song. Nor had Victorio feared death. But he wondered whether Victorio had known how it would end—not only for the warriors, but for the women, and for the children, now all dead, or slaves. The Chihenne had been wiped out, as the Bedonkohe had been, so that soon no one would be left to sing their songs, and tell their stories, and remember the strong things they had done. How had Usen let this happen? Why had he given so much Power to the White Eyes and nothing to The People except courage, and the love of the land they could not keep? How could it be that The People were so useless that Usen would suffer them to be wiped out by such a people as the White Eyes?

So Geronimo resolved to live quietly on the reservation, with his three wives, and his children, so that they could grow up, and grow old, and learn all of the Coyote stories for the long nights of winter, and the songs for painting the Crown Dancers, and the love songs for the fourth night of the ceremonies—the circle, within the circle, in the light of the fire.

He planted crops, as the agent said he should do. And he taught his daughter the right way to behave, so much so that Dohn-say was recognized as one of the outstanding women of her band, which made her father's heart fill with pride.

But it was not to be.

Even when Geronimo set his heart on peace, something always turned his face away. It was /as though his Power tested him always—pushing him first this way, and then that. Perhaps it was so that he would learn some great lesson. Or perhaps it was only the nature of Power—a curious boy with the small bird.

Just so. No matter. As Geronimo sought to live quietly on the reservation, there came word of a medicine man, a small, humble man who had once scouted for the army, but who had prayed a long while, and fasted a long while, and gone up onto the sacred mountain to seek Power. The medicine man had returned from the mountain with a vision and a new idea. His name was Noch-ay-del-klinne, and he was a White Mountain man, but he spoke to all of the bands. He said that Usen had not forsaken The People after all. He said Usen had sent the White Eyes as a test, to see if The People would believe in him, and would do all things rightly, and would not lose heart even when they could see no way through their troubles.

Noch-ay-del-klinne, who many called the Prophet, began to hold dances—Ghost Dances.[26] The people who came to his ceremonies danced for days, arrayed like the spokes of a wheel, shuffling, and chanting, and crying out in growing ecstasy as he moved among them, sprinkling them with *hoddentin*, the sacred pollen of the cattails. Many danced in a kind of trance until they fell to the ground in exhaustion. Noch-ay-del-klinne said he had Ghost Power, and could talk to the spirits of the dead who had promised they would come back in the Time of Large Leaves. They told him the White Eyes would then be gone from the land of The People.

Geronimo, and Juh, and Naiche, and the other leaders did not know what to think about this White Mountain man who said he could speak to the dead. They noted that many people brought the Prophet gifts, which he accepted with grave courtesy. They wondered that he should speak to the dead, when it was not safe for other people to disturb the dead in The Happy Place by so much as speaking their names. And Geronimo and the other leaders wondered at the way the people flocked to the Prophet from all of the bands—Tonto, and Mimbreno, and White Mountain, and Chiricahua all dancing together as though they were one band, and one clan, and one people. This made them think then what The People might accomplish if they were together in this way, instead of divided, one against the other, by old feuds and the tricks of the White Eyes.

So Nana, who was old, and whose people had been nearly all wiped out, and who had come back weary, and lame, and heartsick to live on the reservation, went to see the Ghost Dance for himself. The Prophet took Nana and some others up onto the mountain just at dawn, and prayed a long while, calling to the spirits of the dead for help. Come, show yourselves to us, cried the Prophet, with the medal that he had received from the hand of the Great

White Father dangling from around his neck.[27] Then a fog rose up out of the ground, and while Nana and the others looked they saw three men standing in the fog, rising up out of the earth, looking about, as though surprised that they should be there. Nana looked closely and saw that one of the men was Mangas Coloradas and one of the men was Cochise and one of the men was Victorio. They rose out of the ground only to their knees, as though loath to leave Mother Earth. The chiefs turned to the Prophet and said, Why do you call us? Why do you disturb us? We do not wish to come back. The buffalo are gone. White people are everywhere in the land that was ours. We do not wish to come back. But tell us what we must do! cried his shaken listeners, as the chiefs began to fade away. The spirits replied then: Live at peace with the white men and let us rest, as they sank back into the ground.

Nana went back to Juh, and Geronimo, and Naiche, and the other leaders and told them all of the things he had seen. They talked among themselves and decided that the Prophet had Power after all, and that perhaps Usen had not abandoned The People but was merely testing them in some fashion, as Coyote was forever tested, always failing. Many began going to the Ghost Dances, dancing and singing—even Geronimo, even Juh. They put off talk about leaving, and about raiding, and even put aside their fears of the soldiers, and of treachery, and of the arrest they believed always threatened should the unpredictable White Eyes forget their promises and remember their dead.

Many had gathered for a Ghost Dance at the Prophet's camp on Cibecue Creek, when lookouts came running into camp saying that many soldiers and some scouts were coming from Fort Apache.[28] The warriors ran to get their weapons, talking excitedly, saying they would fight the soldiers if they tried to take the Prophet. But Noch-ay-del-klinne remained perfectly calm, as though he was not worried about the soldiers at all, so that the warriors borrowed his calm, and waited to see what the soldiers would do.

Then one of the scouts, a respected White Mountain man named Dead Shot, came ahead of the soldiers and said the soldiers would not hurt the Prophet, but only take him back to the fort to talk to the agent. The warriors talked excitedly for a while longer among themselves about what they should do. But again the Prophet only sat down in front of his wickiup with no sign of fear, saying the soldiers would not hurt him and that no bullet they had made could harm him. The White Eyes were in Usen's hands, although they did not know it. No warrior of the people need fight them now, because Usen had told the Prophet He would drive out the White Eyes by the time of the summer harvest.

Still, the warriors crowded close around when the soldiers came up to Noch-ay-del-klinne's wickiup. The warriors held their weapons, ready to fight. But the soldier *nantan* said they would not harm the Prophet if he came with them quietly to the fort. Noch-ay-del-klinne said that he would go with them tomorrow, but that he had to help hold a dance. The *nantan* said he could not wait, and the Prophet would have to come along right away, to which Noch-ay-del-klinne said he would come along as soon as he had his lunch, and as soon as his son brought his horse. So the *nantan* nodded in a friendly way, and went away with most of his men, leaving a few with the scouts to bring Noch-ay-del-klinne. But after awhile, the soldiers who had been left became impatient and one of them took the Prophet roughly by the shoulder, pulled him to his feet, and said they must go right away. The warriors who were watching nearly began shooting then, all fingers on a trigger. But again Noch-ay-del-klinne calmed them, saying he would go with the soldiers, and not try to escape, because the soldiers could not hurt him.

So the small group of soldiers went back down Cibecue Creek to where all of the others had stopped to make their camp. They took the Prophet into the middle of the camp and put a guard over him, because the warriors had followed the soldiers and crowded around the camp now. One of the soldier *nantans* walked toward the warriors, shouting at them in a rough way to go away. Then someone started the shooting. Many said the soldiers started shooting first.[29] The warriors shot back, killing the *nantan* and another man right away. All of the soldiers began shooting and some of them shot at the scouts, who had always been loyal, but who the soldiers said were trying to save the Prophet, who was their kinsman, and a White Mountain man like most of the scouts.

The Prophet's wife went to him when the shooting started, begging him to run away before the soldiers killed him. But he said the soldiers would come after him no matter where he went, and it was better to wait to see what would happen there. A soldier came up to the Prophet, drawing out his gun. Noch-ay-del-klinne's wife threw herself on top of her man's body, calling to the soldier not to shoot, but he moved his gun and shot the Prophet anyway. Seeing this, the warriors fired at the soldier, hitting him.[30] The shooting began all over, with more warriors running to help. But then the Prophet woke up and began again to crawl away from the soldiers. Seeing his father fall, Noch-ay-del-klinne's son rode straight into the camp of the soldiers to try and bring his mother and his father out. But the soldiers killed him quickly. When she saw her son fall, the wife of the Prophet ran to one of the saddles of the soldiers to pull out a rifle, but the soldiers also shot her down quickly. Then the soldiers saw the Prophet was not dead after all. So another soldier ran up to him and put his gun against his head, and pulled the trigger. The Prophet fell back again, but after a moment he came to himself and once again began crawling away from the soldiers. So another man shot him a third time, but still that did not kill him, because of the Power of the shirt he wore which protected him from bullets. So finally a soldier ran up to him with an ax, and split open his head, so that the Prophet was finally dead for good. Noch-ay-del-klinne was still wearing the peace medal he had received from the Great White Father. On the back of the medal it said "On Earth Peace, Good Will Toward Men."

The warriors fought all day long, killing eight of the soldiers, but the soldiers had too many guns and too much ammunition and the warriors were all in confusion. Geronimo and some of the others fought, organizing small groups of warriors to keep the soldiers pinned down so they could not escape until more warriors arrived. But even though the warriors were furious the soldiers had killed the Prophet, they would not follow any leader. Each small group of warriors did as they thought best, and none going too close to the trapped soldiers who had so many good guns. During the night, the soldiers slipped away because the warriors could not agree who should watch them. The warriors sent runners to other bands, telling them to set up an ambush in a deep canyon the soldiers must cross to return to the fort. However, the warriors who set up the ambush came late and the soldiers passed across the canyon safely. Other warriors went to watch the fort, shooting at it from behind good cover. But they were taken by surprise when the soldiers who had killed the Prophet returned and so did not prevent them from going on into the fort. Many warriors from many bands gathered around the fort, so incensed the soldiers had killed the Prophet for no reason at all that they attacked the fort a few times—hoping that the medicine of the Prophet might still protect them. They hoped also that the Prophet would come back and bring Cochise, and Victorio, and Mangas Coloradas. But the Prophet did not return, and the soldiers still had their many guns, and their many bullets, so the warriors did not press the attack on the fort very closely. They could not do much with all of the confusion of the bands. Besides, they began to think what the soldiers would do now. Many of those who had come to the fight at Cibecue, and at the fort, thought they should take their families away so the soldiers would not punish them for the fighting.

Geronimo, and Juh, and Nana, and the other leaders of the Chiricahua, and the Nednai, and the few remaining Chihenne,[31] went back to their camps and remained quietly there, wondering that they had so easily believed in the Prophet. The Chiricahua leaders could see now that the ones who had gone would not come back to save them as the Prophet had promised—although he clearly did have Power over guns and bullets, since the soldiers could only kill him with the ax. Still, Geronimo felt foolish he had so easily believed—letting his yearning for an escape from the trap of the White Eyes overcome his good sense.[32]

They remained anxiously in their camps, after gathering up supplies, and weapons, and ammunition they would need to flee should the soldiers come for them. Soldiers poured onto the reservation from every side, because the whites were frightened by the way in which the bands all fought together at Cibecue, and because they had dared even to attack the fort. Soldiers rode back and forth everywhere on the reservation, searching for people who had fought at Cibecue, especially for the scouts who had turned against the soldiers and then run away to hide with their White Mountain relatives.

The Chiricahua leaders went to the agent to ask why so many soldiers had come onto the reservation, and whether they had come to punish people for things that had been done in Mexico before they settled on the reservation. The agent was a man named Tiffany, whom none of the leaders trusted. Many said he did not give all of the rations promised and some saw wagons loaded with their rations and supplies leaving the reservation.[33] The Chiricahua were dissatisfied, because they had not even enough clout to make breechclouts, but they could do nothing because Tiffany controlled the soldiers—as he had shown when he sent them against the Prophet. Tiffany listened to their concerns, but reassured them that the soldiers were only looking for the people who had killed the soldiers at Cibecue, and would not harm the Chiricahua who were living peacefully in their camps.

Still, the Chiricahua did not trust Tiffany, or the soldiers. Many people came to Geronimo and said that they heard the soldiers would imprison all of the leaders. He remembered how the soldiers had seized Cochise under the flag of truce, and how they had killed Mangas Coloradas, and how they had kept him all that time in the small place with iron chains on his legs. And so when the agent sent for the leaders of the Chiricahua for a conference with the soldiers at Fort Thomas, the leaders held a council. Geronimo said it was death to stay now on the reservation, and everyone who heard him could see that it was true because the Power moved now in him. It is more manly, he said, to die on the warpath than to be killed in prison.[34]

So many of the Chiricahua fled from the reservation, thinking to join Juh and his Nednai in the Sierra Madre. But Loco, who had become the principal chief of the Chihenne and the Mimbreno, would not go with them. He said the soldiers would hunt them, as they had hunted Victorio, until none remained. And even though the warriors might prefer such a clean, brave death, the women, and the little ones, would pay the greater price. They could not defeat the White Eyes, and would be ground down like corn between the rock of the whites and the stone of the Mexicans. So they had best stay quietly in this place, and hope that the soldiers would not punish them. But Geronimo and the others said this was the argument of a woman, not a warrior, and went away very angry, their blood hot to fight. Everyone was in fear and confusion, not knowing which way to jump.

Geronimo worked to build up support among the leaders, especially with Naiche, the son of Cochise, who had become the leading man among many of the Chiricahua. He did not have any Power, and some said that he should not lead warriors in battle because of that. But he was liked, and respected, and carried still the authority of Cochise in his face, and in his words, and in his manner. Geronimo knew he must work through Naiche, knowing also that many of the Chiricahua said that the Bedonkohe were nearly all dead and so Geronimo had no right to lead the Chiricahua. Besides, they knew that Geronimo was like a burning stick you dare not take up with your bare hand. So Geronimo often allied himself with Naiche, like two hawks chasing down a jackrabbit in relays. Many trusted Naiche in matters of leadership, and Geronimo's Power in matters of war, so when Geronimo and Naiche moved together many followed. But Geronimo knew he must balance Naiche in his plans carefully, because Naiche would fight only when driven to it because he remembered his promise to his father and hoped to find a space for his people to live peacefully. So Geronimo stood with Naiche, and did not interrupt him in council, and did not criticize him to anyone else, and showed his respect, which was easy because Naiche was a brave man and also kind, easygoing, and loyal. And yet again, Geronimo could not speak too softly in the council in deference to Naiche's doubts—or he would lose influence with the young warriors. The leaders of smaller bands often pushed to gain a following as well, often by talking up war. Foremost among them was Chato, a fierce, arrogant warrior who had pushed hard for leadership and who led a faction of some of the most eager young warriors. Everyone knew Chato was a good man in a fight because he had Power in war. He had fine, fierce features, a quick, sly mind, and a will harder than ironwood, which sinks in water. He was fearless in a fight, impossible to turn from his purpose, and clever as Coyote in his tactics, but his need for respect and influence showed too clearly, like the gash of an ax on a tree that does not heal. Chato had been a warrior in Cochise's band, but left to join Nana when he saw he had no chance to lead the Chiricahua. He fought in many good fights with Nana, and thought that he should lead the band as Nana grew too old for the warpath. But Nana preferred Kaytennae, so Chato joined Chihuahua's band and also went often on war parties with Geronimo.[35] Even so, the resentment simmered between Kaytennae and Chato, which made things complicated for Geronimo, who was Nana's kinsman. So the council discussions went on for a long time, often moving in a circle, like a man following his own tracks.

Still, they waited, hoping that the soldiers contented themselves with killing the scouts who had turned against the soldiers. But then the soldiers came and arrested a White Mountain band that had been living near the Chiricahua, which had been raiding here and there since Cibecue because they had among them some of the scouts who had turned and were now marked as dead men. But then the soldiers released the White Mountain men, and said they could draw their rations after all, which confused everyone trying to decide what the soldiers intended. But then the soldiers went quickly toward the camp of the White Mountain band, so that the warriors scattered. Some ran through the camps of the Chiricahua saying the soldiers were coming to arrest all the leaders and hang them.

So Geronimo, and Naiche, and Juh, and Chato and the others gathered their people and fled toward Mexico, remembering the treachery of the whites in all times past. They had saved up guns and ammunition, and as they left they raided several White Mountain camps to get the guns and ammunition and horses they needed. They killed three soldiers as they were getting away, to get their horses and slow down the pursuit. They came across a wagon train, and killed seven men, and took the supplies they needed so badly now. Soldiers caught up to them, and the warriors stopped to fight and give the women and the children time to get on ahead.

They fought until dark. Geronimo and the others knew the soldiers would expect them to flee in the darkness. But this time the warriors kept up the fighting, sometimes coming to within ten feet of the soldiers. They did this to make sure the soldiers remained in their camp all night long and not chase the women and the children who pushed as quickly as they could run. Finally the warriors scattered, heading for the place of meeting and leaving only a confusion of trails the soldiers could not follow.

They moved through the soldiers thrown out to stop them as wind through the fingers of the trees, leaving only the bodies of the people who saw them and the terrified rumors of their passing. They all came away safely into the Sierra Madre, walking the trails their feet had learned as children, safe from the pursuit of the soldiers.

Geronimo came wearily at last to the place he had arranged with Juh and Nana to meet, riding along confident in the security of this last, great refuge. He had in his band some of the strongest warriors of the Chiricahua. His brother[36] Perico was his *segundo* and helped him lay his plans and direct the warriors. With him also was his brother Fun, who was the bravest warrior among all of the Chiricahua because he seemed an utter stranger to fear, and never hesitated at any risk. Riding with Geronimo also was his brother-in-law Yanosh, a quiet man who never faltered. Geronimo's nephew Kanseah also rode with them, taking the warrior training in the old way from Yanosh. They rode carelessly now, in this refuge.

Of a sudden, they looked up and saw warriors standing on the rocks just above them, holding their guns, and laughing. Geronimo recognized Juh, solid as a grizzly bear, wearing eagle feathers streaming from his skullcap and the elaborately beaded moccasins made for him by Ishton, his favorite wife and Geronimo's sister. He saw also Nana, appearing suddenly as if by some Power of deception, not quite smiling that they had surprised Geronimo.

I knew that you were there all the time, glowered Geronimo. Some other man might have said nothing, knowing that Geronimo had little humor but a long memory. But Nana only laughed, saying, You did not, and you the sly fox of The People. So everyone

Two Apache scouts in chains await hanging for their actions
at Cibecue Creek. The scouts who turned on the soldiers
during the bungled attempt to arrest an Apache religious
leader represented the only such mutiny in the long service
of the Apache scouts. (*Courtesy Arizona Historical Society, Tucson*)

laughed, because Nana remained the most revered leader of the
people, having been a great warrior and war leader in battles with
Victorio, and Mangas Coloradas, and Victorio, and still able to ride
a longer day than any young man although he limped when he
walked.

So the warriors who had left the reservation gathered in the
safety of the Sierra Madre, to consider what they should do. They

saw quickly that things would be hard, even in a place where they had always been safe. They knew that the Mexicans had grown stronger, and had more soldiers out, and more soldiers near the towns, and more soldiers along the trails to watch the wagon trains. They saw also that although the warriors had many good American guns, they had not enough ammunition and so would have to raid back into the territory of the White Eyes to get bullets. So they were caught here, like a man on a rock in the middle of a river. They did not have enough warriors to keep the Mexicans from chasing them, nor enough warriors to do all the raiding they must do. They could only live by sneaking about in their own country, taking a cow here and a horse there, and running always from the soldiers.[37]

The leaders gathered in council to consider what they must do. They talked awhile, and then Geronimo proposed a bold plan. He said they should go back to San Carlos, and bring Loco's people away with them back to the Sierra Madre. Loco had the leadership of more than three hundred people, Chiricahua, Mimbreno, and Chihenne, including perhaps eighty warriors. Chato spoke up then, from the outside ring of the council of leaders, although many said that he had no right to speak. Chato said loudly that Loco was an old woman, and did not deserve to lead The People. But Nana spoke, saying Loco was a strong man, and a strong leader, who should not be criticized by young warriors who had not earned the right. Everyone sat silent, seeing the blow Nana had struck to Chato's pride, and wondering what Chato would do. But he only glared, and walked away from the council because he knew Nana had the respect of all of the warriors, even Geronimo. Even so, the council talked a long while about the idea Geronimo had brought forward, and the more they talked about it, the more the leaders turned toward it. Many had relatives still on the reservation and they yearned for them, and feared for them.

Geronimo and Juh and the other war leaders begin to make their preparations, gathering up supplies, and guns, and ammunition, sending runners to the reservation to go secretly among their relatives to prepare the way. They even sent messages to Loco,

urging him to come away to join them and promising to help him
do it. Geronimo prayed every morning, singing his many songs,
going out to talk with his Power. Others watched him, knowing
they all must rely on Geronimo's Power to undertake such a thing.
Otherwise who would even consider it? They would have to go
through hundreds of miles of territory covered with soldiers,
sneak onto the reservation where more soldiers waited, and bring
away hundreds of people, many of them women and children.

Geronimo and Naiche[38] led the warriors back on the old war
trails toward the White Eyes, taking care to avoid being seen. Chihuahua also came, leading a group of warriors. Two warriors
turned aside to take some horses from a Mexican ranch, then decided to take the horses back to camp in the Sierra Madre. Geronimo could not stop their going, for every warrior had the right to
decide which way he would ride, and when he would fight. He
might have stopped them if his Power had warned him of the consequences of their going, but his Power said nothing because
Power speaks in its own time, for its own purposes.

Geronimo and the others rode four days to San Carlos, covering sixty miles and more each day, taking care that no one should
see them, lest the alarm spread out ahead of them like the ripples
from a stone thrown into water. They came at last to a sheep
camp, near the reservation. Some said they should pass the sheep
camp by, but Geronimo went on, the wolf in his eyes. He had the
war feeling, riding on the old trails, and it burned brighter in him
as they went along, like the fire climbing out of the kindling into
the logs. The sixty warriors[39] came suddenly upon the sheep
camp, and saw it was run by a Mexican whom Geronimo had captured when he was just a boy and raised before trading him to a
white rancher. But Bes-das[40] had become the chief shepherd for
the rancher, and had ten thousand sheep under his care, in this
dangerous place on the edge of the reservation.

The people in the sheep camp looked up in alarm when the
warriors appeared suddenly out of the trees, coming in from all
directions at once so no one could run off. Bes-das was there with
his wife and his three children, along with two other Mexican
women, and three other Mexican men. Bylas, who was a promi-

nent White Mountain man, and his wife and some of his people
were also there, working in the sheep camp. The warriors rode in
among the herders, who stood quietly, hoping the warriors would
let them live. Bes-das came forward and welcomed Geronimo as
an old friend, holding the fear back, knowing that Geronimo
could scent fear like a bear. The warriors began killing sheep, to
replenish their supplies, and to get meat for the people they would
soon be taking away from the reservation. Geronimo shot a pony,
and told Bes-das to cook it for the warriors. So the warriors rested
after their long journey, and ate—watching the Mexican women as
they rushed about to build up the fire, and cut up the meat, and
bring out everything they had for the warriors. The White Mountain men watched this all quietly, wondering what Geronimo
would do. Everyone knew how he hated the Mexicans, but no one
could predict what he might do with the White Mountain men
who had fallen in his path. The Chiricahua and the White Mountain people had never been great friends, or great enemies. But the
White Mountain warriors had often served as scouts against the
Chiricahua, so grudges had grown up between them like catclaw.

Geronimo watched the Mexicans coming and going with
brooding amusement, enjoying their fear. He asked Bes-das for
the fine, embroidered shirt he was wearing, and smiled when the
Mexican hurried to take it off and give it to him. When they had
finished their meal, Geronimo ordered his warriors to seize all of
the Mexicans and tie them up, even Bes-das. Then Geronimo and
several other warriors went among the prisoners, with knives and
clubs and rocks, killing each of them. Other warriors stood aside
uneasily, seeing Geronimo's Power had awakened in him and now
demanded blood. Then someone shouted that Bylas's wife was hiding something, so Geronimo turned on her and went toward her,
with all the blood and fury in his eyes. But Naiche also stepped
forward, and pushed aside her long skirt and found Bes-das's
nine-year-old son hiding there. Geronimo moved forward to take
the child, and kill him, as he had killed all the others, but Naiche
would not stand aside. They argued about the child and everyone
wondered at it, seeing this new strength in Naiche, and seeing also
Geronimo's lust for death—the insatiable need for revenge that

had twisted him so he would argue openly with his friend and ally for the right to kill a boy. Bylas's wife then began pleading for the life of the boy. Geronimo saw then that the warriors' thirst for killing had been slaked, and that Naiche could not back down, so Geronimo yielded and said he would let the boy live.

They decided to move on quickly, leaving two men at the camp to guard the women of the White Mountain men, but taking Bylas and the others along to the reservation so they could not get free and spread the alarm. They camped not far from Loco's people, just off the reservation, in a place where they would not be discovered and sent messengers onto the reservation to tell the people waiting for them to get ready. Then Geronimo went aside to pray, and to consult his Power. He sang four songs, which went on for a long time, his strong, hypnotic voice rising and falling. He spoke to his Power, to see what he should do. His Power said that everything would go well and they would come away with all of Loco's people if they did not falter and did not let Loco's people have any choice, or debate. His Power also promised to lay a deep sleep over Loco's people, so they would all be quietly in their wickiups at dawn and no one would be out to spread the alarm.

Before dawn,[41] Geronimo roused the warriors. He sent some to cut the telegraph wires to delay the arrival of reinforcements from the nearby forts. Then the warriors went to the river where Loco's people were camped, and waited quietly for the light. At length, Geronimo took a white pebble, and threw it into the air, watching its ghostly form fall to the ground. By this he knew they had enough light to start. So he led the warriors out of the trees, and into the river, calling out to Loco's people, telling them to gather up their things, and come away, and warning them that the warriors would shoot anyone who resisted.

Loco's people came out of their wickiups, their heads thick with sleep. They looked fearfully at the warriors who surrounded them, herding them together, demanding that they take only what they could carry. Many of Loco's people did not want to go. They had lived a long time on the reservation. Some of the children had never lived wild, and most of the young men had never taken the warrior training. They had enough to eat on the reservation and they did not want to go out again to be hunted like deer. Others, mostly the young men eager for glory and the older men yearning for the old days, were glad to go. Loco himself was of two minds, seeing how sickness moved through his people, seeing how the young men loafed about, drinking and fighting, seeing how the spirit of The People had faded. But he also knew how the women and children would suffer and that they had no true hope, caught between the White Eyes and the Mexicans. He remembered the days when he had fought the Mexicans, and the White Eyes, and the grizzly bear with his knife and danced proud and erect in many a victory dance. But now he was herded along by Geronimo's Power, moving reluctantly onto the warpath and away from any hope of a peaceful life amid his children, and their children, and their children.

They were all on the move in a short time, with perhaps one hundred warriors and three hundred to four hundred women and children. Geronimo had hoped to send out war parties to kill the forty policemen, warriors who worked for the agent to enforce the White Eyes' laws on the reservation. But he had not enough warriors, and decided it was more important to get away quickly. But he left behind a rear guard to kill anyone who came to investigate. The chief of the police force, a white man whom many of Loco's people considered a friend, came along with several warriors. The rear guard killed them, and came riding quickly back to Geronimo with the boots of the White Eye. Loco's people saw that, and grieved for their friend and for themselves, since they knew now that the soldiers would punish them, whether they had gone along willingly with Geronimo or not.

They all pushed quickly away from the reservation and into the mountains, where it would be hard for soldiers on horseback to follow The People on foot. Geronimo sent out raiding parties in every direction, to bring back guns, and ammunition, and food, and horses for the women and children who would otherwise slow them down. They killed everyone they encountered, until about fifty White Eyes had died. They knew this would stir up all the soldiers against them, but they had no choice because anyone who saw them would spread the alarm so that the soldiers would close quickly in on them.

They waited a day to gather these supplies. As they waited, there came the time for the White Painted Woman Ceremony for one of the girls in Loco's band. Some said they could not wait for the proper ceremony, but Geronimo said that they should have the ceremony, shortened to one night instead of four. After all, why had they left the reservation save to remain The People, and to protect the old ways? They pushed on afterward as quickly as they could, heartened by the songs and the hope that the ceremonies that made the girl White Painted Woman for a time would bring them luck.

And so it seemed. Once, some scouts found their trail and began to follow them, but the warriors ambushed them, killing four, and scattering them. The warriors then pushed quickly on, but the soldiers following on along behind the scouts on their horses overtook the women and the children. The warriors formed a shield between the soldiers and the women and the children, and fought so fiercely that they drove away the soldiers, who had more men, and more guns, but less stomach for the fighting. Nonetheless, they lost two warriors in that fight and had too few warriors to spare even those.[42]

They slipped away from the soldiers in the darkness, and then gathered again to consider what they must do. They could remain hidden in the mountains, but time ran heavily against them. Every day they remained, more soldiers would gather. Their only hope of safety lay in the Sierra Madre. But just ahead of them lay the broad expanse of the San Simon Valley—open, and without cover, where the dust of their passing would draw soldiers from fifty miles in every direction. If they were caught there in the open, the soldiers would slaughter them. But they could not remain where they were. So they set off in the cloaking darkness, moving as quickly as they could.

Geronimo watched the stars wheeling across the sky, calculating the time until dawn, watching as the hours turned against them. Soon he saw they could not make it across and they would be caught by daylight on the open plain. So he turned aside, to consult his Power. He was angry and confused, because his Power had urged him to do this thing, and had said The People would get safely away, but now had led them to this open place in the palm of death. So Geronimo sat down as the people hurried past, and sang some songs, so his Power would explain this thing to him. After a time, Geronimo's Power spoke to him, and they talked back and forth for a time, with Geronimo circling for advantage, trying to move his Power to help without angering it. At length, his Power said he should just go on, and not worry about the daylight, or the soldiers, but just have faith, and go on across the valley as best he could. So Geronimo took up his bag of pollen, and his eagle feather, and his sage, and his turquoise, and his abalone shell and put them in his pouch, and hurried on to catch up with The People who had passed him by. He watched the stars as he rode, and saw they did not move as they had, but remained fixed in the sky. He knew then that his Power had delayed the dawn, and he both rejoiced in it, and feared it.[43] Others saw this also, marveling that Geronimo's Power would do such a thing. It stilled some of the talk that had been growing up against him—even among Loco's band, who began to think they might go safely all the way to the Sierra Madre after all. They began to wonder that they had stayed so long on the reservation and listened to Loco's fears if Geronimo's Power could hold back the day.

They rested half a day in the Chiricahua Mountains, where Cochise had roamed and where no White Eye and no Mexican had once dared to wander. Then they pushed on down into Mexico, rejoicing that they were finally safe from the pursuing American soldiers. They slowed down, laughing and singing as they walked, the young men racing their horses along the long column of people, showing off, savoring their chance to be free warriors of a strong people once again. They camped in Mexico by a good spring at the base of Sierra Emmedio, with a rock ridge behind them and a small hill to the west, and the level plain to the south. They rested for two days, holding dances all through the nights, gathering up the heart of the agave on the surrounding hillsides and making mescal in great baking pits, singing the mescal songs, chanting, and praying, and telling stories. The young men danced, recounting in their movements the fight with the soldiers, when the few warriors had driven away the many soldiers. And for those two days, Geronimo prayed to his Power, watched the women working at the mescal pits, watched the children playing their games in the old way, and drifted over to join in the hoop and pole games. Everything seemed right with the world, and he saw that his Power had led him correctly.

But on the third day, they suddenly heard shooting up on the ridge above the camp. Scouts had fired at Loco's grandson and two women who had gone to tend the mescal pit, killing the women. Shooting broke out all along the ridge, and warriors began to fall on every side. The women and children immediately began running, while the warriors rallied around Geronimo to cover their retreat. Everyone ran to the rocky hill, which provided the only cover on the open plain from the rifles of the scouts on the ridge. Then soldiers also began firing at them, having come up on the plain to cut off their escape. Geronimo saw that he had been careless and overconfident and perhaps too full of pride, so that his Power had taught him this lesson. Geronimo had assumed the soldiers would not cross the border, and so would not continue to chase them. But here they were far down into Mexico. But when his anger at himself had passed, Geronimo considered his situation, counting the guns of the soldiers. He decided that he was not facing the main body of the soldiers, but only the scouts with some soldiers to help them. Most of the soldiers had not caught up with them yet,[44] and they might still escape if they could get into the foothills quickly.

Loco crawled forward to where the scouts on the ridge could hear him, and called out to them to come down from the hill and join them. They should not fight for the soldiers against their own people, he cried out. But the scouts shouted back that the Chiricahua had stolen their horses, and that they all should go back to the reservation where the soldiers would not hunt them. Then an old woman climbed up on a rock and shouted to the scouts, thinking that her son was among them. So she called out to him, pleading with the scouts to stop shooting, and saying that the Chiricahua had made them leave the reservation. But someone in the rocks shot the woman down dead off the rock. Others shot at Loco, so that a bullet fragment gave him a small wound.

Four warriors then decided to go around behind the scouts on the ridge and drive them off so everyone could escape from the trap in which the scouts held them by shooting down from the ridge. So the four warriors moved around behind the scouts and began firing. The scouts had to turn around then to fight the four warriors, so the people among the rocks on the hill could run across the open space and into the foothills. They all began moving south again. The soldiers and the scouts did not follow, because they had been fighting all day, and had used up their ammunition, but they had all of The People's horses, and most of their supplies, and had killed fourteen warriors and at least three women.

The People all pushed on as hard as they could through that night, and by dawn they had covered twenty-nine miles, so that the soldiers were again many hours behind them. Perhaps a dozen warriors pushed on ahead, including Naiche and Chato and Kaytennae, but most of the warriors remained in the rear with Geronimo to protect the women and children from the soldiers, who they knew would keep on following them. The warriors who went on ahead went too far and too carelessly. Some later said the warriors in the advanced guard and Geronimo had fought, disagreeing about what should be done, and placing blame on Geronimo's Power for not having warned them about the soldiers. Chato still festered because Nana had wounded his pride, and Geronimo had not supported him. And anger still lay between Naiche and Geronimo, because Naiche had made him lose face by protecting the Mexican boy back at the sheep camp. So some warriors had split off, angered by Geronimo's arrogance, and the way in which he drove everyone else, and their own pride.[45]

But the worst thing of all still lay just ahead, around the next bend of the wash. The two warriors who had left with their stolen horses back when Geronimo was going to the reservation had fallen into the hands of the Mexicans. The Mexican commander had offered them their lives if they would tell them where the others had gone, and when they would return. So the Mexicans had laid a trap for The People, who straggled now into it in a ragged column of exhausted women and children fleeing from the White Eyes, with many looks back over their shoulder and little thought for the danger that lay just ahead.

The people in the front of the long line of refugees first smelled coffee, and thought the advanced guard had made camp. So they hurried forward. Suddenly shooting broke out all around them as the Mexicans came out of their hiding places in the gullies that cut into the grassy plain. Immediately the air filled with the sound of shooting, and the sound of screaming, and the women and the children turned and ran back away from the soldiers. The soldiers rode in among them, shooting them down on every side, trampling them with horses, cutting them down with swords, piercing them with lances. The women and the children had no weapons, only their legs to keep them running just ahead of death, well mounted.

Then Geronimo came running through them all, calling the warriors to him, calling the warriors by their true names so that they could not leave him there to fight the soldiers alone. Perhaps three dozen warriors rallied, seeing they must slow the soldiers down so the surviving women and children could reach the safety of the mountains. Geronimo led the warriors to a sandy ravine that lay across the path of the soldiers. They began shooting so effectively at the oncoming soldiers that the Mexicans stopped, and fell back, and concentrated their attention on the warriors in the ditch. Some women who sought shelter in the ditch dug out holes for shelter, and water seeped out of the sand into the holes they scooped out, so that the warriors had water. The warriors dug footholds in the side of the gully so they could stand at the edge and shoot at the soldiers with good cover.

They fought back and forth for hours, the 35 warriors in the ditch against the 250 soldiers on the plain. Fun fought alongside Geronimo and so did Lozen, whose aim with her rifle proved deadly. Once when the warriors were nearly out of ammunition, a woman jumped out of the ditch and ran through all of the Mexican bullets to grab a bag of ammunition that had been dropped in the open. She ran nearly back to the ditch before she fell to the ground, the bullets thick as bees about her. But the warriors crawled up out of the ditch, grabbed her feet, and pulled her back to safety. She still held the precious bag of ammunition.

Somehow the Mexicans learned Geronimo was in the ditch, and they began calling out to him, saying that this was his day to die. They called to each other when they charged, saying that Geronimo was there, and they must kill him. Geronimo had waged his war with the Mexicans for thirty years now, avenging his mother, and Alope, and his children, and his other wives each twentyfold. But he had long since stopped counting the Mexicans he killed. Most of them were not worth counting.[46] His name had become something with which mothers in Sonora and Chihuahua frightened their children into good behavior. He had become the nightmare that haunted sleepers in every small village and large town in northern Mexico. So the soldiers now facing him longed for his death, but feared his Power.[47]

During the afternoon, seeing that the soldiers had gathered off to one side, Geronimo crept forward through the ravine and through a connecting gully up close to the lines of the soldiers. The wind blew their words to him. The *nantan* of the soldiers shouted to his men, to give them courage, saying, Officers, yonder in those ditches is the red devil Geronimo and his hated band. This must be his last day. Ride on him from both sides of the ditches. Kill men, women, and children; take no prisoners, dead Indians are what we want. Do not spare your own men; exterminate this band at any cost. I will post the wounded to shoot all deserters; go back to your companies and advance.[48]

Geronimo then rose up a little from his cover, and put a bullet into the *nantan*, laughing as he fired. The soldiers all turned and began firing at him, their bullets tearing up the ground all around him so bits of rock bounced off him. But his Power protected him from the bullets as it always had done. The warriors back in the ravine saw him fire, and raised a war cry of triumph, as Geronimo ran back through the bullets to the warriors.

The Mexicans then charged the ravine, but the warriors' bullets drove them back. The soldiers came forward again and again the warriors drove them back. Still, it seemed that the soldiers would not stop until they had killed Geronimo, and the few warriors could not last much longer against the many soldiers, even though Geronimo had shot their *nantan*. Geronimo looked about him, at the handful of women and children still in the ditch, and at the warriors who remained. He thought of the people who were still running toward the hill, and of the soldiers coming up behind. And he remembered when his Power had kept the sun from rising. He knew then that his Power would not let him remain there in the ravine in a warrior's place. His Power had other uses for him.

So Geronimo turned to Fun, saying, If we leave these women and children, and go now, we can escape.

Fun turned, and looked at him, surprised. And Fun said, Repeat that.

So Geronimo said to him once again, If we leave now, we can escape.

Fun looked hard at him, as though Geronimo had become some other person. Fun replied, saying, If you say that again, I will shoot you.

Geronimo looked a long while at Fun, understanding everything, but held now in the grip of his Power, which would not let him stay to be captured or killed when The People had such need of him. So Geronimo climbed out of the ditch and went back toward the mountains, where the other women and children and warriors would assemble.[49]

The soldiers then came on again, calling Geronimo's name. But Fun jumped up alone out of the ravine and ran toward the soldiers, shooting and shouting. The soldiers could not hit him, and his Power reached out and broke them, so that the line of soldiers wavered and they fled back to cover before Fun's charge.

The remaining warriors drew their strength from Fun, and fought on until dark. They talked then to consider what they must do, knowing that they must escape in the darkness. Some of the women had babies, which might cry out. So the warriors ask the permission of the mothers for the terrible thing they must do. Then mothers gave the warriors their babies, or took the cloths themselves, and smothered their own children, not even able to weep lest the listening soldiers hear. Then they all crawled silently out of the ravine and back away toward the mountains, weighed down by what they had done, even as Geronimo's heart had ached as he crawled away. They each somehow found the strength for the things forced on them with no way to turn aside.[50]

They gathered that night on the hillside, everyone turning eagerly as each new person came out of the darkness, hoping that it would be a mother, or a father, or a child, or a wife. Every family had cause for grief before the morning dawned. Seventy-eight people lay dead down on the plain, including eleven warriors. The soldiers had captured thirty-three others, one of them Loco's own daughter. These prisoners would all soon be slaves far south in Mexico. Perhaps one of every three who had started from San Carlos was now dead, and the survivors had no food, no horses, and only a little ammunition. The survivors huddled through the cold, endless night, not daring a fire. The next morning they watched from the mountain as the White Eyes coming along on their trail reached the battlefield, where the Mexicans rode out to meet them. The warriors hoped the Mexicans and the White Eyes would fight. But the *nantans* conferred, and the soldiers turned back around and went north. The Mexicans then went south, content with their victory, and unwilling to pursue the survivors in the mountains, where the advantage would shift back to the warriors.

Geronimo led the survivors on through the mountains, sending out foragers to bring back cattle, and horses, and supplies. They moved carefully through the mountains, hiding from their enemies, mourning their losses, coming at last to Juh's sanctuary in the Sierra Madre.

And so finally, past all of the grief, and the loss, and the fear, The People returned for this last, short time to this last, free place of upthrust rock, and brooding chasms, rushing streams, and many songs. Geronimo had lost twenty-six of the one hundred fighting men he had with him, but together with Juh's band they had the largest force of warriors assembled in many years, and hundreds of women and children. Now they could at least imagine a future for The People. They could even pretend that they were still a great people, in their own land, and the scourge of their enemies. They knew, in their hearts, that it was not so. They knew they were the last survivors of a free people, who had once roamed as they pleased across a great space, but now hid in this small space. Still, they could light their fires, and sing their songs, dance through the night, and train the young men in the old way. They could make the white buckskin for the girls who would become White Painted Woman, and dance in the circle, and gossip as the mescal baked, and tell Coyote stories, and tell stories of raids and battles as they waited for the jugs of *tizwin* to ferment.

And, of course, they would kill Mexicans, as Geronimo and his Power had always yearned to do.

10

Crook

FIGHTING THE SIOUX

IN LATE MARCH OF 1875, Crook took command of the Department of the Platte, a sprawling jurisdiction that stretched from the Missouri to the western shores of the Great Salt Lake and included Nebraska and the territories of Wyoming, Utah, and part of Idaho. It was also on the brink of an explosion of death and war, the largest-scale, most disaster-plagued Indian conflicts in the nation's history. The long-running, on-and-off-again war with the Sioux and the Cheyenne was now hurtling towards its tragic conclusion, which would thrust Crook and his old rival General George Custer into battle and controversy.

The Sioux moved out onto the Great Plains after the arrival of the Europeans brought them the great boon of the horse. There they pushed aside many other people, and established a sweeping dominance of the northern plains. They often allied themselves with the Cheyenne against traditional enemies like the Crow and the Shoshone. The Sioux were peerless riders and warriors who depended on the buffalo, and migrated with the herds. They initially greeted the whites with wary tolerance, for the most part letting the wagon trains heading for California and Oregon pass unmolested through their territory, although the broad path of the wagon train trail cut the buffalo herds into northern and southern halves. As the pressure from both miners and would-be settlers mounted, conflicts increased. But the government convened a

General George Crook striking an uncharacteristically
Napoleonic pose in 1875. (*Courtesy National Archives*)

great council of the Plains peoples in 1851, where they promised
to supply the tribes with food and trade goods in return for safe
passage for wagon trains across the plains.

The peace was shattered three years later as a result of a stupid incident involving a broken-down cow apparently killed by
Sioux warriors when it lagged behind a wagon train. An arrogant
young lieutenant, J. L. Gratten, marched thirty men into the camp

of Bear That Scatters and demanded return of the cow. Bear That Scatters offered horses as recompense, but the discussions broke down and the soldiers opened fire—killing the chief. The outraged Sioux then killed every man in the detachment. Five of the chief's friends took further revenge by killing three men on a passing wagon train. The army retaliated the next year by attacking a Sioux camp and killing eighty-six Indians, and then demanding the surrender of the warriors who had killed the men on the wagon train. They surrendered to protect their people from retaliation, but were pardoned by President Franklin Pierce.

The first phase of open warfare between the army and the Sioux came in 1862, when the Santee Sioux chief Little Crow led an uprising in Minnesota. The Santee had remained in Minnesota when other Sioux bands had migrated out to the Great Plains, but by 1862 the government had forced them onto a strip of land 10 miles wide and 150 miles long along the Minnesota River. The rise in settlement all around them drove away the game on which they depended. Delays in providing the rations and supplies the Santee had been promised stoked resentment. The spark for a wildfire of violence came when several warriors argued about stealing eggs from a farm. One of the warriors, to prove his manhood, killed the family of settlers. The hunting party rode back to the reservation and reported their actions. The council debated all night, and decided to launch a war before the soldiers came to punish them all for the killings. They struck quickly, killing hundreds of whites who were caught completely unprepared. The army gathered its forces and crushed the uprising. The majority of the most warlike bands fled to the Great Plains, where they joined other Sioux bands. The army summarily executed hundreds of Sioux who remained behind, including many who had refused to join the uprising.

The fighting in Minnesota terrified the settlers on the Great Plains, who appealed frantically for troops to protect them. The arrival of these troops sharply increased the clashes, although the Sioux managed to keep an uneasy peace. However, the ambitious, Indian-hating Colonel John Chivington seized the pretext of a probably fictitious livestock theft to attack four peaceful Cheyenne villages in Colorado, which triggered a bloody war with the Cheyenne and Arapaho. The war with the Cheyenne eventually drew in the Northern Sioux under Red Cloud and others on behalf of their Cheyenne allies. Hampered by the Civil War, the United States in 1865 sought a truce with the tribes that had been prodded into warfare, and several years of uneasy peace prevailed.

A belligerent Army officer provoked a fresh round of battles in 1867, which led to another peace conference involving an array of tribes who roamed across the Great Plains, including the Sioux, the Cheyenne, the Arapaho, the Comanche, the Kiowa, and others. However, renewed fighting soon broke out. The Sioux harassed wagon trains and killed off prospectors who ventured into their territory. In 1866, Sioux warriors lured an eighty-man detachment led by Captain William J. Fetterman out of Fort Phil Kearny and wiped out the entire force. The United States responded by sending out a peace commission, which met with the Sioux in 1868, and ceded to them a reservation that embraced the western half of South Dakota plus the Powder River country. In addition, everything between the North Platte and the Yellowstone was classified as "unceded Indian territory" from which all whites were excluded. The government also agreed to close the Bozeman Trail and abandon the forts along that route through Sioux territory. The Sioux also ceded a large chunk of territory, and the government established agencies on the newly defined Sioux reservations to distribute supplies and food promised in return for the tribe agreeing to give up a portion of their land and to stop raiding the wagon trains and settlers. This marks perhaps the only time an Indian nation ever won a war against the United States—although the victory proved temporary.

Settlers, prospectors, the railroad, and buffalo hunters soon began to press in on the vast territory the government had promised to the Sioux. The government came under pressure to renege on the agreements that had ceded so much land to the Sioux and their Cheyenne allies. Only sporadic incidents marred the peace for the next eight years. But the simmering conflict boiled over in 1874 after General George Armstrong Custer led an expedition into the Black Hills and reported "gold from the roots down" in that area held sacred by the Sioux. This made war with the Sioux all but inevitable. Miners immediately rushed into the Black Hills. Initially the army drove off the miners, anxious to maintain peace with the Sioux, who had adhered to the treaty terms. However, prospectors returned as quickly as the army could brush them away.

The government called a council in 1875 and attempted to buy the Black Hills from the Sioux for $6 million. But the Black Hills Commission nearly met disaster in a stormy meeting that drew thousands of Sioux to the Red Cloud Agency. Sitting Bull boycotted the commission, saying he could never agree to the sale of the Black Hills. "Are you the Great God that made me?" he sent back in response to the summons from the commission. "Or was it the Great God that made me who sent you? If He asks me to come see him, I will go, but the Big Chief of the white men must come see me. I will not go to the reservation. I have no land to sell. There is plenty of game here for us. We have enough ammunition. We don't want any white men here."[1] Other war leaders attended the session in full war gear and threatened to kill any Sioux who agreed to surrender the Black Hills. Spotted Tail, the uncle of Crazy Horse, narrowly averted a massacre of the peace commission, and the commissioners then hastily decamped and reported the failure of their mission.

Seeing that the Sioux would fight for the mineral-rich Black Hills, the army gathered its forces—recalling its top Indian fighter from Arizona and sending him immediately into the field.

Crook's first job upon arrival in 1876 was to evict the miners from the Black Hills. Crook went straight to the Black Hills, moving through the mining camps in an attempt to talk them into leaving. Crook appeared to harbor no illusions that the government would let the Sioux keep the Black Hills, now that they proved valuable. He told the miners he had no personal feelings as to whether they were there, but he would follow his orders and force them to leave. He then suggested they agree on some system to register their claims, a clear indication they could return as soon as the government compelled the Sioux to surrender the Black Hills.

Bourke voiced Crook's weary disapproval of the government's policy, although Crook's doubts did not deter him from serving as a weapon in the hands of the policy makers. "It is hard to make the average savage comprehend why it is that as soon as his reservation is found to amount to anything, he must leave and give it up to the white man," wrote Bourke, who noted that even the Spanish had allowed Indians to patent and lease mineral claims on their lands. "The policy of the American people has been to vagabondize the Indian, and throttle every ambition he may have for his own elevation."

Meanwhile, Crook received orders to compel any outstanding bands of Sioux or Cheyenne to return to the reservations. Once-defiant Sioux leaders like Red Cloud and Spotted Tail complied, understanding the long odds the Sioux faced. But the insistence of these moderates that the Sioux make the best deal possible was fervently opposed by rising war leaders like Crazy Horse and Sitting Bull. The defiant Sioux bands pursued buffalo without regard to reservation boundaries, and killed any whites they found in the Black Hills.

The War Department ordered Crook to mount a winter campaign in 1876 directed at driving back to the reservations the defiant bands camped in a largely uncharted territory bounded by the Bighorn Mountains and the Tongue and Yellowstone Rivers. Crook's superiors had no idea how many Indians had actually taken refuge with the hostile bands, and dramatically underestimated the difficulty of the task assigned to Crook. Crook set out with twenty companies of cavalry and two companies of infantry, supported by eighty-six mule-drawn wagons, four ambulances, and a four-hundred-mule pack train. He enlisted as his chief scout Frank Gruard, a part white, part Indian man who had lived in Crazy Horse's camp and who had since passed himself off as a native of the Hawaiian Islands.

Crook soon found himself slogging through snow and blizzards, harassed intermittently by Sioux warriors seeking to drive off his horses, or to provoke a fruitless chase to break down his command's horses. After Crook reached the ruins of Fort Reno, abandoned in 1867, he shed the wagons, ordered each man to take a minimum of gear and fifteen days' worth of half rations, and set out on a series of night marches in the teeth of a vicious snowstorm. He knew his success depended on surprising an Indian village and destroying the summer-gathered cache of supplies that made it possible for the Sioux to survive the severe winters of the northern plains.

Bourke penned another description of Crook in this campaign, noting that the rumpled general was dressed in brown corduroy trousers burned at the end, a heavy brown wool shirt, a blouse of the old army style, a brown Kossuth felt hat "ventilated at the top," an army overcoat with red flannel lining, and a wolf-skin collar from one of Crook's own kills. He also wore a leather belt with fifty copper cartridges, held to the shoulders by two leather straps. The general "was six feet tall, 170 pounds, spare, straight, limbs long and sinewy; complexion, nevro-sanguine; hair, light brown; cheeks, ruddy, without being florid; features delicate and firmly chiseled; eyes, blue-grey; nose, a pronounced Roman and quite large; mouth, mild but firm, and showing with the chin much resolution and tenacity of purpose."

Crook's command labored on through the snow and freezing temperatures for a week, rations already growing slim. Seeing that his column was moving too slowly to surprise the wary Sioux, Crook detailed Captain. J. J. Reynolds to take six companies of the Third Cavalry to follow the trail of a band of hunters they had found on the march. Crook ordered Reynolds to attack any village he found and to rejoin the main column on the Powder River. The resulting battle was to determine the course of that winter campaign, and once again reveal the frictions that marked Crook's relationships with other officers, both superiors and subordinates.

Reynolds followed the trail to an apparently slumbering Sioux village, and planned his attack. He divided his force so he could hit the village from three directions at once, assuming the Indians would flee at the first shot. However, the leading detachment had to attack prematurely when they stumbled across a boy herding horses in a ravine. The Indians in the village ran for a rocky bluff.

Soldiers were supposed to have occupied that bluff, but in the predawn darkness they had occupied the wrong hill, taking themselves out of the battle. Bourke charged the camp along with the lead detachment, although their exhausted and malnourished horses could barely run. The soldiers captured the Indians' seven hundred horses and tons of buffalo robes, meat, and other supplies, but they soon came under telling fire from the Indians on the bluffs. The soldiers found what cover they could and returned fire. Many had shed their heavy clothing for the charge, and now struggled to stave off frostbite in the debilitating cold. Reynolds ultimately decided to pull out of the village before the Indians could muster additional reinforcements and cut off his retreat. He burned most of the captured supplies, and set off in a rapid retreat under the continued fire from the Indians on the bluff. Bourke noted, "We fell back at such a rate that our dead were left in the hands of the Indians and, as was whispered among the men, one of our poor soldiers fell alive into the enemy's hands and was cut limb from limb. I do not state this fact of my own knowledge, and I can only say that I believed it to be true."

The Indians pursued and sniped at the retreating soldiers. The Indians recovered most of their horse herd at night, in part because Reynolds failed to post adequate pickets. Reynolds pushed on to the Powder River, then settled in to wait for Crook. On his way to the Powder, Crook encountered the Sioux with their recaptured horse herd. The Indians fled, and Crook recovered about one hundred ponies. He was furious when he learned that Reynolds had abandoned his position in the village and destroyed the huge cache of captured supplies. Crook's command, out of food and suffering from the cold, desperately needed the Sioux's food and buffalo skin blankets. Lacking those supplies, and knowing that every Indian within miles would soon know of their presence, Crook now had little choice but to break off the campaign. Crook slaughtered the captured ponies to keep them from falling into Indian hands, and turned back toward Fort Fetterman.

Crook noted in his autobiography that "serious complaint was made against Captain Reynolds and Captain Moore [who had occupied the wrong bluff] for mismanagement and misbehavior in the face of the enemy." A court ultimately found Reynolds guilty and suspended him from rank for a year. Captain Ptian Alexander Moore was found guilty of neglect of duty and suspended from command for six months. Lieutenant Henry Noyes was also reprimanded. It is unclear whether Reynolds deserved the reprimand, since it was possible his command could have been wiped out had he remained in the village. The army continued to badly underestimate the Sioux, an arrogance that would soon lead Custer to his death. The court-martial revealed that a feud had existed within Crook's command. At the court-martial, Captain Anson Mills testified that bitter feelings divided the officers, and that Reynolds was old and feeble, and so disobeyed Crook's order to hold the village. Again, as throughout Crook's career, his gruff, uncommunicative disdain for ceremony, adherence to his own ideas, and unconventional manner had won the fervent loyalty of some officers and the sullen resentment of others.

In the spring, Crook initiated a series of conferences with the Sioux on the reservation, using his old tactics of divide and conquer to enlist the more peacefully inclined chiefs against the war chiefs such as Sitting Bull and Crazy Horse. The chiefs at the Red Cloud Agency promised to provide forty warriors to help drive the hostiles back to the reservation, but here Crook was hindered by the old specter of divided control. Throughout the West, the War Department and the Interior Department fought a fierce bureaucratic struggle for control of the reservations. The War Department often assumed control when actively fighting the Indians, but lost control to the Interior Department as soon as the Indians stopped fighting. That gave the political appointees in the Interior Department control of millions of dollars in contracts and patronage. When the Interior Department agent heard the reservation chiefs had promised Crook scouts, he convinced Red Cloud to renege on the promise.

Crook narrowly avoided death on this tour of the reservations. Warriors had slipped away from the agency when they learned that "Three Stars" was there, hoping to bring back a force of warriors that could kill Crook as he left the reservation. Crook normally traveled with a small escort, a perhaps foolhardy display of confidence among the Sioux. By sheer coincidence, Crook on this occasion traveled with an additional detachment of soldiers and a group of miners. When the warriors assembled to ambush him, they didn't like the odds and instead attacked a supply train.

The army now readied a campaign for the summer of 1876, determined to break the resistance of the Sioux and the Cheyenne, who were leaving the reservations in increasing numbers. The offensive was directed by Lieutenant General Phil Sheridan, Crook's old classmate and sometimes rival, who set three columns in motion with orders to converge on the suspected position of the hostile camps in the Powder River country. Colonel John Gibbon was to command the first column of five hundred men who would set out east from Fort Ellis in western Montana. Crook set out from Fort Fetterman with about one thousand men on May 29, with orders to find the hostiles and link up with the other columns. General Alfred H. Terry set out with another force of about one thousand men, marching west from Fort Abraham Lincoln in Dakota Territory. His force included the seven hundred soldiers of Lieutenant Colonel (Brevet Major General) Custer's Seventh Cavalry.

Crook's command consisted of ten troops of the Third Cavalry, five troops of the Second, two companies of the Fourth Infantry, and three companies of the Ninth Infantry, a total of 47 officers and 1,002 men. Crook also hoped to link up with Crow and Shoshone allies, traditional enemies of the Sioux. The long column of troops, which seemed virtually invulnerable to the traditional hit-and-run Sioux tactics, set out from Fort Fetterman on May 29, 1876, headed toward one of the most surprising and controversial battles of Crook's career.

Charles King, who wrote a fascinating account of the campaign and later became a best-selling novelist, penned a vivid description of Crook: "This utterly unpretending party, this undeniably shabby looking man in a private soldier's light blue overcoat, standing ankle deep in mud in a far-gone pair of soldier's boots, crowned with a most shocking bad hat, is Brig. Gener. George Crook, of the United States Army & Bourke, the senior aide and adjutant general of the expedition, is picturesquely gotten up in an old shooting coat."[2]

Henry Dalyh, writing later in the *American Legion Monthly*, also described the general. "In a populous place General Crook would have worn the regulation uniform, but it probably would have needed pressing. A battered slouch hat would have been carelessly thrust on his head and his boots would have been dusty. In the field, except that everybody knew him, General Crook might have been taken for a Montana miner. The only part of his uniform he wore was an old overcoat, except in wet weather he wore moccasins, and his slight, bushy beard would be gathered in a series of braids. He was a silent man, but good-natured and philosophically humorous. I have seen him walk up to a cook fire, where the troops were getting their coffee, take his turn for a cup, and then walk away and sit down on the ground and blow it off and drink it without saying a word."[3]

Crook had received word through his spies on the reservation that Crazy Horse, who had a large force of warriors, had sent warning that he would attack any soldiers who crossed the Tongue River. The expedition proceeded without incident for several days, although Crook did discover that a soon-to-be famous frontier character known as Calamity Jane had posed as a man and gotten a job as a packer on his eighteen-hundred-mule train. Bourke noted that she was revealed as an imposter by her "lack of swearing." Crook had her arrested and sent back to the nearest settlement. Meanwhile, anxious to add the knowledge and numbers of the Crow and Shoshone warriors to his force, Crook dispatched his two best scouts to find them and guide them to his column.

As promised, a small force of Sioux warriors attacked Crook's advanced line shortly after the soldiers crossed the Tongue River. Crook brushed off the attack, and the warning it represented. Moving without his scouts, who were still off looking for the absent Indian allies, Crook had wandered into the wrong valley, a fact he discovered only upon reaching the Tongue. He had to swing around on a detour to the east to get back on course for a linkup with Gibbon and Terry, from whom he had received no word at all since setting out. Gruard and scout Louis Richaud finally returned with about three hundred Crow and Shoshone warriors, gorgeously arrayed, and spoiling for a fight with the

Sioux, who had largely driven their people out of the prime buffalo hunting grounds before the whites arrived.

Crook's whole strategy was to strike the main Sioux village by surprise, destroying their supplies, scattering their warriors, capturing their women and children. By demonstrating the army could reach them in their most secure places, he hoped to convince them to return to the reservation. No one believed the Sioux would stand and fight, much less take the offensive against such a large force. Therefore, Crook pushed his men as hard as possible. At one point he mounted the infantry on mules, to the amusement of the cavalrymen and scout Frank Gruard: "I never saw so much fun in my life. The valley for a mile in every direction was filled with bucking mules, frightened infantrymen, broken saddles, and applauding spectators. Having nothing else to do, the entire command took a half holiday to enjoy the sport, and some of the most ludicrous mishaps imaginable were witnessed. But the average soldier is as persevering as the mule is stubborn and in the end the mule was forced to surrender."[4]

John Finerty, a newspaper reporter traveling with the column who later published his collected dispatches as *War-Path and Bivouac*, left a vivid account of the campaign and the frontier army, composed in large measure of immigrants in the ranks and well-educated West Point and Civil War veterans in the officers corps. He wrote: "The great mass of soldiers were young men, careless, courageous, and eminently light hearted. The rank and file, as a majority, were of either Irish or German birth or parenting, but there was also a fair sized contingent of what may be called Anglo-Americans, particularly among the noncommissioned officers. Taken as a whole, Crook's organization, and its officers, four-fifths of whom were native Americans and West Pointers, were fully in sympathy with the ardor of their men. . . . Crook was bristling for a fight."[5] The force was later augmented by a group of sixty-five miners and prospectors, well-armed with long-range rifles.

Crook advanced with front, flank, and rear guards moving a good distance from the main column to protect against surprise and to keep the Indians from determining the size of his force. He also indulged his fascination with the natural world on the long march through the emerald green hills of that beautiful country, triumphantly collecting the nests and eggs of some rare birds and unusual butterflies. He also adopted a "wonderfully tame" owl he dubbed "Sitting Bull." But mostly Crook was concerned about keeping the size and the direction of his command hidden from the Sioux. Therefore, he was irritated and frustrated when the column encountered a herd of buffalo, upon which his Indian allies immediately leaped on their horses and dashed off after the animals, shooting with expert abandon. The jubilant warriors returned to camp with plenty of buffalo meat. Crook ordered the command to light no fires, but the warriors lit great fires anyway to cook their meat, talking, and singing, and celebrating through the night. "The general was angry enough to punish the recalcitrant savages severely," observed Finerty, "but it would never have done to make them enemies at that stage of the game. He therefore submitted with characteristic philosophy to the inevitable."[6]

The command roused at 3 A.M. on the morning of June 17 and was on the march by 6 A.M., now a total of thirty-five miles from the slow-moving wagons that constituted Crook's supply base. At mid-morning, Crook ordered a halt, passing word for the soldiers to unsaddle their tired horses and rest. They were in a broad valley near Rosebud Creek in Montana, with hills and bluffs on all sides. A Crow scout rode in saying that the Sioux were near, so Crook immediately threw out strong pickets on all sides of the main force. He then sat down beside a small spring with Bourke and several other officers to play cards. The rear of the long column of soldiers continued to move up for the half-hour halt, as the tension caused by the scout's warning ebbed.

Suddenly, a group of Crow scouts galloped into camp, yelling that the Sioux were upon them. The excited scouts reported that they had been hit by a strong force of Sioux warriors about ten miles down the Rosebud. Even as the scouts made their report, Sioux warriors charged in among the advanced pickets, engaging them in hand-to-hand fighting.

Crook immediately raced to the crest of a nearby hill to gain an overview of the battle, which was breaking out along the ridgeline just in front of his main force. He hoped to get some idea of the location of the Indian village he assumed the warriors had ridden out to protect. His decision to move to the high ground to gain a sense of the battlefield would prove controversial later, since it left his subordinates to make crucial early decisions that would determine the entire course of the battle.

Crook did not realize until much later that he was facing a new enemy and new Sioux tactics. Crazy Horse, the charismatic, spiritually powerful, and fearless war leader of the Sioux, had to an unprecedented degree won the loyalty and leadership of the normally independent war leaders of the Sioux and Cheyenne. The gigantic Sioux and Cheyenne village was actually some twenty miles from the battlefield in the valley of the Little Bighorn, and had grown to somewhere between two thousand and five thousand warriors. Crazy Horse had set out the night before in the vanguard of a force of about fifteen hundred. He warned his warriors that they should not bother to count coup by riding in close to touch a living enemy with their weapon, a practice that among the Sioux carried more honor than simply killing an enemy. Instead, they should fight as the soldiers fought, focused only on killing as many as possible. Some of the Sioux were actually better armed than the soldiers, with Winchester repeating rifles pitted against the soldiers' single-shot, .45 caliber Springfield rifles.

Still convinced he faced a few hundred warriors trying to give the people in the nearby village time to escape, Crook's command quickly rallied to meet the attack. Major George Randall charged with the Crow and Shoshone warriors into the ranks of the oncoming Sioux, who had swept the pickets off the high ground and were now spilling over the bluffs. Accounts of the role played by the Indian allies differ. Some officers reported that the Shoshone and the Crow fell back in the face of the Sioux attack. More convincing accounts maintain that the initial charge of the Indian allies bought the soldiers a precious twenty minutes in which to organize, and may have prevented a rout.

Bourke rode with the Shoshone warriors. The Sioux fell back before the attack, thereby luring the Shoshone further from the support of the soldiers. "I went in with this charge, and was enabled to see how such things were conducted by the American savages fighting according to their own notions," wrote Bourke. "There was a headlong rush for about two hundred yards which drove the enemy back in confusion; then was a sudden halt, and very many of the Shoshones jumped down from their ponies and began firing from the ground; the others who remained mounted threw themselves alongside of their horses' necks, so that there would be few good marks presented to the aim of the enemy. Then, in response to some signal or cry which, of course, I did not understand, we were off again, this time for good, right into the midst of the hostiles, who had been halted by a steep hill directly in their front. Why we did not kill more of them than we did was because they were dressed so like our own Crows that even our Shoshones were afraid of mistakes, and in the confusion many of the Sioux and Cheyenne made their way down the face of the bluff unharmed."[7]

The unfolding battle gave Crazy Horse the opportunity to test out the new tactics he and the other war leaders had devised for a running battle with the well-armed soldiers. His warriors would dash in, hanging over the sides of their horses and firing under their mounts' necks to present an impossible target. As soon as the soldiers charged, the warriors would spin about and retreat, hoping to draw their enemies away from the main force so they could then turn and destroy the exposed contingent. The Sioux therefore fell back as the Shoshone charged, drawing them a mile from the main force before turning. The Shoshone saw the shift, and retreated so abruptly that Bourke and his bugler were for the moment left almost alone facing the Sioux charge. The pair turned and fled just in time. "Scarcely had I mounted my horse and mechanically loaded my carbine, when I called out to Bugler Snow to mount at once as the Sioux were charging up the ravine on the left of the hill. Sure enough, they came to the number of thirty or more, poor Snow being still on the ground. I gave them the contents of my carbine at more than 30 yards, at the same time yelling to make them believe there were still many of us there. . . . They halted for one brief space, long enough, however, to let Snow and myself spur our horses, and rush after our commands nearly 400 yards away. My usual good fortune attended me, but poor Snow rode back to our lines badly shot through both arms near the elbows."

The Ninth Infantry was then ordered forward to occupy the bluffs, driving the Indians ahead of them with fire from their long-range rifles. When the soldiers reached the rim of the bluff, they were dismayed to find the plateau ahead of them swarming with well-mounted, well-armed warriors. "When we reached the crest of the plateau, there appeared in our front a formidable band of those justly celebrated Sioux and Cheyenne Warriors, magnificently mounted, and in all the splendor of war paint and feathers," recalled Captain Azor Nickerson, an aide to Crook who was to perform heroic service that day in carrying Crook's orders to other commanders. "Every hill appeared to be covered with their swarming legions, and up from every ravine, and out of every little vale, more seemed to be coming. . . . Many wore the long Sioux war bonnet of eagles' plumes, which floated and fluttered in the air, back of the wearer, to the distance of five or six feet; while others wore half masks of the heads of wild animals." As the soldiers closed with the warriors, Crazy Horse divided his forces, sweeping around both flanks of the suddenly beleaguered infantry. However, the soldiers took cover at the crest of a small hill and drove off the encircling attack.

Crook had by now returned from the bluffs to discover that in his absence Captain Nickerson had divided his forces, responding to the rapidly developing Sioux attack. In retrospect, the deployment seems a plausible effort to occupy high ground and respond to the confusing fluidity of the Sioux attack, but it had the effect of scattering Crook's forces, making the separate parts vulnerable to the piecemeal destruction that was soon to befall Custer at the hands of these same warriors. One small detachment crossed the Rosebud and drove warriors off a plateau, firing from the high ground to protect the pack train. Another detachment had been sent forward to clear the Sioux from a high point later dubbed Crook's Hill. Most critically, Colonel William B. Royall with fifteen companies of the Third Cavalry and infantry support was sent to the rear to fend off another attack developing from a series of hills in that direction. Royall advanced perhaps a mile, driving the

Indians before him until suddenly the Sioux turned, augmented by fresh forces pouring in from every direction. Royall was forced to fall back and fortify a ridge, under fire from higher hills on three sides.

Crook had meanwhile returned and regained control of the battle. He moved his main force to Crook's Hill and sent orders for Royall's command to rejoin the main body of troops. However, Royall, under heavy fire, responded by sending only a small detachment back toward the hill. It took a full three hours before Royall's entire command returned to Crook's Hill, after fighting through heavy Sioux resistance and repeated attacks. Crook later maintained that he had sent Nickerson three times to order Royall to rejoin the main command so that Crook could push down the Rosebud to locate and destroy the Sioux village. Royall insisted he received only one order to "close the gap" between his exposed force and the main command, and that he immediately moved to do so. Another officer supported Royall's insistence that he received only a single command to fall back. Moreover, despite his claim that Royall had delayed in obeying repeated direct orders, Crook never preferred charges. On the other hand, even if Royall received only one command, his action in sending a small detachment off to occupy a position partway back toward Crook's Hill seems a delayed, halfhearted, and dangerous attempt to "close the gap."

In the meantime, Crook struggled to salvage the battle—still not fully understanding the dimensions of his danger due to Crazy Horse's new tactics. Crook remained convinced the Sioux were fighting a desperate rearguard action to cover the flight of the women and children from the village that contained the horses and supplies necessary to sustain them off the reservation and through the winter. His real goal remained the destruction of those irreplaceable supplies. Therefore, as soon as he had consolidated his position in the center, Crook dispatched a strong force under Captain Anson Mills to move up the Rosebud toward its junction with Indian Creek, where he believed the Sioux village lay. In fact, the Sioux village was twenty miles from the battlefield, and ten miles beyond the junction of the Rosebud and Indian

Creek. Crook ordered Mills to move down the Rosebud, locate the village, and press the attack, ignoring, as much as possible, attacks on his column by the Sioux trying to lure him away from the village. Crook promised Mills he would move the main command off the hill as soon as Royall reinforced him and then move as quickly as possible along behind Mills's cavalry. Crook also recalled the detachment that had occupied the plateau on the opposite side of the river.

Mills moved off, and Crazy Horse took the opportunity to press the attack on the now-diminished force on Crook's Hill and on Royall's isolated command. Royall was by now battling from ridge to ridge trying to rejoin Crook, struggling to prevent the stubborn, costly retreat from turning into a disaster. In the meantime, a force of Sioux warriors swept completely around Crook's command, demonstrating to the anxiously watching general that he was surrounded now by a larger enemy force. The number of wounded soldiers had mounted steadily, and Crook soon saw he would have to leave a substantial part of his force behind to protect the wounded. In addition, he realized he could not effectively support Mills if Crazy Horse attacked him in the relatively narrow confines of the Rosebud valley. Seeing that he faced a far larger force of warriors than anyone had expected, Crook dispatched the redoubtable Nickerson to recall Mills.

Nickerson reached Mills about eight miles down the canyon from Crook's Hill just as Mills was about to take his force into a narrowing of the canyon. Some descriptions of the terrain suggesting that the canyon of the Rosebud had one-thousand-foot walls and formed a perfect trap for Mills's force do not actually match the topography. Most of the half-mile-wide river valley through which Mills rode in search of the Sioux village was flanked by rolling, wooded hillsides that provided good cover for an ambush, but would not have trapped Mills's command on the riverbanks. However, Nickerson turned Mills back at one of the narrower portions of the canyon. Bourke maintained that Crazy Horse later told him the Sioux were waiting just down the canyon in great numbers, intending to fall upon Mills's command once the front half of the column had passed through the narrow portion, cutting the column in two and wiping out the leading detachment. However, other Sioux accounts of the battle cast doubt on the idea that an effective ambush had been prepared for Mills's force. Although Crazy Horse had a certain loose control over the Sioux warriors, mostly they fought in independent swarms. While the fluid, mobile tactics of dash and retreat had frustrated Crook's efforts to concentrate his command against a force of warriors willing to stand and fight, those tactics also made it difficult for the Sioux to organize something as complex as a well-hidden, long-delayed ambush. In any case, Mills remained convinced the village was almost within his grasp, and questioned the orders to fall back before reluctantly complying. Crook's decision probably saved many of the men in Mills's command who could have been ambushed or cut off from reinforcement had they advanced much further in a futile search for the still-distant village. Breaking off his advance, Mills left the canyon and circled back toward Crook's Hill.

The decision proved fortunate for Crook's command as well. As Mills's weary troopers approached Crook's Hill, they came upon a large group of warriors Crazy Horse was rallying for a renewed attack on Crook. Mills charged the gathering of warriors, scattering them. Seeing that Crook had finally reunited his command, the Sioux broke off the attack. They were weary, their horses were nearly played out, and their ammunition was low. Most had ridden twenty miles through the night before throwing themselves into the battle, and Crook now had his full force gathered on high ground. The Sioux withdrew toward their distant village, with Crook moving warily in pursuit for some miles before breaking off and returning to his camp to protect his supplies and his wounded men.

Crook stubbornly claimed victory at the Rosebud for the rest of his life, pointing out he had stood off a stronger enemy force with modest casualties. Crook reported ten killed and twenty-one wounded, while Bourke reported a total of fifty-seven killed or wounded. Crook's Indian allies collected thirteen Sioux scalps. All told, the casualties were astonishingly low considering the duration and intensity of the fighting and the number of shots fired on both sides. Crook had remained coolheaded, calm, and flexible in the midst of heavy fighting, despite having had his horse killed beneath him. The Sioux probably had one thousand to fifteen hundred warriors engaged in the opening stage of the battle, which would have made the Sioux force about equal to Crook's. But reinforcements had continued arriving from the Sioux village throughout the battle. It is unclear how many warriors were involved at the peak of the battle. Bourke later quoted Crazy Horse as saying he had more than five thousand warriors, which would have given the Sioux a three to one advantage in the middle stages of the six-hour battle. Although the initial division of his forces opened the door to disaster, Crook reassessed the shifting conditions, redeployed his forces, avoided heavy losses, and ultimately drove the Sioux from the field. Crook's official report of the engagement observed, "My troops beat these Indians on a field of their own choosing, and drove them in utter rout from it, as far as the proper care of my wounded and prudence would justify. Subsequent events proved beyond dispute what would have been the fate of the command had the pursuit been continued beyond what judgment dictated."[8] The latter observation referred to the disaster that befell Custer just a week later when he divided his force to attack these same warriors. The loyal Bourke also depicted the battle at the Rosebud as a victory, noting that Crook had outfought a superior enemy force led by the greatest warrior in Sioux history, adroitly avoiding the traps set for him.

However, other officers and commentators faulted Crook's conduct of the battle, arguing that he effectively squandered the half hour between the first warning of the approaching Sioux and the onset of the battle. The command was still resting and largely unsaddled when the first Sioux attacked, and might have suffered disaster had not the Shoshone and Crow warriors bought time for the soldiers to get organized. Moreover, Crook lost control of the early stages of the battle by climbing to the top of the hill to reconnoiter in the first moments of the attack. The resulting division of his forces took three hours to repair. Of course, that might have actually been an advantage, as it kept Crook from moving up the Rosebud with his unified force, which might have simply moved him into the jaws of Crazy Horse's trap, assuming such a trap had actually been set.

Big Bat, Crook's Crow interpreter, also criticized Crook's conduct of the battle in interviews in 1907 with E. S. Ricker, a Nebraska justice of the peace and amateur historian. Big Bat maintained that he was with Crook on the hill in the center as Royall's command struggled to retreat up to the hill. One of Royall's officers fell from his horse, shot through the face. The Crow warriors wanted to rescue the officer, but Crook called them back, which disgusted the Crow and played a role in their decision to return home after the battle. Big Bat also maintained that only the strong advice of the Crow prevented Crook from falling into a fresh trap as he pursued the retreating Sioux warriors. Crook hesitated at the mouth of a canyon leading back down to the Rosebud, still wondering whether he might recover the battle by finding the village. "The general said he wanted to get to the Sioux village and fight them there," said Big Bat. White Face answered that "the force you have been fighting is only a little war party; if you go to the village you will find as many Indians as the grass. If you go down there you can never get out of the trap; you will all be killed."[9] The warning prompted Crook to send back a runner to determine how much ammunition was left. He discovered that his soldiers had fired 10,000 rounds, nearly exhausting his supply of bullets. Crook then turned away from the canyon and returned to the wounded and the pack train, reluctantly abandoning the quest for the village.

However, despite Crook's own assessment, there is little doubt that the battle and its aftermath amounted to a great tactical victory for Crazy Horse, both for protecting the distant village and for halting Crook's advance.

Moreover, Crook's decision to retreat thirty-five miles to his supply train to await reinforcements set the stage for the Custer disaster. The dashing but fatally reckless and ambitious Custer stumbled onto the huge Sioux and Cheyenne encampment at the Little Bighorn just eight days after Crook's battle on the Rosebud. Custer divided his 600-man force into three contingents, determined to attack the Sioux village from several sides at once on the arrogant assumption that the Sioux would flee with the first shot. Instead, Crazy Horse and Sitting Bull rallied the surprised Sioux warriors and turned back a frontal assault on the village, forcing that third of Custer's command to flee back across the river and dig defensive positions on a hill where they remained besieged for three days. Thousands of warriors then converged on Custer's 231-man command and wiped them out to the last man, as they might have done to Mills's detachment had Crook not recalled him.

Many blamed Custer's annihilation on Crook's retreat from the Rosebud. Crook also came in for criticism for remaining in camp for a month after his retreat. Crook decided not to move out blindly after the Sioux, since he could get no information about the positions of the other two columns with which he was supposed to coordinate the offensive. Crook sent out several scouts and detachments attempting to make contact and find out what was happening, but roving bands of Sioux warriors drove the couriers back into Crook's camp. Crook himself left camp with a small detachment and climbed the Bighorn Mountains, looking for some distant sign of Gibbon's force, but returned on July 4 without any useful information. On July 10, a three-man detachment from Gibbon's command finally brought Crook word of the Custer disaster, which had occurred perhaps forty miles from Crook's position.

Captain Mills watched as Crook read the dispatch with the news of the slaughter. "He read the dispatch, and while all of us were horrified and oppressed with mortification and sympathy for the dead and wounded, there was with all, particularly in General Crook's expression, a feeling that the country would realize that there were others who had underrated the valor and numbers of the Sioux. While General Crook was a cold, grey-eyed, and somewhat cold-blooded warrior, treating his men perhaps too practically in war time, there yet ran through us a feeling of profound sympathy for his great misfortune, while at the same time we had a still more profound sympathy for the other gallant and more sympathetic Custer—at least, most of us. There were some there, I regret to say, who had ranked him and over whom he was promoted, that would insinuate 'I told you so,' and for the majority of us had no respect."[10]

The territorial press heaped criticism on Crook in the deep shadow of the destruction of Custer's command. "The officers of the post speak in terms of unmeasured condemnation of Gen. Crook's behavior, and denounce his retreat in the face of the savage enemy as cowardly," thundered the *Helena Daily Independent*'s June 30 edition. "It is also reported that the Crows refused to stay with Crook any longer, and have gone off in a body to Gibbon on the Yellowstone. They call Crook the 'squaw chief' and say he's afraid to fight. . . . The idea of two regiments of American cavalry being stampeded by savages and having to rally behind friendly Indians is regarded as incredibly revolting to the pride and honor of the Army. . . . It is now clearly evident that General Crook was not the man to be entrusted with the conduct of the military expeditions in the Powder River country. . . . Crook has delayed for months after the others were ready, and in his eager desire to monopolize the honors of the campaign has suffered two defeats, both of which have been more or less disastrous. . . . he may outgeneral the indolent Apache, but he is no match for the daring and aggressive Sioux."[11]

However, others defended Crook's decisions. Robert Stahorn, a correspondent for the *Rocky Mountain News* who was with Crook throughout the fight, observed, "He said that with all those wounded on our hands, and with an ambuscade clearly in sight, he would not take his men down into that hole & he was on the offensive the whole time throughout the fight, took his time to return to his base and wasn't whipped. . . . I was with Crook in every foray or movement throughout the Sioux war, and am sure that his undoubted courage, absolute devotion to duty, and unequalled experience in Indian warfare, would have led him to persist in his march to a junction with Terry on the Yellowstone except for the needless sacrifice of troops involved in certain further encounters with the savages, whose overwhelming numbers were absolutely unknown until then. Crook was actually in nearly as poor shape to advance as was Custer when he rode to his doom a week later."[12]

Moreover, General Sheridan, Crook's commander, approved his decision to remain in camp and await reinforcements and re-supply before going out again after the now-retreating Sioux. Nonetheless, the Rosebud was widely considered Crook's only major defeat in his decades of warfare with the Indians, and he remained defensive and indignant about that perception for the rest of his life.

Crook was reinforced by 213 new Shoshone allies on July 11, immediately after he received news of Custer's disastrous defeat. Nonetheless, Sheridan advised him to wait for reinforcements commanded by General Wesley Merritt, who had been delayed by a series of clashes which had prevented 800 Cheyenne warriors from leaving the Red Cloud Agency. Crook continued to send out scouts, who reported that the Sioux had left their position along the Little Bighorn and were moving toward the Powder River.

Crook finally received reinforcements on August 3, some fifty-six days after the fight on the Rosebud. He now had a force of 2,000 men and 160 supply wagons, plus several hundred Indian allies. Determined to overtake the fleeing Sioux, Crook left his wagons behind, ordered each man to carry a minimum of rations, and hurried off. He still hoped he might drive the Sioux into Terry's force, which had also been resupplied and reinforced.

The two-month campaign that followed was a nightmare of hunger and exhaustion. Crook pushed the men to the limits of endurance. "We had in our mess eight individuals, including the General, who could live on a very small amount of food and sleep," noted Captain Walter Schuyler. "After many hardships, we reached the Powder River for resupply by steamers. Have seen men become so exhausted that they were actually insane, but there was no way of carrying them." The pace of the advance was such that Crook's men were already suffering its effects by the time they linked up with Terry on August 11.

Bourke noted the difference between the charming, outgo-ing Terry and the somber Crook. "In his manner, Terry was the antithesis of Crook. Crook was also simple and unaffected, but he was reticent and taciturn to the extreme of sadness, brusque to the verge of severity. In Terry's face I thought I could sometimes detect traces of indecision; but in Crook's countenance there was not the slightest intimation of anything but stubbornness, rugged resolution, and bull-dog tenacity. . . . I thought that within that cleanly outlined skull, beneath that brow, behind those clear, glancing, blue-grey eyes, there was concealed more military sagacity, more quickness of comprehension, and celerity to meet unexpected emergencies, than in any of our living generals excepting Grant."

Crook quickly decided to move on separately with his force, not wanting to be tied to Terry's slow-moving supply wagons. But the hardships only mounted as Crook pushed on along the trail of the Sioux, which had begun to split into a welter of diverging trails as the great camp of Sioux and Cheyenne which had overwhelmed Custer and stymied Crook at the Rosebud broke up. August 23 brought the first in a series of violent storms, and a week later the midsummer temperatures had dropped so sharply that some men nearly froze to death. The horses also began to falter, used up by the pace of the advance and the lack of grass. The Sioux had burned off much of the grass as they moved, knowing it would hinder the inevitable pursuit. Soon the whole command began to subsist on horse meat, to the consternation of the cavalry and the gallows-humor satisfaction of the infantry.

Crook sent a strong force ahead of the main column under Captain Mills, knowing that only a relatively small, mobile force had any chance of striking any of the Sioux villages. Mills finally overtook a small village of about thirty-seven lodges on September 8 at a place later known as Slim Buttes, striking them at daybreak. Captain Emmett Crawford, who would play a leading role in the Apache struggles still to come, led a force of twenty-five men into the village, capturing two hundred horses and five thousand pounds of food. The women and children fled, covered stubbornly by the warriors, many of whom fell back into a ravine, from which they poured fire back on the soldiers. Mills sent for Crook and settled in to hold the village, with its precious supplies of food and blankets. Crook came up and directed the soldiers to flush out a group of warriors trapped in the ravine. Bourke and a group of soldiers moved carefully around the ravine, trying to get behind the defiant warriors. But as Bourke and several others moved to the edge of the ravine, the ground gave way beneath their feet and they tumbled down into a terrified group of women and children. At about the same time, one of the scouts, Charley White, a close friend of Buffalo Bill Cody's whom the soldiers had nicknamed Buffalo Chips, stuck his head up to investigate the commotion. One of the warriors in the ravine shot him, and he fell mortally wounded crying, "O, Lord! O, Lord! They've got me now, boys." Fortunately, the place where Bourke and the others had fallen into the ravine was protected from the fire of the warriors, and Bourke sent the frightened women and children back to Crook as prisoners. Crook learned they were members of a Sioux band led by American Horse. Crook reassured the women they would be well treated and returned to the reservation, then sent one of them back into the ravine to convince the warriors to surrender. When the warriors refused, Crook appealed to them to send out any remaining women and children before he resumed his attack, going personally to lead a handful of women and children to safety. The soldiers then resumed firing. "Our troops reopened with a very rain of hell upon the infatuated braves, who, nevertheless fought it out with Spartan courage against such desperate odds for nearly two hours. Such matchless bravery electrified even our enraged soldiers into a spirit of chivalry and General Crook, recognizing the fact that the unfortunate savages had fought like fiends in defense of wives and children, ordered another suspension of hostilities and called upon the dusky heroes to surrender,"[13] reported newspaper reporter John Finerty.

American Horse, mortally wounded by a shot in the stomach, emerged from the gully and offered to surrender if Crook would spare the lives of the surviving warriors. Men who had lost friends cried out against the proposal, but Crook hesitated for a minute and then said, "Two or three Sioux, more or less, can make no difference. I can yet use them to good advantage. Tell the Chief that neither he nor his young men will be harmed." Only three or four warriors emerged, with only a handful of bullets left between them.

American Horse, whose intestines protruded from his wound, walked quietly to the women and children, without so much as a groan. He died during the night, biting down on a stick so that he would not give voice to his pain.

Finerty noted that Crook "displayed to the fullest extent his eccentric contempt for danger. No private soldier could more expose himself than did the General and the officers of his staff. I expected to see them shot down every moment, for Charley White, the well-known scout, was shot through the heart just across the ravine, not ten paces from Crook. Kennedy of the Fifth Cavalry and Stevenson of the Second were wounded, the one mortally and the other dangerously, beside him, while many other soldiers had hair-breadth escapes."[14]

Crook had taken up strong positions by the time fresh Sioux reinforcements from Crazy Horse arrived and began sniping from nearby high ground. But the great Sioux concentration of warriors that had destroyed Custer had now scattered, and Crazy Horse could not hope to challenge Crook's large force. On the other hand, the soldiers had no chance of overtaking the better-mounted Sioux. Crazy Horse's warriors had vanished by morning. Crook released his female prisoners, telling them to tell Crazy Horse that no harm would come to anyone who returned to the reservation, but that Crook and the soldiers would kill anyone who remained out, no matter how long it took. Crook then again took up the trail of the Sioux, who were moving south toward Deadwood. The warriors harassed the now struggling column of soldiers. The firsthand accounts of the march testify to Crook's almost obsessive persistence, and to the appalling hardships that he shared with his soldiers. Through mud, sleet, and storms, they struggled to remain on their feet, saved from starvation only by horseflesh. Hardened campaigners grew so exhausted and starved that they simply sat down along the line of march and wept. But instead of pushing for the nearest cache of supplies, Crook resolved to drive his command on to Deadwood, which he feared would be vulnerable to Sioux attack without army protection. Crook maintained screens of skirmishers to keep the warriors from getting in close enough to run off his pack train or horses. He also sent a detachment to Deadwood to organize a relief column with supplies, and return to the Plains to meet his starving command.

Not surprisingly, the starvation march spurred bitter resentment in the ranks. The correspondent for the *New York Times* reported on September 22 that "the general impression in this command is that we have not much to boast of in the way of killing Indians. They kept out of the way so effectually that the only band which was struck was struck by accident, and when, by the subsequent attack upon us, it was discovered that another and much larger village was not far off, the command was in too crippled and broken down a condition from starvation and overmarching to turn the information to any good account."[15]

Lieutenant Charles King, normally a staunch defender of the general, wrote in a letter home: "I fear that even the 5th (Cavalry) cannot uphold their old chief as they did in Arizona. He certainly is greatly altered and while in the 2nd and 3rd Cavalry & the Infantry of his command he has not a friend left, there are still two or three in the 5th who are hoping that certain things may yet be explained before they lose respect and confidence."[16]

One soldier quoted in the press accounts observed, "There would not have been a murmur of disaffection among the troops, had there been a shadow of a cause for the existence of such a state of affairs; but as it was merely to satisfy a fleeting fancy of General Crook, who was endowed in the premises with discretionary and unlimited authority, the greatest discontent, want of energy, and carelessness existed in the command. I have no doubt that more favorable results would have been attained, and the people of the United States would probably not be obliged to replace about 300 horses abandoned since the 5th of August."[17]

On the other hand, the bedraggled and nearly beseiged citizens of Deadwood greeted the starving troops as saviors. Bourke noted that the Sioux had been picking off prospectors and travelers around Deadwood for months, leaving bodies scattered in canyons and gullies all around the rough-and-tumble frontier town. Whenever one of the resident roughnecks managed to kill an Indian, he would return to town in triumph with the skull and sell the scalp at auction to the highest bidder.

Granted, Crook's campaign had yielded only modest results. But it had started the disintegration of the Sioux and disrupted their efforts to gather up a summer surplus to see them through the coming winter. Certainly, Crook's command was the only one to make any sort of a show against the Sioux that summer. Moreover, his reliance on pack trains, his insistence on remaining in the field with a mobile force, and his use of a surprise dawn attack proved the only effective tactics against the wary, highly mobile Sioux. As Finerty noted, "All other commanders had withdrawn from the pursuit . . . but Crook resolved to teach the savages a lesson. He meant to show them that neither distance, bad weather, the loss of horses nor the absence of rations could deter the American army from following up its wild enemies to the bitter end."

The disasters of the summer had roused the nation and doomed the Sioux. Reinforcements poured into the territory, and Crook hastened to confer with Sheridan. They prepared another winter campaign, knowing that a year of fighting had worn the Sioux down. Now Crook prepared to hit them again, just as he had pursued the Apache through the winter in Arizona. The tactic capitalized on the overwhelming material and logistical advantages of the soldiers in a sustained campaign against Indians who had to both fight and support their families through the grueling winters.

Once again, Crook demonstrated his personal disregard for hardship and discomfort, and his willingness to subject his men to the most grueling of conditions. He kept his men moving doggedly all through blizzards, temperatures that plunged far below zero, deep snow, and dangerous ice. It stormed twenty-six of the fifty-two days of the campaign. "There should be no stopping for this or that thing," he observed. "The Indians cannot stand a continuous campaign . . . the best time to strike the Indians is in the winter. They cannot remain together in large bodies at that season. The necessities of subsistence compel them to separate, and then is the time to throw a large force on each band, and crush them all in detail."[18] Crook had also learned the hard lessons of his previous winter and summer campaigns against the Sioux. "The system of moving without a wagon train is the only proper one for a campaign of this character. A mule train can go anywhere, there is no rear to protect at the cost of largely reducing your fighting force. Our train was not large enough [on previous campaigns]. That will be remedied. We were unable to carry enough provisions to give us time to scout the country when we cut loose from our base. We had to make straight for another base as soon as we left the last, because our rations were not sufficient to allow us to wait on the way and search the country. . . . We were almost without guides or scouts."[19] Crook remedied that problem this time by enlisting scouts from among the Sioux and Cheyenne on the reservation.

Crook's advanced cavalry force led by Cheyenne and Sioux scouts hit one large Cheyenne village, capturing seven hundred ponies. Crook hurried forward with the infantry on a twenty-six-mile night march through snow and ice upon receiving word that the cavalry had pinned down a large number of Cheyenne warriors. During the daylong battle, Dull Knife begged the Sioux and Cheyenne scouts to go home, saying that he could not fight both the soldiers and his own people. Dull Knife and his band slipped away during the night, leaving behind the bodies of eleven infants who had frozen to death in their mothers' arms. However, when Crook arrived with the main force, the Cheyenne surrendered, starving and freezing and without hope. Crook promptly enlisted them to help him locate and fight the dwindling number of Sioux who remained defiant under the leadership of Crazy Horse and Sitting Bull.

Crook continued the march through the worst of the winter, but never managed to locate either Crazy Horse or Sitting Bull. However, circling back to the reservation he met with reservation leaders of the Sioux and Cheyenne and with other groups, building a powerful Indian alliance against the shrinking number of warriors who remained defiant. Spotted Tail agreed to find Crazy Horse, who was his nephew, and convince him to come in. Crazy Horse finally surrendered on May 6, 1877, with three hundred warriors, twenty-five hundred ponies, and about eight hundred women and children.

Bourke was impressed with the "Strange Man" of the Oglalas. "I saw before me a man who looked quite young, not over thirty years old, five feet eight inches high, lithe and sinewy, with a scar in the face. The expression of his countenance was one of quiet dignity, but morose, dogged, tenacious, and melancholy. He behaved with stolidity, like a man who realized he had to give in to Fate, but would do so as sullenly as possible. All Indians gave him a high reputation for courage and generosity. In advancing upon an enemy, none of his warriors were allowed to pass him. He had made hundreds of friends by his charity toward the poor, as it was a point of honor with him never to keep anything for himself, excepting weapons of war. I never heard an Indian mention his name in any save terms of respect."[20]

However, once again the politics on both sides of the struggle would make a mockery of Crook's effort to deal fairly and honestly with the Indians he fought, frustrating his determination never to make a promise he couldn't keep. Crook soon found himself in the midst of overlapping conflicts. On one hand, the Interior Department moved to regain control of the reservations and the patronage they represented. Bourke observed that the Indian Bureau was a "stench in the nostrils of decent people." In addition, Crook soon found himself sucked into the complex politics of the Sioux, as the tribal leaders maneuvered for influence on the reservation. By his very existence, Crazy Horse challenged the authority of the other Sioux leaders. His influence grew, although he did little to cultivate it. His aloof dignity, reputation for spiritual power, the adulation of the young warriors, and his quiet refusal to bow to the whites who controlled the reservation all contributed to his aura. Soon, rumors raced across the reservation suggesting that he planned to lead up to two thousand warriors off the reservation to join Sitting Bull, who had taken his band across the border into Canada.

In August of 1877, the peaceful Nez Percé Indians under Chief Joseph protested an effort to seize their land and move them to a different reservation by heading for Canada, with much of the U.S. Army in pursuit. On August 16, at a council on the reservation, the army asked Crazy Horse and a contingent of his warriors to help track down the Nez Percé. Conflicting accounts of that conference have survived. Bourke maintained Crazy Horse agreed to enlist as a scout, but confusion in the translation gave the impression that he intended to break out and fight the whites. The error was apparently straightened out, but confusion persisted. Crazy Horse evidently at first refused to fight, and then in exasperation said he would, without ever intending to actually ride against the Nez Percé—in part, because Crazy Horse suspected Crook's real target was Sitting Bull in Canada. On August 31, Crazy Horse evidently changed his mind and said that he would take his warriors and head north if the army persisted in trying to enlist them against either the Nez Percé or Sitting Bull. Lieutenant Colonel L. P. Bradley telegraphed General Sheridan warning of a possible breakout, and Sheridan telegraphed Crook, who was preparing the campaign against the Nez Percé.

Crook arrived at Camp Robinson on September 2, 1871, and ordered the Sioux leaders to convene in a great council. Crazy Horse refused, saying he wanted nothing to do with Crook.

Crook headed for the place selected for the council on September 2, having just learned that the Nez Percé had passed through Yellowstone and reached the Bighorn River. On his way to the meeting, Crook was stopped by a Sioux named Woman's Dress, wearing the uniform of a scout. Woman's Dress insisted that Crazy Horse planned to kill Crook at the council. In the past, Crook had faced down such threats. But this time he hesitated, and then decided to return to his headquarters and order the chiefs to come and meet him there. Red Cloud, Spotted Tail, and the other agency chiefs came as commanded, and warned Crook that if they helped him to track down the Nez Percé, Crazy Horse would make trouble back on the reservation. They reportedly urged Crook to simply have Crazy Horse killed, lest he start a civil war among the Sioux. Crook rejected that advice, but suggested the agency chiefs arrest Crazy Horse, with the backing of the troops. Crook then hurried off after the Nez Percé, anxious to take over command of that effort from Colonel Nelson A. Miles, a tall, imposing, politically astute officer Crook was already beginning to dislike.

On September 4 the agency chiefs set off to arrest Crazy Horse with four hundred warriors and eight companies of cavalry. Crazy Horse first fled to the Spotted Tail Agency, where he insisted he had never threatened to murder Crook or planned to leave the reservation. He then agreed to return to the Red Cloud Agency. There, Crazy Horse was stabbed when he drew back at the door to the guardhouse, perhaps by one of his own people, perhaps bayoneted by a soldier. He was taken to an officer's room where he died a short time later, saying to his father, "It is no use to depend on me. I am going to die."

Crook returned hastily to the reservation, and managed to prevent the reaction to the death of Crazy Horse from spurring a new breakout. Ironically, he had again been maneuvered into betraying a fellow warrior whose courage and determination he respected. In truth, Crook probably had more in common temperamentally and ethically with both Crazy Horse and Geronimo than he had with the politicians and bureaucrats and politically minded generals who repeatedly controlled and reaped the benefits of the victories Crook won in the field.

Bourke observed, "Crazy Horse was one of the great soldiers of his day and generation; he never could be friends of the whites, because he was too bold and warlike in his nature; he had a great admiration for Crook, which was reciprocated; once he said of Crook that he was more to be feared by the Sioux than all other white men."[21]

But one final betrayal of the Sioux still awaited, including leaders such as Red Cloud and Spotted Tail who had turned on Crazy Horse to win the favor of the whites. Crook's adroit policy of divide and conquer yielded the same bitter fruits among the Sioux as it would among the Apache. Crook had promised the Sioux he would do everything he could to secure for them a reservation at the mouth of the Tongue River, which included much of their most-loved territory. Once again, he had mistakenly assumed that his superiors and the politicians would prove as just and reasonable as he. Instead, as soon as the Sioux had surrendered and given up their weapons, they were removed to a much smaller, less suitable reservation on the Missouri River. Crook later wrote to the Sioux chiefs who had accepted his promises and helped him end the Sioux wars, "I tried very hard to get your reservation established at the mouth of the Tongue River, as you wished, but I was not able to do it, and had much trouble in getting you sent back to the Missouri River to the place you now occupy. I will at all times be glad to help you all I can. You know that I am your friend, and friends must help each other. When I needed soldiers to preserve order on the reservation and bring in the Indians whose hearts were bad, you helped me, and I have not forgotten you. The grievances of which you complain ought to be redressed by the Secretary of the Interior, as I cannot do much to assist you about them."[22]

Crook served for five more years on the plains. He was a sharp tool used to cut away the claims of the Indians to their lands, although his sympathies often remained with the Indians. He was called out to fight the Bannock in 1879, after settlers drove them off the land providing the camas roots that were their chief source of food. The Bannock decided to fight back rather than starve quietly. Crook noted, "Starvation is staring them in the face, and if they wait much longer, they will not be able to fight. They understand the situation, and fully appreciate what is before them & I do not wonder, and you will not either, that when these Indians see their wives and children starving, and their last source of supplies cut off, they will go to war. And then we are sent out to kill them. It is an outrage. All the tribes tell the same story. They are surrounded on all sides, the game is destroyed or driven away, they are left to starve, and there remains but one thing for them to do—fight while they can. Some people think the Indians do not understand these things, but they do . . . and fully appreciate the circumstances in which they are placed."[23] Crook could only dispatch troops, offer the Indians the choice between surrender and extermination, and do his best to provide adequate rations and land for those who surrendered.

Crook also helped direct the campaign to recapture several bands of Cheyenne who left their hated, malaria-infected reservation in the Indian Territory in 1878 and fought their way back five hundred miles to the Tongue River, hoping they might be given the land originally promised to them. Dull Knife and 149 members of his band were finally captured and confined for seventy days at Camp Robinson while Crook pleaded with the Indian Bureau to let the Cheyenne settle on a reservation in their old home territory. The Indian Bureau ultimately decreed that the Cheyenne would have to return to the reservation they had been assigned to in Indian Territory, whereupon the Cheyenne produced a few weapons they had managed to keep hidden for two months and make a hopeless escape into a snowstorm. They killed eleven soldiers and wounded another nine before the seventy-eight survivors finally surrendered again. Crook concluded sadly that "among these Cheyenne Indians were some of the bravest and most efficient of the auxiliaries who had acted under General MacKenzie and myself in the campaign against the hostile Sioux in 1876 and 1877, and I still preserve a grateful remembrance of their distinguished services, which the government seems to have forgotten."[24]

Trouble also broke out on the Ute reservation in Colorado, where whites continued to encroach on the Indians' land. Agent N. C. Meeker appealed for soldiers to restrain the Indians, and Crook dispatched troops although the area was not actually under his jurisdiction. The Ute ambushed the soldiers and killed Meeker, convinced the army was coming to hang them. As a result, the Ute White River Reservation was thrown open to settlement, and the tribe was forced to move to a reservation in Utah. A commission demanded the Ute turn over the warrior who had murdered Meeker, but not the Indians who had attacked the soldiers and killed Major T. T. Thornburgh. Crook noted bitterly that a soldier's life seemed of less importance than the life of an Indian agent.

Crook also helped corral the Ponca Indians when two hundred left the Indian Territory and returned peacefully to their homeland in South Dakota. The Ponca, who had never resisted the whites, had been forced from their homelands to make way for a new reservation for the Sioux. Malaria took a heavy toll of the tribe on the new reservation, and after losing his daughter to disease, chief Standing Bear led thirty followers off the reservation on a trek toward home. They harmed no one, and begged for food along the way. They arrived at the Omaha agency on March 4, and began farming peacefully on their old land. Although Crook's sympathies lay entirely with the Indians, he was ordered to arrest them and return them to the reservation. However, a crusading newspaper editor in Omaha, backed by churchmen and leading citizens, petitioned for their release. The reformers served a writ of habeas corpus, which provoked the case of *Standing Bear v. Crook*. A local judge ruled in favor of the Indians after a two-day trial in April 1879, and commended Crook for his attitude toward the Indians. The Interior Department appealed the ruling, since it raised the alarming prospect of extending at least some constitutional rights to the Indians. It also established a presidential commission, on which Crook served along with Colonel Miles. The commission recommended that the Ponca be allowed to remain on the land that had once been theirs, which effectively made the lower-court ruling moot as a precedent. One of the chief outcomes of the case for Crook was that it introduced him to the Indian Citizenship Committee, for whom he would become a major advocate in the years to come.

Repeatedly, Crook tried to convince his superiors, politicians, and the public that the Indian wars could be ended by treating the Indians with simple justice, and giving individual Indians land, cattle, crops, and other resources that would wean him away from dependence on the tribe. "The Indian is a child of ignorance, and not all innocence. It requires a certain kind of treatment to deal with him and develop him. One requisite in those who would govern him rightly is absolute honesty—a strict keeping of faith toward him. The other requisite is authority to control him, and that the means to enforce that authority be vested in the same individual. . . . As it is now you have a divided responsibility. It is like having two captains on the same ship. For this reason, I think there can be no question but the management of the Indians should be placed under the control of the War Department." He also insisted that the solution to the "Indian problem" was economic.

There is no reason the country should sustain or support any portion of its population in idleness. The Indians can be made self-sustaining, and they are willing to do so, all they want is the proper facilities and the proper instruction. Of course, you have got to use a little force. I have twenty-six years experience with the Indians, and I have been among the tribes where I spoke their language. I have known the Indians intimately, known them in their private relations. I think I understand the Indian character pretty well. They talk about breaking up their tribal relations. I might as well try breaking up a band of sheep. Give these Indians little farms, survey them, let them put fences around them, let them have their own horses, cows, sheep, things that they can call their own, and it will do away with tribal Indians. . . . When once an Indian sees that his food is secure, he does not care what the chief or any one else says. . . . The great mistake these people make is that they go looking after the spiritual welfare of the Indians before securing their physical welfare.[25]

He concluded that the corruption or misconduct of the Indian agents or the government's broken promises lay at the root of virtually every Indian trouble.

But Crook's pleas for justice and an end to dual control of the reservations were fruitless, a small shouting into the wind of greed, economics, and racism that controlled the nation's Indian policy. Throughout Crook's service, he found he had influence only so long as he was actively fighting warriors who had left the reservation. As soon as he had restored peace, control shifted to corrupt agents and the politicians whose chief interest was in opening the West to settlers and prospectors.

In the meantime, Crook continued to travel ceaselessly throughout the West, hunting every chance he got. Once he fell through thin ice in a blizzard, and would have died there if his companions had not pulled him out. On another occasion, a grizzly bear he was stalking charged out of a tule swamp, but Crook coolly dropped the beast with a single shot that passed through its gaping mouth and severed the spinal cord. He also made several attempts to get rich, yielding to the example set on every side. He had speculated unprofitably in real estate in California in the late 1860s. Now he and several other officers, including Bourke, invested in several California gold mines. Crook dispatched his aide and his nephew, Oliver Crook, to oversee the operations of the mine. The investment seemed about to pay off with the introduction of a new refining process that tripled the yield of ore from the mine. Crook enlisted other investors, including General Sheridan—his commander and classmate. As the mine shaft sank deeper following the inconsistent ore vein, the expenses mounted until the investors were forced to sell out in March 1881, recovering just about enough money to cover their investments, but not enough to pay dividends.

In many ways, it must have seemed to Crook that his life had reached its logical fulfillment. In the course of an adventurous thirty-year career, Crook had fought Indian wars throughout the West, commanded troops in the greatest and most terrible war in the nation's history, and played the leading role in the destruction of the Sioux.

He could not know then that the most controversial, frustrating, and dangerous time in his life lay just ahead. Back in Arizona, the seven years of peace Crook had won back in 1875 had been squandered through mismanagement, corruption, and confusion.

And so Brigadier General George Crook was about to confront the one enemy who would finally defeat him.

The enemy destined to become the most famous Indian in the nation's history.

Geronimo.

Part Five

1883–1909

THE FOX FACES THE WHIRLWIND

11

—————— **1883**

Geronimo
THE LAST DAYS OF A FREE PEOPLE

GERONIMO AND THE OTHER LEADERS who had assembled in
the Sierra Madre now began to go out with small raiding parties to
gather up cattle, and horses, and things they could trade. The
divisions had started to form almost immediately among the tat-
tered remnants of many bands that had been gathered together.
The Nednai remained, and many other people viewed them as
wild men whose ranks included warriors who had been cast out of
other bands for murder, or witchcraft, or bad behavior. The Chiricahua mostly followed Naiche and Geronimo, who had once again
made their peace with one another. The Chihenne and Mimbreno
followed Loco and Nana, who had been reunited as old friends
and comrades. Loco grieved for all of the losses in their escape
from the reservation, but admitted to Nana that they would probably have lost even more to the diseases of the White Eyes if they
had remained on the reservation.[1]

Geronimo and Chato and Naiche and others gathered up all of
the things that they could trade with the Mexicans at Casas
Grandes, and took perhaps one-third of the band there to trade—
as they had in the old days. The people at Casas Grandes greeted
them with open arms, traded for their goods, and invited all of
them to a fiesta. The warriors entered the town with their weapons,
very wary, but the Mexicans smiled at them, and made good trades
and brought them food. Geronimo remained for a time on his

guard, but the Mexicans smiled, and laughed, and brought him the strong tequila, which he loved. Sometimes it seemed that the tequila, and the *tizwin*, and the strong whiskey of the White Eyes provided the only answer to the questions that had haunted him all his life. When he drank these things, the future did not matter, the past did not matter, and he felt that he would never die, that Alope had never died, that nothing had ever changed and The People would live forever as they always had. And if this was not a solution to the riddle of the White Eyes and to the mystery of Usen's purpose, it did make all of the questions seem unimportant, at least for a few hours. Besides, he had a craving, like grief, like helpless lust, like the yearning for killing. He thought of it at unexpected moments sometimes so that his hands trembled. So among the friendly people of Casas Grandes, who had more often than not remained at peace with the Chiricahua, he drank some, and then some more, until it filled him so with courage that he could not remember the bitter lessons of his life.

And so when most of the warriors lay drunk in their camp outside of town, men with guns and clubs who had come from some other town[2] attacked the camp, killing those too drunk to rise, and chasing the others out into the bushes. Geronimo escaped, as he always escaped, because his Power would not let him die. But the Mexicans killed twenty and captured thirty-five to sell as slaves, including two children of Chato and Geronimo's beautiful wife Chee-has-kish, whom he never saw again after that day.

The survivors returned to the Sierra Madre, camping at the edge of the great canyon of the Yaquí River, where they could not be attacked. Geronimo prayed, and fasted, and consulted his Power, seeing that he had once again failed his People because he had trusted the Mexicans. He had fallen away from his war with the Mexicans as though weary, and so had fallen once more into their old trap.

The bands camped together for a time, and Geronimo took for a wife a Nednai girl named Zi-yeh, whose father was named Dji-li-kine, a White Eye that had been taken as a child and raised by White Mountain people. But even in the midst of their enemies, even after all the things that they had seen, even though they had taken such risks to bring the last free People together, the bands could not remain long together. They followed too many leaders. They harbored too many old grudges, one against the other. A warrior was not a soldier. A warrior was a free man. He could go, and come, and make his own decisions. He could go alone among his enemies, and travel a thousand miles alone, and make his weapons and find his food, and take what he wanted from weaker people who were meat to his needs. The soldiers had no heart, no mind, no spirit. They were like ants, or bees—creatures of the colony and hive. They moved all together. They came always in great numbers. They were slaves to the commands of their *nantans*. They could not survive alone in even a place with lots of game and plenty to eat. They were like the innumerable fingers of a single hand, useless when cut off, but crushing as a fist. But the very strength of The People seemed to count against them in this struggle. So long as every warrior was free, and free to choose, they could not fight all together for more than a battle or two. Even the different bands of the same people could not fight long together, much less the bands of different people, the Chihenne, and the Mimbreno, and the Chiricahua, and the White Mountain, and the Nednai, and the Tonto, and the Coyotero, and the Mescalero. The Prophet had brought them all together, and the White Eyes had killed him for it, seeing their danger. But the Prophet had died, and the dead warriors he had promised had not rallied to the need of the people. Now they could only hide far from the soldiers with only the evidence of Geronimo's Power to show they had not been forgotten altogether by the supernatuals who had given them this land so long ago. Now the leaders vied with one another, and the warriors each made their choice about whom to follow, based on family ties, and on reputation, and on Power.

So they split apart. Juh led his Nednai back to the heart of his territory, far up in the Sierra Madre where the Mexicans rarely went. But Geronimo wanted to kill Mexicans, and take cattle, and return to raiding, as though he were still a young man, and the world still belonged to the warriors of The People. Chihuahua went with him, anxious to build his reputation in war. Chato went with them also, still grieving his lost children, but eager for glory.

Kaytennae went along, with Lozen, whose Power to locate the enemy every warrior valued.[3] They took with them about eighty people, most of them women and children. But they rejoiced in their freedom, and in having their families with them. As they traveled, one of Geronimo's wives gave birth, and so they stopped for a little while to celebrate. He sang over the baby, buried the umbilical cord so that the earth would remember the child, and held up the infant to the four directions in the place that would always remain sacred to the child.

They moved easily through the mountains, then down into the lowlands to attack ranches and villages, taking what they needed, and killing those who resisted. They raided south to Ures, and then turned and moved north toward Arizona. Rumors had come down to Geronimo that Gray Fox had returned to take command of the soldiers. This news made him cautious, because Gray Fox was a hard enemy, but an honorable one, so that he could win over the leaders of the people still on the reservation and enlist many scouts. Gray Fox was a careful man, and he would have his soldiers out watching the water holes. He would leave nothing undone. But still, Gray Fox was far away, and he could not know where Geronimo had gone, or where he would strike. And they had now a great need for ammunition for their American-made guns, so they moved back toward Arizona and even raided into Arizona. Geronimo's Power led them to plenty of bullets so that they would have enough to last them for months to come. And Lozen's Power led them safely through the enemy, so that the soldiers scarcely knew they were there. So Geronimo thought that perhaps he had overestimated Gray Fox, and should not worry so much about his return.

But then one San Carlos man ran away from the band, taking his wife to go back to the reservation. The defection angered Geronimo. He sent out warriors to hunt them down and kill them, but they escaped. Some of the warriors wondered at this, because they believed that each warrior could choose when he would fight and where he would go. But they also knew that they had not enough warriors, and no place to get more. Every loss was telling and Geronimo could not let them trickle away, like a deep wound bleeding slowly. The word had spread that Gray Fox had returned, and had charge of the reservation again. This made many people turn their minds toward returning. Other White Eyes cheated them, gave them barely enough wormy meat to eat, and barely enough cloth to make a shirt, but Gray Fox had always treated The People fairly. So Geronimo watched his warriors carefully as they moved through Arizona, so close to the reservation. He knew each of them, especially which of their wives talked yearningly of the reservation where they could sleep peacefully in the same bed each night and need not spring up ready to flee each time a raccoon made a noise near camp in the night.

They returned finally to the Sierra Madre, and were camped near Oputo, when Geronimo's Power saved them once again. He rose before dawn to pray and sing. Suddenly his Power spoke to him saying, Take care, Geronimo. He turned to his Power, which was nowhere and everywhere, and said in reply, I always take care. His Power laughed, seeing his pride, and liking this in him. The soldiers are coming, said his Power. Which soldiers? asked Geronimo. The Mexicans, said his Power. I am not afraid of the Mexicans, Geronimo said in return. His Power replied, Of course not, but you must have a care. Geronimo asked, Where will they be? Outside of Oputo, going east, coming toward you when the sun is about halfway to the top, said his Power. Enuh, grunted Geronimo in approval, already thinking of the trail leading east out of Oputo, recalling the best place there for an ambush. Geronimo returned to the camp and assembled the warriors and told them that they would go to kill the soldiers east of Oputo, and that the soldiers would come through a certain ravine in the middle of the morning. The warriors looked at one another, and nodded.[4]

They went to the ravine and waited, well hidden. In the middle of the morning the soldiers came along with plenty of supplies just as Geronimo had said they would. The warriors opened fire, killing the soldiers and taking their horses and their supplies. That night they held a great victory dance, for they had taken many supplies and suffered no losses. Geronimo danced when they called out his name, but mostly he watched the others, seeing the pride in the young warriors, even some of those from the reservation who had never raided before. His Power had led him correctly, and he understood then that they could not be The People, and could not know themselves, except in this way. They must give and take death so that their courage, and their strength, and their cunning, and their Power would all be tested. Then a young warrior and a young woman danced out into the circle of people, all laughing, and singing, and full of joy. The warrior put his rifle awkwardly on his shoulder and marched about like a stick man, so that everyone laughed and shouted. And the woman put a shawl around her shoulders and simpered, and swished, and pranced about like a Mexican woman so that everyone laughed twice as loudly as before.

So they returned in triumph to the place where they had arranged to meet Juh, and camped across a deep gorge from the Nednai. Each camp played their drums through the night, and the warriors shouted across the canyon, safe in their own country. The next day they crossed the great canyon, climbing thousands of feet down into the bottom that was so narrow and tangled that it was like evening in the midst of the day, then out again to the other side. Juh's people met them with news of their own great victory. They had encountered a large force of Mexican soldiers, and fought them all day, until they ran out of ammunition. They then retreated up a steep trail out of a deep canyon, and waited at the top for the soldiers to follow. When the soldiers came on against them, the warriors sprang up with logs to pry loose large boulders that they had set in place, sending the boulders crashing down among their enemies. Those who were not crushed by the rocks turned and fled. The triumphant warriors went down among the dead and gathered their guns and their ammunition. They lost not a single warrior.

Flushed with this success, the leaders met in council to decide what they should do. Nana spoke and everyone listened in respectful silence, for his Power was great and he had fought longer, and harder, and with more distinction than any of them gathered. He said they should go, all together, to attack Galeana. Geronimo's eyes glittered when Nana said this, because he believed that soldiers from Galeana had attacked his camp outside of Casas Grandes and had taken Geronimo's wife, and Chato's children, and killed many others. Then Nana said the *nantan* at Galeana was Juan Mata Ortiz, who had helped kill Victorio and all his people. The leaders all quickly assented, accepting the duty of revenge.

But Geronimo saw that Juh remained pensive and somber, despite all of their success. Geronimo and Juh had always been of the same spirit, so Geronimo watched him carefully, knowing that Juh would always push for war, even as Geronimo did. So now Geronimo took Juh aside, to see why he was troubled. Juh said that he had seen a vision. He had been camping on the sacred mountain, and had been awakened, and gone to the edge of a great canyon. A cave opened up in the side of the canyon, which Juh had not seen before. Soldiers started coming out of the cave, an endless line of them, one after the other, with horses, and guns, and mules loaded with ammunition. They came out of the cave without pause, like the lake that stretches to the horizon so that all of The People could be lost in the sea of them without trace. Juh knew then that they were doomed, that they were already Indeh—the dead. He knew that they could not win against the White Eyes, they had only a choice of deaths. Juh would choose the warrior's death. Geronimo nodded, and thought on it, and realized Juh's vision was true, as he had always known it was true.[5]

They went all together to Galeana, taking care that no one should see them, and prepared an ambush in a ravine outside of the town. Then they sent a few warriors on fast horses right up to the city. They drove off a herd of grazing horses, making sure that they were seen so the soldiers would come out of the town to chase them. The soldiers did as expected, riding out in a group to chase the few warriors right into the ambush. When the hidden warriors began firing, the soldiers saw they could not ride through the bullets back to the town, but they kept their discipline and rode all together to the top of a rocky hill. On the hill they shot their horses or made them lie down, so they could take cover behind the horses and shoot down on the warriors. Juh, and Nana, and Geronimo, and a few others, each with good rifles, took up a position beside a cedar tree where they had a view of the hilltop and began firing to keep the soldiers down. The other warriors went all around the bottom of the hill, each selecting a rock as big as their heads. Each man lay down behind his rock, and began crawling up the hill, pushing the rock in front. The soldiers saw the warriors moving up the hill toward them, and began firing faster and faster as their fear grew, but they could not hit the warriors behind their rocks. By the time the warriors reached the top of the hill, the soldiers had used almost all of their ammunition. So the warriors fought them hand to hand, until all of the soldiers lay bloody and still, with just one warrior killed. Only one soldier escaped, pulling up his horse and riding down the hill in a way that inspired the admiration of those who saw it. Geronimo called out to the warriors to let him go, saying he would bring more soldiers for them to kill. The warrior who had led the others attacking the hill rushed forward, and seized the *nantan*'s horse, which had a fine saddle and bridle. But one of the soldiers, who had not been dead after all, rose up on his elbow and shot the warrior dead out of his sddle. The other warriors quickly killed the man, but the deaths of two warriors had spoiled the victory, even though they had killed twenty-two soldiers. One of the dead soldiers was Ortiz, who had helped to kill Victorio. The warriors turned back to the town, waiting for more soldiers. But when the approaching soldiers saw the warriors, they stopped and took cover in a good place, so the leaders decided not to risk further losses. They went back then to the Sierra Madre, content in having killed the soldiers, but sorrowing in the loss of warriors they could not replace.

They did not know then that this was their last great victory and that everything would soon turn against them. Even Geronimo's Power could only fight a hopeless rearguard action now, holding off death, and slavery, and the silencing of all their songs.

They soon split up once again. Juh and his Nednai went off along with many of the Chihenne, including Nan and Kaytennae and Lozen. Geronimo and Naiche and Chihuahua and Chato camped with the Chiricahua at the headwaters of the Bavispe.[6]

The Chiricahua continued to raid, leaving the women and children in camp and moving through Sonora with only warriors and capturing a pack train heavily laden with goods. But the Mexican soldiers surprised Juh in his camp, and killed most of his people. They killed even Ishton, who had ever been Geronimo's favorite sister and who had been Juh's chief counselor and his great source of strength. Her loss was a great blow, to both Juh and to Geronimo. She had often helped Juh make his plans and was respected by everyone in his band. It was while he was praying for Ishton that Geronimo's Power had first spoken to him, and now her death also killed a part of him. Fortunately, Nana and Juh and Kaytennae and others escaped, and returned to rejoin Geronimo. But many of the warriors now turned against Juh, saying his Power was gone and he could not protect his people. Wounded in heart and spirit, and grieving for Ishton, Juh camped away from the rest—with only three warriors and a few women and children. Once he had been one of the greatest war leaders of The People, but now he was a remnant of himself—his Power broken. Perhaps it had been his vision. It had not weakened Juh, but it had perhaps weakened the warriors who followed him. Few men could fight without hope.

The united band could now boast more than one hundred fighting men, and Geronimo, Naiche, and Chihuahua were the principal war leaders, although strong factions of warriors followed Kaytennae and Chato and several others. They decided to leave the women and children in a secure camp once again, and to mount two raids—one through Sonora for cattle and horses and the other into Arizona to get more ammunition. Geronimo took leadership of the raid into Sonora, while Chihuahua and Chato and Naiche led twenty-six warriors into Arizona. Before they went off, Geronimo cautioned them to be careful about the water holes. Gray Fox had command of the soldiers now, and would watch the water holes, and would have the White Mountain scouts with them. But Chappo, Geronimo's son, said he was not afraid of Gray Fox, and did not need instruction in raiding.

Geronimo led his large party of warriors toward Ures. They killed almost everyone they encountered, but did not find any pack trains. The Mexicans fled at his approach, calling on their God, and crying Geronimo's name. His pride and his arrogance grew. In one town, the people all went up on the flat roofs of their homes, and Geronimo lined up his warriors, who jeered and laughed at the people huddled on their roofs. But the Mexicans would not come down to fight and Geronimo would not risk an assault for so poor a reward. No soldiers came against them on the raid, so they enjoyed the journey, feeling the power of so many warriors together. Chappo rode proudly with his father, and was also his father's pride.

One night they stopped to rest and wait for the moon. The warriors took the saddles from their horses and set them down. Chappo draped his saddle across a small rock. But when they were ready to continue, the rock with his saddle on it was gone. Chappo thought someone had stolen his saddle, and looked about in growing anger, thinking they were mocking him as a safer way to mock his father, who had no humor about anything that made him look foolish. Then one of the warriors shouted out that he had found the saddle, laughing as he said it. Everyone rushed over and found Chappo's saddle walking slowly along in the moonlight, because he had put it on an armadillo. Everyone laughed so that they fell over one another, saying Chappo had a fine pony now. Chappo took the teasing with a good face, because he had not yet the pride of his father.

Heading back to the encampment where the women were waiting, they had good luck and found a pack train. The mules were loaded with mescal, so the warriors drank until they passed out, with only the apprentices standing guard.

They returned to the camp at about the same time as Chato and his warriors, who had ridden more than four hundred miles through Arizona. They had killed twenty-six people,[7] and brought back ammunition and some horses, and a boy. They had killed the parents of the boy on the road near Lordsburg. Chato said the boy's father had been a brave man who got down from the carriage he was driving to try to fight off the warriors alone so that his wife and son could escape. They killed the man, and then caught up with the carriage and killed the woman, taking the boy because he was young enough to learn the ways of a warrior and because of the courage of his father. Perhaps if they had known what trouble the boy would cause, they would have killed him and left him with his mother.[8] They had lost one warrior, Chihuahua's son-in-law, in an attack on a camp of cowboys. Then Tsoe, who was the good friend of the dead warrior, lost his heart for fighting. With tears standing in his eyes, he stood a long time looking back, and then turned to the warriors and said that he was going back to the reservation. He was a White Mountain man, who had married a Chiricahua woman who had been killed, so he said that now he wanted to return to his people on the reservation. Geronimo might not have let him go, loath to reduce their fighting strength. But Chato was Tsoe's friend, and so gave him supplies for his journey and let him ride away, saying that each warrior was free to choose his own path. In time to come, Geronimo had great cause to wish that he had been with them then, and that Chato had killed Tsoe instead of letting him go.

Reunited, they rested for a time, and then sent out new raiding parties, this time looking for cattle. The warriors brought back about one hundred cattle, which would feed The People for a time, but the warriors watching the back trail of the raiders soon saw soldiers coming along behind them. So the warriors went back and set an ambush for the soldiers near the top of a steep trail leading out of a canyon. They hit the soldiers and drove them back down a ways, then rolled boulders down on them, as Juh had done, killing many.[9] The rest fled. Geronimo lost not a single warrior.

The leaders conferred again, each speaking in his turn in the council. They decided they should go into Chihuahua to find prisoners to trade for the people the Mexicans had captured in the attack near Casas Grandes on Geronimo's camp and the attack in the Sierra Madre on Juh's camp. They held another war dance, the warriors dancing out into the firelight to show that they would go with Geronimo on this dangerous raid for prisoners. They danced in the old way; they danced the high steps and thrilled to the chanting of the women and the children and to the sound of their names.

Geronimo watched them with grim pride, thinking ahead to the raid. He did not know that the world would change forever-more by the time he returned. Gray Fox had set his sights now on Geronimo, like a man with a good rifle and the sun behind him. He was coming on, already.

12

Crook
A Bold Gamble

GERONIMO'S RAID on the San Carlos Reservation that had brought away Loco's band caused near hysteria among press and public. It also prompted the army to recall Crook to resume command against the Apache. He had broken the Sioux, but Custer's death, Rosebud, and the death of Crazy Horse had all cast a pall over his service against the Sioux. Although he remained outwardly unaffected by the criticism he had drawn, Crook was prickly and defensive on the subject for the rest of his life. He returned to Arizona with mixed feelings, confident that his knowledge of the Apache and of the terrain would yield victory, but also weary after thirty years of hard service on the frontier. Moreover, he fully understood the campaign that lay ahead—a war of endurance and attrition against an elusive foe. He knew the Apache would do everything possible to deny him a decisive battle that would bring the campaign to a quick end and mute the outspoken criticisms of the territorial press, now calling for the quick extermination of the Apache, both on and off the reservation. Crook immediately conducted an exhaustive tour of the reservations, interviewing officers and soldiers and listening for hours to the complaints of the chiefs. He found himself mostly in agreement with the Indians, and appalled at the corruption of the reservation system. Near the end of San Carlos Indian agent Joseph Tiffany's tenure a grand jury issued a scathing review of his administration, concluding it was "a disgrace to the civilization of the age . . . As honest American citizens [we] express our abhorrence of the conduct of Agent Tiffany and that class of reverend peculators who have cursed Arizona as Indian officials, and who have caused more misery and loss of life than all other causes combined. . . . With the immense power wielded by the Indian agent almost any crime is possible. There seems to be no check upon his conduct."[1] However, Tiffany was never brought to trial.

Crook found widespread abuses. He documented instances in which Indians who questioned the wagon loads of supplies leaving the reservation were imprisoned without charges for more than a year at a time. He found that most of the supplies the government provided for the Indians were sold off the reservation, so that twenty Apache had to live for a week on a shoulder of beef and twenty cups of flour. Nonetheless, Tiffany persistently refused to allow the starving warriors to hunt off the reservation.

"Everywhere, the sullen, stolid, hopeless, suspicious faces of the older Indians challenge you," wrote Lieutenant Britton Davis in *The Truth about Geronimo.* "You felt the challenge in your marrow—that unspoken challenge to prove yourself anything else than one more liar and thief, differing but little from the procession of liars and thieves who have preceded you."

Bourke observed, "There is a coincidence of sentiment among all people whose opinion was worthy of consultation, that the blame did not rest with the Indians; curious tales were flying about from mouth to mouth of the gross outrages perpetrated upon the men and women who were trying faithfully to abide in peace with the whites. No one had ever heard the Apaches' story and no one seemed to care whether they had a story or not."[2]

Crook met with the leaders remaining on the reservation, many of them friends from his previous service in Arizona. Meeting with twenty-six White Mountain Apache leaders on the Black River, he made a point of asking Bourke to take down everything that was said. "I want to have all that you say here go down on paper," Crook told the chiefs, who were led by Alchise, who had scouted with Crook against the Tonto Apache in the early 1870s, "because what goes down on paper never lies. A man's memory may fail him, but what the paper holds will be fresh and true long after we are all dead and forgotten. This will not bring back the dead, but what is put down on this paper today may help the living. What I want to get at is all that has happened since I left here to bring about this trouble. I want you to tell the truth without fear, and to tell it in as few words as possible, so that everybody can read it without trouble."

Alchise replied with simple dignity. "When you left, there were no bad Indians out. We were all content; everything was peace. The officers you had here were all taken away and new ones came in—a different kind. The good ones must have all been taken away and the bad ones sent in to take their places. We couldn't make out what they wanted; one day they seemed to want one thing, the next day something else. Perhaps we were to blame, perhaps they were. But, anyhow, we hadn't any confidence in them. We were planting our own corn and melons and making our own living. The agent at San Carlos never gave us any rations, but we didn't mind that, as we were taking care of ourselves." He continued, "One day the agent at San Carlos sent up and said that we must give up our own country and our corn-patches and go down there to live, and he sent Indian soldiers to seize our women and children and drive us all down to that hot land. Uclenni and I were doing all we could to help the whites, when we were both put in the guardhouse. All that I have ever done has been honest; I have always been true and obeyed orders. I made campaigns against the Apache-Yumas, Apache-Tontos, Pinaleos, and all kinds of people and even went against my own people." He ended with a plea for a return of the officers whom Crook had put in charge of the reservations in the 1870s.

Old Pedro, another chief, echoed Alchise's plea for justice. "When you were here, whenever you said a thing we knew that it was true, and we kept it in our minds. . . . Our children were happy and our young people grew up contented. When you were here we were all content; but we can't understand why you went away. Why did you leave us? Everything was all right when you were here."

Bourke concluded, "Had the Apaches a little more sense they would have perceived that the whole scheme of Caucasian contact with the American aborigines was based upon that fundamental maxim of politics so beautifully and tersely enunciated by the New York alderman, 'the boys are in it for the stuff.' The 'Tucson Ring' was determined that no Apache should be put to the embarrassment of working for his own living; once let the Apaches become self-supporting and what would become of 'the boys'? Therefore they must all be herded down onto the malaria-reeking flats of the San Carlos, where the water is salt, and the air poison, and one breathes a mixture of sand blizzards and more flies than were ever supposed to be under the care of the great fly-god Beelzebub." In tones heavy with frustrated sarcasm Bourke concluded, "They had only to report that the Apaches were 'uneasy,' and 'refused to obey the orders of the agent,' and a lot more stuff of this same kind, and the Great Father would send in ten regiments to carry out the schemes of the ring, but he would never send an honest, truthful man to inquire whether the Apaches had a story or not."[3]

Crook took immediate action. He reinstituted military control of the reservations, initiating a count that demonstrated that more than eleven hundred men of fighting age remained on the reservation, four or five times as many as had left. He fired many of the previous contractors. He also expelled all unauthorized people from the reservation—chasing out whiskey sellers, prospectors, traders, and others. He put honest, sympathetic officers like Lieutenant Britton Davis and Captain Emmett Crawford in charge of the reservations. Davis soon discovered that the scales used to weigh beef cheated the government, and the Apache, of fifteen hundred pounds of beef each week. He issued metal identification tags to each Indian, but also allowed them to settle anywhere on the reservation, instead of forcing them to cluster in mutually hostile groups near military posts. He banned the making of *tizwin*, the traditional, relatively weak Apache beverage. He also decreed that the Apache could no longer cut off the noses of unfaithful wives.

"I believe that it is of far greater importance to prevent outbreaks than to attempt the difficult and sometimes hopeless task of quelling them after they do occur. Bad as the Indians often are, I have never yet seen one so demoralized that he was not an example in honor and nobility to the wretches who enrich themselves by plundering him of the little our government appropriates him," he wrote in a letter to the U.S. district attorney.[4]

Crook advocated justice and unfettered military control of the reservations. "The commanding general regrets to say that he finds among (the Indians) a general feeling of distrust and want of confidence in whites, especially the soldiery. Officers and soldiers serving in this department are reminded that one of the fundamental principles of the military character is justice to all—Indians as well as white men—and that a disregard for this principle is likely to bring about hostilities, and cause the death of the very persons they are sent here to protect." He called on his officers to set the example. "In all their dealings with the Indians, officers must be careful not only to observe the strictest fidelity, but to make no promises not in their power to carry out; all grievance arising within their jurisdiction should be redressed. Grievances, however petty, if permitted to accumulate, will be like embers that smolder and eventually break into flame. When officers are applied to for the employment of force against Indians, they should thoroughly satisfy themselves of the necessity for the application, and of the legality of compliance therewith, in order that they may not, through the inexperience of others, or through their own hastiness, allow the troops under them to become the instruments of oppression."[5]

Crook established a system of Indian courts with Indian judges and juries, and also handed over the task of policing the reservations to an Apache police force. He directed the officers in charge of the reservation to do everything possible to make the Indians self-supporting. Captain Crawford's 1883 report indicated that the White Mountain Apache raised 2.5 million pounds of corn, 180,000 pounds of beans, 135,000 pounds of potatoes, and 200,000 pounds of barley that year, as well as pumpkins, watermelons, cantaloupe, and enough seeds for the next year's crop.

Crook soon came under fire in the territorial press for taking the part of the Indians and not moving aggressively enough to hunt down the raiders. Bourke noted, "General Crook at this time was made the target of every sort of malignant and mendacious

General George Crook with Apache scouts Dutchy and Alchesay. Crook usually rode a mule and wore a pith helmet in the rugged territory in which he battled the Apache and perfected the art of pack trains. (*Courtesy Arizona Historical Society, Tucson*)

assault by the interests which he had antagonized. The telegraph wires were loaded with false reports of outrages, attacks, and massacres, which had never occurred. These reports were broadcast with the intention and in the hopes that they might do him injury. Crook made no reply to these scurrilous attempts at defamation, knowing that duty well performed will in the end secure the recognition and approval of all fair-minded people, the only ones whose recognition and approval are worth the having. But he did order the most complete investigation to be made of each and every report, and in each and every case the utter recklessness of the authors of these lies was made manifest."[6]

Having pacified the Apache still on the reservation, Crook also began military preparations, knowing that the Chiricahua would eventually raid back into the United States. He improved the pack trains and dispatched independent, roving patrols to the border, looking for raiders. He posted guards on most of the water holes, knowing that the Chiricahua would eventually renew raiding into the United States. He also doubled the number of Apache scouts to a total of 250, knowing that the key to defeating Geronimo lay in turning his own people against him.

The expected raid soon came. A band of perhaps two dozen Apache led by Chato and Chihuahua swept through Arizona and New Mexico in March of 1883, covering four hundred miles in six days. The raiders killed twenty-six people, while losing only one warrior. They also killed a prominent local judge and his wife, kidnapping their little boy—Charlie McComas. The killing and kidnapping sparked outrage throughout the territory. But the war party also suffered a fateful defection. Tsoe, known to history as Peaches, left the war party and returned to the San Carlos Reservation to rejoin his relatives there. Crook soon learned of his return to the reservation, arrested him, and convinced him to guide an expedition into the Sierra Madre. Tsoe seemed willing enough, explaining that he had never felt comfortable among the Chiricahua, especially after his Chiricahua wife had been killed. Another commander might have been reluctant to gamble on the word of a warrior who had so recently been killing whites. But Crook did not abandon his reliance on the loyalty and reliability of the Apache scouts, who he believed were the key to defeating the hostiles. Tsoe offered to wear chains to demonstrate his reliability, but other scouts pleaded with Crook to give Tsoe his weapons and promised to vouch for him. Thus reassured, Crook resolved to risk his future on Tsoe's faithfulness.

Seeing his opportunity to strike a decisive blow, General Crook took a train into Mexico, where he met with the governors of Sonora and Chihuahua and federal officials to win permission to cross the border to hunt down the Chiricahua in their Sierra Madre hideouts. The Mexican officials approved the invasion and told Crook they were preparing their own offensive.

General Crook returned to the United States and quickly assembled his force. He took 6 officers and 42 men of Company I, Sixth Cavalry. But his main fighting force consisted of 193 Apache scouts from many different bands, including the Chiricahua, under the command of Captain Crawford, Al Sieber, and Lieutenant Charles Gatewood. The company of scouts also included a translator—Mickey Free. Years ago, the kidnapping of this same half-Mexican, half-Apache boy had led to Cochise's decade-long war with the Americans.

Guided by Tsoe, Crook's force made its way through the devastated northern provinces of Mexico and into the heart of the Sierra Madre. They passed abundant evidence of the toll imposed by the Chiricahua on every hand—discarded supplies; the bodies of cattle walked to death, butchered, and abandoned; and even the sun-bleached skeletons of Mexican soldiers left where they had fallen in their pursuit of the Apache into their most secure fortress. Bourke came to admire the fighting style and independence of the Apache warriors, who trotted tirelessly up the rugged mountain range, easily outwalking the laboring horses of the cavalrymen. "To the veterans of the campaigns of the Civil War, the loose straggling methods of the Apache scouts would appear startling, and yet no soldier would fail to apprehend at a glance that the Apache was the perfect, the ideal, scout of the whole world. When Lieutenant Gatewood, the officer in command, gave the short, jerky order, Ugashe—Go—the Apaches started as if shot from a gun, and in a minute or less had covered a space of one hundred yards in front, which distance rapidly widened as they advanced at a rough, shambling walk."

He also admired their odd, very unmilitary discipline. "They moved with no semblance of regularity; individual fancy alone governed . . . Their chests were broad, deep, and full; shoulders perfectly straight; limbs well-proportioned, strong and muscular without a suggestion of undue heaviness; hands and feet small and tapered but wry; heads well-shaped, and countenances often lit up with a pleasant, good-natured expression, which would be more constant, perhaps, were it not for the savage, untamed cast imparted by the loose, disheveled, gypsy locks of raven black, held away from the face by a broad, flat band of scarlet cloth. Their eyes were bright, clear, and bold, frequently expressive of the greatest good humor and satisfaction."[7]

He glimpsed the humanity in the scouts, who cheerfully confronted every hardship. "In the presence of strangers the Apache soldier is sedate and taciturn. Seated around his little apology of a campfire, in the communion of his fellows, he becomes vivacious and conversational. He is obedient to authority, but will not brook the restraints that, under our notions of discipline, change men into machines. He makes an excellent sentinel, and not a single instance can be adduced of property having been stolen from or by an Apache on guard." Bourke also observed and appreciated their culture and quirks. "He has the peculiarity of not caring to give his true name to a stranger; if asked for it, he will either give a wrong one or remain mute and let a comrade answer for him. This rule does not apply when he has been dubbed with a sobriquet by the white soldiers."

And he admired their skill as warriors. "Approaching the enemy, his vigilance is a curious thing to witness. He avoids appearing suddenly on the crest of a hill, knowing that a figure projected against the sky can at such time be discerned from a great distance. He will carefully bind around his brow a sheaf of grass, or some other foliage, and thus disguised crawl like a snake to the summit and carefully peer about, taking in with his keen black eyes the details of the country to the front with a rapidity and thoroughness the American or European can never acquire. In battle he is again the antithesis of the Caucasian. The Apache has no false ideas about courage; he would prefer to skulk like the cayote (cq) for hours, and then kill his enemy, or capture his herd, rather than, by injudicious exposure, receive a wound, fatal or otherwise. But he is no coward; on the contrary, he is entitled to rank among the bravest."[8]

The column made its way into the foreboding recesses of the Sierra Madre, guided unerringly by Tsoe. The faint tracework of a trail led in and out of sheer-sided canyons with trails so steep that even the surefooted pack mules sometimes missed their footing and plunged into the canyon below. "Climb! Climb! Climb!" recalled Bourke. "Gaining the summit of one ridge only to learn that above it towered another, the face of nature fearfully corrugated into a perplexing alternation of ridges and chasms. [The terrain] seemed to consist of a series of parallel and very high, knife-edged hills, extremely rocky and bold; the canyons all contained water, either flowing rapidly or else in tanks of great depth. Dense pine forests covered the ridges near the crests, the lower skirts being matted with scrub oak. Trails ran in every direction, and upon them were picked up all sorts of odds and ends plundered from the Mexicans—dresses, made and unmade, saddles, bridles, letters, flour, onions and other stuff."

The scouts increased their vigilance and preparation as they penetrated further into the territory of the Chiricahua, depending heavily on the advice and ceremonies of their medicine men. As Bourke observed in *An Apache Campaign in the Sierra Madre*, "The 'medicine men' gathered together for the never-to-be-neglected duty of singing and 'seeing' the Chiricahua. After some palaver I succeeded in obtaining the privilege of sitting in the circle with them. All but one chanted in a low, melancholy tone, half song and half grunt. The solitary exception lay as if in a trance for a few moments, and then, half opening his lips, began to thump himself violently in the breast, and to point to the east and north," declaring that the Chiricahua were close.

Crook soon realized that the pack train could never move quickly enough through the maze of precipitous trails to surprise the Chiricahua, so he sent 150 Apache scouts on ahead under the command of Crawford and Sieber. Tsoe guided them to Chato's camp. The scouts attacked immediately on May 15, 1883, killing nine and capturing five—although most of Chato's warriors were away hunting. The scouts found no sign of Charlie McComas, the boy whose kidnapping had spurred such outrage in Arizona. Years later, an Apache revealed that the scouts had killed an old woman, whose enraged son seized the white child and dashed his brains out with a rock. The Apaches then hid the body, for fear of retaliation. The victorious scouts destroyed the thirty wickiups in the village, and collected their plunder, including forty-seven horses and mules.

Crook hurried forward and occupied Chato's camp. But Crook now found himself in a delicate situation, deep in the Sierra Madre, beyond any hope of relief. In fact, he was betting heavily on the demoralizing effect of his appearance here—guided by kinsmen of the Chiricahua. But he knew that if war leaders like Geronimo convinced the warriors to fight, he would be lucky to escape from the remote, rugged country along endless mountain trails perfect for an ambush. He had grimly noted the ample signs of fighting between the Mexicans and the Apache on the way in, and knew the Apache warriors could make him pay dearly for having ventured so far into their domain. Moreover, he knew that anything less than full success against the Chiricahua would ignite a firestorm of protest against him in Arizona. Therefore, he resolved to bluff his way through the confrontation to come, relying on talk and the politics of divide and conquer to win the battle.

Fortunately, the most warlike of the leaders were not in the vicinity. Geronimo was some three or four days' travel away, returning with a dozen Mexican women he had seized as hostages to trade for Apache captives, including his wife.

Jason Betzinez, Geronimo's cousin, who had been reluctantly pressed into service as a warrior from the ranks of Loco's abducted band, related an unsettling display of Geronimo's Power in his absorbing *I Fought with Geronimo*. "Geronimo was sitting next to me with a knife in one hand and chunk of beef . . . in the other. All at once he dropped the knife, saying 'Men, our people whom we left at our base camp are now in the hands of the U.S. troops! What shall we do?' This was a startling example of Geronimo's mysterious ability to tell what was happening at a distance. I cannot explain it to this day. But I was there and saw it. No, he didn't get the word by some messenger. And no smoke signals had been made. Every one of us replied to Geronimo that we wanted to go back right away. We believed what he had told us."[9] They hurried to cover the 120 miles back to camp, although hampered by the pace of their women prisoners. At daybreak, the party stopped for breakfast, but the women wouldn't eat. "Geronimo urged them to eat," recalled Betzinez, "so that they would have strength for the journey. He explained that we were in a hurry. But they remained stubborn. Then to our amazement, a slight, short Apache strode up, pretending that he was a chief. He spoke to the women something like this, 'Now, women, if you want to live, you must eat.' He walked back and forth talking loud and threateningly. Becoming frightened, they called for roast beef, which they ate with good appetite. The pretended chief walked away smiling."[10]

They reached the place where they had left their families after two days of travel, and found many of the women already preparing to rejoin the main band. That evening in council, Geronimo provided another demonstration of his Power, saying, "Tomorrow afternoon as we march along the north side of the mountains we will see a man standing on a hill to our left. He will howl to us and tell us that the troops have captured our base camp." The next day, just as Geronimo predicted, the band heard a howl from a hilltop to the left. "There stood an Apache calling to us. He came down through the rocks to tell us that the main camp, now some fifteen miles distant, was in the hands of the U.S. troops. General Crook with some cavalry and Indian scouts had taken all the rest of the Apaches into custody. Thus the event that Geronimo had foretold when we were still several days' journey away, and had repeated last night, came to pass as true as steel. I still cannot explain it," concluded Betzinez.

Crook had made full use of Geronimo's absence. He welcomed surrendering women and children into his camp, giving them food freely from his dwindling supplies and urging them to go back and tell the warriors that no harm would come to them if they surrendered. Several of the leaders then came cautiously into Crook's camp. Bourke described Chihuahua as "a fine-looking man, whose countenance betokened great decision and courage." Chihuahua assured Crook that he wished to surrender and promised to gather his people and return, no matter what Geronimo and the others decided. Crook's camp was soon full of surrendering Chiricahua women and children. "The women of the Chiricahua showed the wear and tear of a rugged mountain life, and the anxieties and disquietudes of a rugged Ishmaelitish war. The children were modest of grace and beauty, which revealed themselves through dirt and rags," observed Bourke.[11]

By the time Geronimo returned, Crook had already accepted the surrender of some 120 of the Chiricahua, nearly half of their total force. However, the arrival of Geronimo, Kaytennae, and other hard-liners brought a deadly tension to the proceedings. "A fearful hubbub was heard in the tall cliffs overlooking camp," recalled Bourke. "Indians fully armed could be descried running about from crag to crag, evidently much perplexed and uncertain what to do." Betzinez noted that Geronimo stationed his men on high ground overlooking the camp, and sent two old warriors down to talk to Crook, telling them that if they did not return in a certain time the thirty-six warriors he had gathered would begin firing on the soldiers. But the two old warriors returned only partway up the mountain, calling on Geronimo to come down and talk to Crook.

Upon learning that Geronimo had arrived, General Crook hit upon a daring stratagem—designed to intimidate the hard-liners among the Chiricahua with a show of nonchalant personal courage. As Crook later noted, "It is not advisable to let an Indian think you are afraid of him even when fully armed. Show him that at his best he is no match for you."[12] Taking his shotgun, Crook wandered away from camp alone—ostensibly to hunt birds. Warriors led by Geronimo and Kaytennae quickly surrounded him. Seemingly unconcerned, Crook sat down and opened negotiations. "[Geronimo] and his warriors were certainly as fine-looking a lot of pirates as ever cut a throat or scuttled a ship," observed Bourke in *An Apache Campaign in the Sierra Madre*. "Not one among them who was not able to travel forty to fifty miles a day over these gloomy precipices and along these gloomy canyons. In muscular development, lung and heart power, they were, without exception, the finest body of human beings I had ever looked upon. . . . They are men of noticeable brain power, physically perfect and mentally acute—just the individuals to lead a forlorn hope in the face of every obstacle." Crook's gambit for opening negotiations with Geronimo remained largely covered up for decades following, coming to light in the 1930s with the publication of the recollections of John Rope, a White Mountain Apache scout who accompanied the expedition. Bourke made no mention of it in his various accounts of the expedition into the Sierra Madre, perhaps because of the controversy that later arose when the territorial press claimed Crook had granted generous terms to the Chiricahua because they had actually captured him.

Surrounded by warriors who could easily kill him and spur a disastrous attack on the scouts and their handful of supporting soldiers, Crook bluffed boldly. He knew that the Chiricahua could simply melt away into the mountains and inflict heavy casualties on his retreating troops. But he affected an air of unconcern— explaining that he had merely come to give them a chance to surrender and return peacefully to the reservation. He would return soon with the Mexican army, American soldiers, and with more Apache scouts to hunt down every remaining renegade. "Crook declined to have anything to do with him [Geronimo] or his party beyond saying that they had now an opportunity to see for themselves that their own people were against them; that we had penetrated to places vaunted as impregnable; that the Mexicans were coming in from all sides; and that Hieronymo could make up his mind for peace or war just as he chose."[13]

Crook then returned to his camp, the picture of calm confidence. He made no effort to prevent the hostiles from moving in and out of his camp, counting on their conversations with the scouts to wear down their objections and reinforce their fears. Many of the Apache were relieved when this trusted enemy offered them a chance to surrender. "I am sure this was one of the happiest days of the year for General Crook," observed Betzinez. "We Apaches felt the same way about it. It was a great relief to give up to superior authority, to have someone take charge. No more worries, no more sleepless nights, fearing attacks by an enemy." Crook's arguments won over most of the leaders, who were strongly influenced by the great majority of the women, who saw only death and hardship in remaining at war. Increasingly, Geronimo found himself isolated. He returned repeatedly to talk with Crook in the next several days, trying to determine whether this was a White Eye that he could trust. Crook remained blunt, unflappable, and remote, insisting he did not himself care whether Geronimo surrendered or not. "You may fool others as to your intentions," Crook observed, "but you can't fool the Indian. He has no books nor newspapers, and so he has to draw on nature for his knowledge. This training has made him wonderfully sharp. He will sit looking at you with the expression of those old-fashioned crocks—you've seen them—you can't tell by their looks whether there is honey or vinegar inside. But all this time he is reading you as if you were an open book. He can almost tell from your expression what you had for breakfast."[14]

But Geronimo had one more desperate plan. When the leaders gathered to discuss surrendering, Geronimo urged them to hold a social dance and invite all of the scouts. The Chiricahua women would dance on the inside of the circle, each opposite one of the scouts. Then the Chiricahua warriors on the outside of the circle would rush forward, each killing a scout. The Chiricahua debated the plan, with Geronimo arguing that even if it touched off a battle in which many of the Chiricahua were killed, they would have a chance to kill the treacherous scouts who had turned against their own people. The desperate plan underscored how effectively Crook's enlistment of the scouts had destroyed the whole basis of the Chiricahua strategy—their ability to elude their pursuers and find safe refuge in the Sierra Madre. Geronimo turned for support to Dji-li-kine (also known as Jelikine or Pine Pitch House), the white captive turned warrior who was also Geronimo's father-in-law and who had relatives among the White Mountain scouts. Geronimo said, "My father-in-law, we mean to do as we told you tonight. That's why we told you. Whenever we have gone to war before, you have gone with us. But now you won't make up your mind to say yes or no." Dji-li-kine answered. "I told you already that I would not help you do this," he said, turning on his heel to walk away. Then he turned back, saying to the council, "You chiefs don't mean anything to me. I have been with you many times and helped you kill lots of Mexicans and whites, and that's the way you got the clothes you are wearing now. I am the one who has killed these people for you and you have just followed behind me. I don't want to hear you talking this way again."[15] Dji-li-kine's opposition undercut support for Geronimo's plan, which would have certainly caused great casualties, both among the scouts and among the Chiricahua, and would have turned Crook's gamble into an unmitigated disaster. In addition, the wary Al Sieber forbid the scouts to attend any more social dances with the Chiricahua, mostly because it was traditional for a warrior to present a gift to the woman he danced with and one warrior at a previous dance had given his partner a handful of rifle shells.

In the end, Geronimo had no choice but to yield. Crook accepted Geronimo's promise to surrender, never realizing how close he had come to disaster. "I am not taking your arms from you," said Crook imperturbably, "because I am not afraid of you with them. You have been allowed to go about camp freely, merely to let you see that we have strength enough to exterminate you if we want to; and you have seen with your own eyes how many Apaches are fighting on our side and against you. In making peace with the Americans, you must also be understood as making peace with the Mexicans, and also that you are not to be fed in idleness, but set to work at farming, or herding, and make your own living."[16]

Geronimo replied haughtily that he had no fear of the Mexicans, and could kill them easily enough with rocks. But he said that he would go back with General Crook and farm—asking only that he be treated fairly. He then added craftily that it was unfair to expect him to start back immediately, when his people were still so scattered. Moreover, if Crook could delay his departure, then Geronimo himself would search for the McComas boy. Geronimo had already gleaned from Crook's repeated questions about the boy that the captive offered valuable leverage. Why not wait a week, asked Geronimo, so that Loco and the others still out could come to join them? But Crook could not wait any longer. He was low on supplies, worried that the Mexican offensive might scatter the Chiricahua, and concerned about the reaction in Arizona to his long disappearance. Therefore, Crook said he would start out immediately and Geronimo could join the column as it moved back toward the United States.

Just as Crook was preparing to strike camp and return to the United States, the exhausted and terrified Mexican women captives Geronimo had abandoned miles from the encampment staggered into the camp of the Americans. "The women had suffered incredible torture climbing the rough skirts of lofty ranges, fording deep streams of icy-cold water, and breaking through morasses, jungles and forests," recalled Bourke. "The gratitude of these poor, ignorant, broken-down creatures welled forth in praise and glorification to God. It brought tears to the eyes of the stoutest veterans to witness this line of unfortunates, reminding us of our mothers, sisters, and daughters."

Crook set out on May 23, 1883, with 52 warriors and 273 women, including Loco, Nana, Kaytennae, Lozen, and Bonito. However, Geronimo sent word that his people were still widely scattered. He promised to come to the reservation within two months.

Crook returned to discover that his command had largely been given up for dead. Newspaper pundits insisted that the scouts had turned on Crook and slaughtered his command, adding their numbers and guns to the hostiles. Crook's dramatic reappearance with the bulk of the Chiricahua was greeted with initial astonishment and rejoicing. But then the newspapers learned that Geronimo and many of his warriors remained at large and, in many quarters, fulsome praise for Crook's triumph turned to bitter criticism.

Undaunted, Crook escorted the Chiricahua to the reservation, where he split them up into smaller bands and scattered them across the land. He then journeyed to Washington, D.C., for a political confrontation with the Indian Bureau, which he blamed for most of the problems he had found on the reservations. Crook and the secretary of war met with the secretary of the interior and the commissioner of Indian affairs on July 7, 1883, insisting that the War Department assume complete control over the reservations.

Crook returned to Arizona in seeming triumph, having secured the surrender of almost all of the remaining hostiles, having won control of the reservations, and having quelled the troubles that had plagued Arizona before his arrival. Moreover, his policies received additional vindication when Geronimo arrived at the border in February 1884, muting some of the criticism that had risen against Crook.

However, almost as soon as the Chiricahua returned to the reservation, Indian agents began a fierce political struggle with the officers Crook placed in command of the reservation. First, Interior Department officials began to spread the rumor that Crook had actually been captured by Geronimo and the renegades in the Sierra Madre and forced to offer them generous surrender terms.

The struggle between Crook and the Indian agents seeking to regain control of the lucrative contracts and appointments connected to the reservation flared anew, now that Geronimo had surrendered. Crook threatened to resign if he didn't retain full control of the reservation, but instead the Interior Department regained in 1885 the control Crook had wrested away in 1883. Crook noted in his annual report of 1885 that he had maintained the peace for two years without a single incident. "The whole country has looked to me individually for the preservation of order among the Apaches. The Chiricahua have been to a great extent scattered all over the reservation . . . at the same time trusted Indians of the peaceful bands are better enabled to keep the scattered Chiricahua under constant surveillance . . . as the right of control has now been withdrawn from me, I must respectfully decline to any longer be held responsible for the behavior of any of the Indians on that reservation. Further, I regret being compelled to say that in refusing to relieve me from this responsibility and at the same time taking from me the power by which these dangerous Indians have been controlled and managed and compelled to engage in industrial pursuits, the War Department destroys my influence and does an injustice to me and the service I represent."

Crook also came to the defense of the Indians, even at this moment when the press was calling out for their extermination, renegades and peaceful women and children alike. However, he could not set aside the racial blinders that prevented him from seeing the contradictions in his own argument, which held simultaneously that the Indians were a morally inferior race but that most of the problems had been caused by the immoral behavior of the whites. His annual report of 1885 observed, "It should not be expected that an Indian who has lived as a barbarian all his life will become an angel the moment he comes on a reservation and promises to behave himself, or that he has that strict sense of honor which a person should have who has had the advantage of civilization all his life, and the benefit of a moral training and character which has been transmitted to him through a long line of ancestors." He blamed the continued troubles more on unscrupulous whites than on the Apache. "I do not wish to be understood as in the least palliating their crimes, but I wish to say a word to stem the torrent of invective and abuse which has almost universally been indulged in against the whole Apache race. This is not strange on the frontier from a certain class of vampires who prey on the misfortunes of their fellow men, and who live best and easiest in time of Indian troubles. With them peace kills the goose that lays the golden egg. Greed and avarice on the part of the whites—in other words the almighty dollar—is at the bottom of nine-tenths of all our Indian troubles."

And so it had come finally to politics, and to Geronimo's wary suspicion and unbroken spirit.

Having won all his battles, General George Crook was about to lose the war.

And Geronimo—his grim nemesis—was about to lose everything.

13

Geronimo

RETURN TO THE RESERVATION

GERONIMO CAME across the border into Arizona carefully, his twenty-six warriors herding the 350 head of cattle he had taken from the Mexicans. He came also with seventy women and children, including his three wives and children. One of his sons had died on the journey, which caused Geronimo to wonder whether he had offended his Power by agreeing to go in, and seemed to him perhaps a warning of the diseases of the White Eyes that waited for them on the reservation. Nonetheless, the idea of living on the reservation had begun to appeal to him in the months that he spent moving through Mexico and assembling his cattle herd. He had been shaken first by the death of Juh, who had been the only one whose will to fight had burned as fiercely as Geronimo's own. Juh had fallen suddenly from his horse and died in the arms of his son, as though witched by the Power of his enemies. Geronimo was certain that Gray Fox had great Power, because he had come so easily into the middle of the Sierra Madre where the Mexicans could never touch them and where the White Eyes had never been. Gray Fox clearly had Power in war, for he seemed to know the place of his enemies and his plans seemed proof against mischance and circumstance. Moreover, Gray Fox had Power over the hearts of men, because he could make the Mexicans let his soldiers pass through their territory, and he could make even strong leaders of The People work for him and trust him. Clearly, they could not remain safe in the Sierra Madre with so many women and children as long as Gray Fox was after them, with his great Power in war. But Gray Fox had promised that they would have good land, and that they would not be bothered by the soldiers or by the settlers, and that all past grievances of the White Eyes against him would be forgotten. Everyone said Gray Fox was a man of his word, like a warrior, and not at all like the other White Eyes, who could not be trusted. The White Mountain scouts who had come with Gray Fox said things were much better on the reservation now that he had come. They went to bed early and got up late and had nothing to fear. They cooked their food in fine metal pots and pans and skillets, instead of on sticks over the fire. Moreover, Gray Fox had promised that all past problems would be forgotten and no one would speak badly of him anymore so that he could live peacefully among the White Eyes, even on the reservation. The idea of settling down, growing his food like a Pima, and living on the small rations of the White Eyes did not appeal to him. But then he thought of the cattle. Herding cattle was not beneath the dignity of a warrior. The Navajo lived by herding, and they were good fighters and honorable men. So Geronimo had spent the past month gathering up cattle and moving them carefully through Mexico. Near the border he had to push the cattle quickly, so they began to lose their body fat. But he knew that once he crossed the border he could slow down and save the cattle, since Gray Fox had promised that they could pass safely from the border to the reservation where the rest of the Chiricahua were already waiting.

But things began to go wrong quickly, as they always did when he was foolish enough to trust a White Eye.

A stout young *nantan* met him shortly after he crossed the border, at a spring where he had stopped to rest the cattle from the long, fast push out of Mexico. The man said that his name was Lieutenant Britton Davis, and Geronimo eyed him suspiciously, because Gray Fox had said nothing about the need for soldiers to escort him to the reservation as though he were a prisoner, and not a war shaman of the Chiricahua coming here of his own will. Davis said he came along only to protect Geronimo and to make sure he made it safely to the reservation because so many people had cause to hate him. Geronimo considered turning around and returning to Mexico, thinking Davis was holding something back from him, and wondering whether Gray Fox intended to hang him after all. But his Power whispered no warning, and the idea of living peacefully on the reservation with his relatives, and his children, and his grandchildren, and raising cattle, had taken him by the imagination. So he decided to go on with Davis, although Geronimo insisted on resting the cattle for several days instead of pushing on quickly as Davis demanded.

But after a day, two White Eyes came to talk to Davis. The warriors watched them carefully, their weapons close at hand. The three men argued, and Geronimo wondered at the meaning. The two men were not soldiers, but one was a policeman. After a while, another *nantan* came and Davis greeted him like an old friend and then the *nantans* started drinking together with the two others, so it seemed they had all become friends again. Geronimo could not decide if this was good for him or bad.[1]

Davis came to Geronimo in the night and said the white men had come to take his cattle, and so they must take the cattle and leave quickly in the darkness without waking the two white men. Geronimo's anger rose up in him, that this boy and these men should play with him, promising one thing and then changing their words. He said he'd had nothing but trouble since he had come here as he'd promised, and perhaps he should go back to Mexico. Then Davis said it would be a great joke on the White Eyes if they woke up from their drinking in the morning and found the warriors and all the cattle simply gone. However, he said he did not think that Geronimo could leave quietly enough with so many cattle to fool the white men. Geronimo studied the young *nantan* suspiciously as the scout translated his words, then smiled slowly when he understood. It would be a great trick on the White Eyes who wanted to take his cattle, and would show them how quietly warriors could move. Besides, he was not quite ready yet to give up on the promises Gray Fox had made. So Geronimo gave directions, and the warriors rose silently, and moved the cattle carefully, and by daylight they were so far from that place that not even the dust of the cattle smudged the horizon.

They rode without further trouble to San Carlos, where Geronimo met with Captain Emmett Crawford, who was one of the leading *nantans* of the White Eyes, and one of the chiefs the scouts most respected. Geronimo had been thinking a long time what he should say to Gray Fox. He had decided he should give himself up to Gray Fox. But he remembered how it had been on the reservation, and wanted to make sure that the Chiricahua had a good place to live, away from the other people who had made trouble for them in the past. When he had talked with Gray Fox in the Sierra Madre through the translator,[2] Gray Fox had promised they could live on Eagle Creek or someplace similar instead of in the bad country around Fort Apache among other bands who hated them now. But when he arrived at San Carlos, everything seemed uncertain.

So Geronimo spoke to Crawford in this manner:[3] Before, when I lived at San Carlos, everything was wrong. But now everything is carried on straight; I will not think as I did before. We have all come like wild mules, which may be tamed, little by little. Before, when I was living at San Carlos, I felt as if I were standing in a big hole, covered as far as my chest. But now I have surrendered entirely, and any orders given to me I will obey without thinking of resisting them. And if in the future someone tells anything bad about me, I want to know right away who is telling these bad things about me. But here in San Carlos, it does not seem very good—there is no grass, no good water, and there is sickness here, too. I would like to live in a place where there is lots of water, lots of land, and lots of wild animals. I know where there is such a place, but want to know where we are to live, and whether we will have enough land to live all together. And now that there is no war, you can take away the line around the reservation, so that we can go where we will. Let us live at Eagle Creek, where there is plenty of land and plenty of grass, so all my people can live there. Can you not buy the land from the Americans who live on Eagle Creek and give it to the Indians? We will take great interest in good land, and can farm and live like white men. Eagle Creek would be good for us. Now that we are here and you have us in your power, you can do as you please with us, and ought to let us do as we wish. We all have the same things as white men, hands, legs, arms, just as white men. We are surprised that we are not given the same things as white men when we ask for them. This peace you promised was a legal peace and we expect to get the land we want on account of having made peace. Tell Gray Fox that I beg him as if he were my father. Write the paper so that the general will give them this land. All the Indians here know what I have said and are very anxious to get this land. They want Gray Fox to know this so he will give it to them. At Camp Apache it is not good to live as there is not game around there, and all the Indians come around for their rations, and there is not land enough for the Chiricahua. We want to plant melons, squash, corn, and everything, but if we are made to stay at Camp Apache we will starve. After we raise one or two crops, the land will be taken away from us. Besides, there is no mescal to bake around Camp Apache. Let us live at Eagle Creek, and if you think that I am going to steal anything, soldiers can be put to watch over me. In the Sierra Madre, the interpreter told us that we could live on Eagle Creek or on one of the creeks that come out of the mountains there. But if we cannot go to Eagle Creek, we want to go to Ash Creek and see what the country is like around there. And also tell Gray Fox that we want all our captives here. They are in Mexico and we believe that General Crook can get them for us. We believe that he can do anything. If these Indians around San Carlos come here after I leave and talk about me, I don't want you to believe them. We are going out to look for some land to farm and we don't want any of these Indians around here with us. We want to be alone. And have no Indians but Chiricahua with us. Where we are going to live we would like to have a store so that we can buy what we want. We only want a little one, just for ourselves, he added, thinking how they could arrange things now that they had given themselves up, and forsaken raiding, and war.[4]

Crawford listened to him carefully, writing everything down, and promised that all of Geronimo's words would go to Gray Fox. But the words were scattered and useless, like seeds on rock. First, to Geronimo's deep outrage, Gray Fox took away the cattle Geronimo had brought back with him from Mexico. Geronimo protested that he had taken these cattle from Mexicans, not from White Eyes. He said Gray Fox had no right to take away the cattle they needed to start a herd. Then Gray Fox sent them to live at Turkey Creek, instead of Eagle Creek. He said Eagle Creek had been taken out of the reservation, and settlers already lived there. Geronimo protested this decision as well, saying that The People lived there a long time before the White Eyes came, and that Eagle Creek had originally been part of the reservation. Besides, although Turkey Creek had tall pines, and clear streams, and much game, they could not get water onto the land there and so could not farm much. Moreover, they had to live too close to the White Mountain bands, who hated them. But Gray Fox would not listen, and Geronimo began to see that he was not really so much different from the other whites, and that his promises were marked down in the same sand as the rest of them.

Nonetheless, Geronimo had promised to go to the reservation, and to live in peace, and so he would keep his promise. Besides, everyone was weary, and afraid of the Power of Gray Fox, and so no one would go out with him again if he returned to Mexico. So he decided that he would try it here and hope that Gray Fox was a man to be trusted after all. Also, Gray Fox had put Archie McIntosh over them, to issue their supplies and speak for them. McIntosh was a good man, for a White Eye, and he had married a Chiricahua woman. He had been a *nantan* of the scouts for Gray Fox, and had hunted the Chiricahua a long time, but he was an honorable man, who treated the Chiricahua like human beings. McIntosh had become a friend, and had been the one to suggest that Geronimo ask Gray Fox for a store for the Chiricahua, which McIntosh could run to be sure the Chiricahua would get all the supplies they needed.

Soon McIntosh gave them one hundred wagons and two hundred plows, and two hundred sets of harnesses so their ponies could pull the plows and the wagons. But the harnesses did not fit the small, sturdy ponies, and the ponies did not know anything about plowing. Once the ponies were tied to the plows they started off running, throwing the warriors riding the plows in all directions. Everyone gathered to watch this, laughing so hard it brought tears to their eyes. The plows bounced up into the air with the warriors and everyone had a good time, but the plows did not cut up the earth, and were useless for farming. Nonetheless, they set out quickly from Fort Apache for Turkey Creek, which was seventeen miles to the southwest, using the wagons like boats to cross over the Black River, which was high with the spring floodwaters. They numbered 521, including 127 men and boys of fighting age.

At first, Geronimo thought maybe he had been wrong and that Turkey Creek would be a good place for The People. It had tall trees, and deep streams, and lots of game. Gray Fox himself came to see them when they first arrived there, and put Lieutenant Davis in charge over them. Geronimo studied Gray Fox carefully, trying to determine what sort of man he was and whether he could be trusted after all—although they had taken the cattle and put them in this place after promising them Eagle Creek. Gray Fox seemed gruff, and short, and rumpled, not dressed up like a quail in the way of many of the *nantans*. He did not waste words, and spoke directly and without guile. More importantly, he moved about with assurance—as a man who knew the source of his Power. Most White Eyes had no personal Power, and did not understand it. But Gray Fox seemed like a man who could talk to Power as an equal, and make It listen. He seemed like a man who could command the sun, even as Geronimo had done. Perhaps that was why Gray Fox had no need to puff himself up. But he seemed also harsh, and cold—a man who would not hesitate to kill his enemies, and break their bones, and slaughter their children. This was a dangerous combination, and Geronimo could see now why Gray Fox had such Power over both the soldiers and the Indians—and why the leaders of The People feared him, and turned to him to protect them. Among all the White Eyes he had seen, Gray Fox was most like a warrior—most like a man Geronimo could understand.

Lieutenant Davis set up his tent near the stream, and Geronimo and Naiche settled several miles away where the soldiers would not always be watching him. But Kaytennae settled on a ridge where he could watch the young *nantan*, and Nana settled nearby. Chihuahua and Mangus, the son of Mangas Coloradas, also settled near Davis where they could keep track of what happened.

The leaders all agreed Davis was a good man, although young and inexperienced. He seemed fair and he laughed easily, and appreciated a good joke. Everyone remembered how he had laughed and laughed when they had first attached the ponies to the plows, not in the way of White Eyes, who considered The People stupid savages, but in the way of a good-hearted man.

Nonetheless, things soon began to go wrong. First, Gray Fox sent away McIntosh, who was a man that the leaders all liked and trusted. Gray Fox said McIntosh had not given them all of their rations, but had kept some of them for himself. But the leaders did not believe this, and did not care, because the White Eyes who were in charge of them had always taken the supplies due to them—most of them much more than McIntosh. McIntosh appealed to the leaders for help, and they signed a paper that said he was a good man to have charge over them. But Gray Fox did not listen to them, and sent McIntosh away anyway, although McIntosh had fought with Gray Fox for a long time. This made them all wonder what sort of a man Gray Fox really was.[5]

Davis also picked as his principal translator Mickey Free, whose history had been all tangled up with the Chiricahua like a snake among tree roots. Mickey Free was the boy whose kidnapping a long time ago had started all of the trouble between the Americans and Cochise. He was the son of a Mexican woman and a warrior. The Mexican woman had gone to live with a white rancher after her husband was killed. So the boy was living with the white rancher when a Coyotero band kidnapped him. The Coyotero had raised him awhile then, so he spoke English, and Spanish, and Apache. But his heart had grown up crooked, so he was neither one thing nor the other, and loyal to no one. He was a sly, resourceful, and skillful warrior, and he became a great manhunter. He hated everyone alike, and the leaders soon became convinced he was twisting their words to convince Davis they were troublemakers and untrustworthy, turning Davis against them. Moreover, they could soon see that Chato had finally found his opportunity to be a big man, by becoming Davis's camp dog.[6] Chato became a great friend with Tsoe, who had betrayed The People and led Gray Fox into the Sierra Madre. Chato became the leading man among Davis's scouts and police force. So Geronimo told Chappo, his son, and Perico, his cousin, to join the scouts also—to keep an eye on Chato and on Davis. They reported that Chato went often to Davis's tent, speaking to the *nantan* in secret. Kaytennae and others who were watching said Davis had spies among The People, who brought back to him words about what each of the leaders was doing. Kaytennae said Chato and Tsoe and Mickey Free were all bringing back lies, poisoning Davis against the rest.

Then Davis called them all together and said he had orders for them from Gray Fox. He said they could no longer make *tizwin*. Moreover, Gray Fox had said they could no longer punish their wives who were unfaithful. The People honored women, and a woman was free to leave a marriage simply by putting her husband's things out of the wickiup. But they also had no respect for those who slept around, and believed that a husband and a wife should be faithful to each other. If a woman was not faithful, and made a fool of her husband for everyone to see, that man had a right to cut off her nose so others would know what kind of woman she was. But Gray Fox said he would no longer allow this, as though he were their father to order them about. The leaders protested, saying they were not children to be told what they might drink, and how they must treat their wives. Chihuahua spoke the loudest, growing red in the face, his voice rising almost to a shout. Kaytennae glowered, saying little, but killing Davis with his eyes. Geronimo watched them all, saying only a little, but seeing how things had gone. It was always this way with the whites—their words were like sandbars in a wide river, shifting every day to a different place.

The leaders went away from the conference very angry, even Mangus, who was respected because of his father, and his courage, but who was a kind and mild-mannered man, very slow to anger. He had married Huera, a Chihenne woman of great Power, who had survived the massacre of Victorio's band and been sold into slavery in Mexico. She had waited for more than a year for her opportunity, and then escaped with two other women and gone alone with only a knife through a thousand miles filled with the enemy to come back to her people. She had been attacked by a mountain lion, and killed it with her knife. She had been struck by lightning, and now had Lightning Power as well. So she was feared and respected, having Power in childbirth and in healing and in the making of *tizwin*. Some said she pushed Mangus into opposition when she learned that Gray Fox had banned the making of *tizwin*. The leaders agreed that Chato, and Tsoe, and Mickey Free had turned Davis against them all, and agreed they should find some way to break the ban. They had agreed to live on the reservation, and give up war, but they had not agreed to be as children. Kaytennae said they must think ahead to what other things the White Eyes would take away from them, and what other promises they would break.

Kaytennae went to the top of a hill with some of his warriors to have a *tizwin* drink, insisting that no boy could tell him what he should do. As they sat on top of that hill, they heard someone coming up the hill, through the bushes. They crept to the edge of the hill and looked down, and saw Davis coming with his gun. So they got their guns, and prepared to fight him. But before he reached the top of the hill, he heard a turkey calling in the ravine below, so he turned, and went down carefully through the bushes as though stalking the turkey. They talked excitedly among themselves for a time, but decided he had only been hunting turkey, and not coming after them at all.

But that night, Chihuahua lay hidden outside of Davis's tent, trying to find out who among them were the spies. As he waited, he saw Chato and Mickey Free come into Davis's tent.[7] They told the young *nantan* that Geronimo and Kaytennae were planning a breakout, and that Kaytennae had laid a trap for Davis when he was turkey hunting, from which Davis had turned aside just in time.

The next day,[8] Davis called Kaytennae to his tent, and the other leaders came as well, gathering around with their guns. They were dismayed to see four troops of cavalry, about 140 men, well-armed, waiting also with Davis. The *nantan* confronted Kaytennae, who had behind him the 32 warriors of his personal following, well-armed themselves. But Davis faced Kaytennae fearlessly, saying he knew Kaytennae had been working against him, and planning a breakout. Kaytennae protested that he had done nothing wrong, and demanded the name of his accuser. But Davis only took his gun, and said there would be a trial to determine the truth of things. Geronimo watched this all from the edge of the circle of warriors, his eyes shifting back and forth from the soldiers to Davis, seeing how easily Davis could take one of the leaders out from among the rest—like wolves cutting one elk out of the herd. Later they learned that the White Eyes had chained Kaytennae to a great rock in the middle of the ocean, near one of their great cities thousands of miles away.[9]

The leaders resolved then to do their best to satisfy Gray Fox, knowing that if they went out again it would be much worse than before. Geronimo in particular devoted himself to farming, growing melons and squash and corn. The Chiricahua raised forty-five thousand pounds of crops that year, and even Crawford said Geronimo and Chato were both among the best farmers in the group.

But despite the efforts of the leaders, things grew steadily worse. Chato and Mickey Free grew more and more arrogant, sure of their position with Davis. They knew that the war leaders like Geronimo and Naiche and Nana and Mangus still had the respect of The People, and so they worked to undermine them. The traitors talked often with Davis. When they saw Geronimo walking about, they would catch his eye and draw their fingers slowly across their throats to show that the soldiers would soon come for him. The soldiers did the same thing. They would come and say, Which one is Geronimo? Which one is Naiche? And then they would go to them, and draw their hands across their throats. Geronimo and Naiche and the other leaders talked about this. They did not trust Chato, but they thought that maybe some of the soldiers were good men after all, and they were trying to warn them that they were going to get their heads cut off as had been done to Mangas Coloradas. Huera also came to Geronimo, and told him that she had heard that the soldiers were coming soon to arrest him.[10]

Davis came then[11] to Geronimo and said Gray Fox was trying to decide whether to let Kaytennae come back to the reservation.

Geronimo considered this, looking for the trap in the offer. He thought perhaps Davis was testing him, to see if he wanted to have Kaytennae come back so that they could break out together. He also wondered whether Kaytennae would come back angry, insisting on going out right away. Geronimo knew that everything was balanced like a spear in a warrior's hand, and that Kaytennae could tip things in a bad direction. So he advised Davis not to bring Kaytennae back yet and wondered after he said it whether that had been the right thing, and whether Davis would send the soldiers next for him.

Next Geronimo heard that Crawford had been sent away. He wondered what this meant, because Crawford was a good man, who had treated The People fairly, and had been a loyal man of Gray Fox. None of the leaders understood why Crawford had been sent away, but wondered what it would mean to them.[12]

Then Davis began to arrest more people. He arrested one man who got drunk and beat his wife, who had been with another man. He had to beat her because he could not cut off her nose, and because he had lost respect among everyone who knew that his wife had made a fool of him and he had done nothing.[13] The leaders protested, but Davis ignored them. He then arrested another man who had made *tizwin*. Chihuahua and Mangus protested loudly, but Davis could not be swayed. Then the leaders held a conference to consider what to do. Chihuahua said they should all drink *tizwin* together, and then go to Davis and confront him. Davis could not arrest them all, and he would see that he must not forbid the making of *tizwin* anymore. Mangus agreed and so did Geronimo, whose voice swayed Naiche as well. So by consensus they remained in council all night, drinking *tizwin* that Huera had made.

They assembled thirty followers the next morning in front of Davis's tent, squatting in a half circle until he came out to talk with them. Loco started to present their case, because he was still a man of influence and because he had always been mild and cooperative with Davis—so Davis would see how serious was the situation when Loco spoke out against him. But Loco spoke slowly, and carefully, and Chihuahua, who was still drunk, ignored rules of good conduct and jumped up to interrupt Loco—saying that Loco could speak all day, but he would speak plainly. They had agreed to come here, Chihuahua said, to live peacefully on the reservation. But Gray Fox had never said anything about regulating their behavior on the reservation, he had never said anything about forbidding *tizwin* and how they treated their wives and husbands. They had done all they had promised to do. They had kept the peace and never hurt anyone. But now they were being punished for things they had a right to do so long as they did no harm to others.

Davis started out talking again, lecturing them in an arrogant way as Mickey Free translated. Nana glowered as Davis spoke, then rose up in anger and said to Mickey Free, Tell *Nantan* Enchau [Stout] that he can't advise me how to treat women. He is only a boy. I killed men before he was born. Then Nana turned and walked out. Davis turned to Mickey Free to learn what Nana had said, insisting on a translation. His face grew red when he heard it. Then Chihuahua said, We all drank *tizwin* last night, all of us in the tent and outside, except the scouts; and many more. What are you going to do about it? Are you going to put us all in jail? You have no jail big enough if you could put us all in jail.[14] Geronimo, watching, said nothing—letting Chihuahua go out front like the first man riding into a suspected ambush.

Then Davis said he would have to send word on the talking wires to Gray Fox, to see what he should do with the leaders and the others who had broken the rules. He left then, leaving the leaders all looking one to the other in front of his tent, wondering if they had made a great mistake.

The day passed. Then another. And so did the next.[15] Geronimo waited in his camp, praying and consulting his Power. His Power warned him that he should prepare for bad times ahead, and chided him for sitting so long, doing nothing. So Geronimo began to think what he would do if the soldiers came to arrest him. He knew that the talking papers of the White Eyes were full of lies about him, and full of calls for the army to hang him. He remembered the time when the soldiers had put the chains on him, and resolved he would not let them do that again. So he talked to Chappo and Perico about what they might have to do, and began carefully to sound out which warriors might go out, and which of their families might go out with them. Then the rumors ran through the camp saying the soldiers were coming with an order from Gray Fox to take the leaders, especially Geronimo, and cut off their heads.

Geronimo consulted his Power about this, and learned that it was true.[16] He sent Perico and Chappo to watch Davis, and to kill him if the *nantan* began to gather up soldiers or scouts to lead against them. Geronimo then went to Naiche, and Chihuahua, and Mangus, and Nana, saying that the soldiers were coming against them and that Chappo had killed Davis and also Chato, who was a traitor to his people. The other leaders considered this, realizing that killing Davis had decided everything. They must run now whether they wished it or not because Gray Fox would surely punish them all for the killing of Davis. These principal leaders of the Chiricahua decided to leave with as many warriors and their families as they could gather, mostly kinsmen of the leaders. Nana took with him his wife, who was Geronimo's sister. They had with them 35 fighting men, 8 boys old enough to help the warriors, and 101 women and children. But only one in four of the Chiricahua agreed to go. The others knew they could never hope to defeat the White Eyes and could not hide forever even in the Sierra Madre. Loco said that even if Gray Fox punished the leaders, it was better to stay than to take the women and children out to be hunted until the soldiers, and the scouts, killed them all. Trust Gray Fox, said Loco. But Geronimo had heard enough of Gray Fox's lies. Then Nana told the warriors to cut the telegraph wires, but to tie them back together with strips of rawhide in places where the wires passed through trees. That way, the soldiers could not find the break.

Geronimo and the others got free of the reservation before the soldiers could follow them, gaining a lead of more than half a day. They killed anyone they encountered,[17] and seized a wagon train they came across to supply themselves for the flight into Mexico. After a time, Perico and Chappo joined them. They said Davis had been very careful and they had no opportunity to kill either

Davis or Chato. Chihuahua and Naiche then turned on Geronimo, and on Mangus—who also knew that when Geronimo had spoken, Davis and Chato were not yet dead. The argument between Geronimo and Chihuahua came almost to knifepoints[18] when Chihuahua realized that Geronimo had tricked him into running. Geronimo did not flinch, saying his Power had told him the soldiers were coming to kill them and that he had done what was necessary. But Chihuahua would not be calmed and broke off with his own people, thinking that he could circle back and return quietly to the reservation.

Geronimo and his band moved carefully through the mountains, while the country all around filled up with soldiers. In three weeks, they had moved down into Mexico. The soldiers chasing them did not stop at the border, but came on without pause as Gray Fox had promised. *Nantan* Crawford came back again to hunt them, and the traitor Chato led the scouts against the people who had gone out. Chato's scouts hit Chihuahua's camp (on June 23), killing one woman and capturing fifteen women and children, including Chihuahua's daughter. They captured also Perico's wife, and Huera and many others. After that, Chihuahua gave up any idea of returning to the reservation, and headed for Mexico as well.

But a far greater disaster awaited. A few weeks later (on August 7), the scouts found Geronimo's camp, since they were led now by Chiricahua warriors who knew all of his hidden places. The seventy-eight scouts attacked quickly, killing one woman and two boys and capturing perhaps fifteen other women. The people captured included Geronimo's wives Zi-yeh and She-gha and five of his children as well.[19] When the scouts attacked, the warriors fought only briefly before seeing that they faced too many scouts, with too many bullets. So the warriors scattered. Geronimo ran alone through the rocks, leaving his family behind, as he had done before, as he had to do, as his Power demanded. Once he was safely away, he sat down, grieving to have lost his wives, and his children, and everything for which he had been fighting. He turned about then, speaking angrily to his Power, asking how his Power had let such a thing happen without warning him. Why had his Power insisted he leave the reservation, and led him so far through his enemies, only to give over Geronimo's own children to his enemies? Had he not prayed aright? Had he not done everything demanded of him? But then his Power spoke back, saying Geronimo sounded foolish and weak, and not like a warrior at all. Did he not know that he was the last warrior, the keeper of the spirit of his people? Who else remembered what it meant to be a warrior of The People? Only Geronimo's personal following seemed willing still to fight, seemed to understand that it was better to die as warriors than to live as slaves of the White Eyes. Geronimo held Naiche to the fight by the thread of his Power. He knew that Chihuahua was a weak stick, eaten by the termites of hopelessness. Mangus was determined to stay out, but he had no will to fight, only to hide away from his enemies in the mountains. Nana remained unquenched, but he was an old man now, with his Power flickering. Only Geronimo remained, to remind his people who they were. It did not matter so much what happened to him now, he was the bent bow in the hands of Power. All that mattered was that they should fight, and that The People should remember who they were.[20]

After the warriors had reassembled, Geronimo selected four men who had lost family members and set out for the reservation, knowing the soldiers would take his wives and his children there. They traveled for several weeks, while the soldiers continued to hunt them in Mexico. They moved quietly onto the reservation. They captured one woman, making her tell them where the soldiers had taken Geronimo's family. They went then in the middle of the day (on September 22) to the camp, and came away with She-gha and her three-year-old daughter—taking also another woman so that Perico would have a new wife. On the way back down to Mexico, they found some Mescalero women and their children gathering piñon nuts. Geronimo took Ih-tedda as his wife, and adopted also her son, who was nearly of the age to take training as a warrior. In the weeks that followed, Geronimo began to teach the boy the ways of a warrior as they fled from the soldiers, hiding in the mountains. They passed safely through the soldiers Gray Fox had thrown out to guard every watering hole between the reservation and the border. They killed a few more White Eyes, captured a horse herd, and escaped again into Mexico.

They rested for a time in the Sierra Madre, avoiding the places Chato would expect them to go, keeping lookouts posted constantly on the high places so that they could not be surprised. They moved constantly, leaving little trace of their passing. The leaders conferred, seeing that they had not enough bullets for hunting or to protect themselves against the Mexicans, or the White Eyes, who continued to chase them through Mexico, as though it was their own country. Everything had happened just as Gray Fox had threatened. It seemed the White Eyes and the Mexicans had forgotten all of their wars so they could work together to exterminate The People.

The leaders sent a party of ten warriors led by Ulzana, who was Chihuahua's brother, back into the United States to get more ammunition and supplies. They also wanted to take revenge on the families of some of the warriors who had ridden with the soldiers, hunting them. They also needed to replace the children and the women the soldiers had taken. The raiding party struck the reservation, killing seven men and eleven women, and capturing six women and children and many horses. Chato and the scouts chased them, killing one warrior. But they came safely through all of the soldiers back into Mexico, killing many whites and capturing many horses.[21]

But while the warriors were gone, Crawford's scouts again found Geronimo's camp. This time the lookouts gave the alarm in time, and everyone slipped away, but the scouts captured their horses and all of their supplies. When they reassembled, the leaders again conferred. They were discouraged now, seeing that so many Chiricahua warriors rode as scouts for the White Eyes, and that Crawford and the scouts could move freely into their best hiding places. True enough, a party of warriors like Ulzana's could still slip through the fingers of the soldiers and stay ahead even of the scouts. But it was much harder for the women and the children, and they could not remain in any one place long enough to get the supplies they needed to survive. Even worse, most of the warriors had by now lost their wives and their children, who had been captured by the soldiers. They yearned for the touch of their wives, and the sound of their children. They could not see the point of fighting, if they could never see their families again. So Naiche said they should talk to the soldiers, and see if perhaps they could come in—for the sake of the women and the children. Geronimo listened, seeing the will to fight going out of his men the way water eats at a sandy bank. He reluctantly agreed that perhaps they could send Lozen to talk to Crawford, to see if the soldiers would let them return to the reservation without punishment although they had killed many people since leaving. Lozen went bravely to Crawford's camp and returned saying Crawford wanted to meet with Geronimo and the others to talk.[22]

The warriors moved to a hillside where they could look down on Crawford's camp but retreat quickly if he proved treacherous. While they waited, they saw coming up quickly a group of Mexican soldiers with Indian auxiliaries. As they watched, the Mexicans fired a few shots. Crawford climbed up on a large rock, crying out that they were American soldiers and the scouts who were hunting Geronimo. But one of the Mexicans shot Crawford down off the rock, and so all of Crawford's scouts began shooting, killing many Mexicans. Geronimo watched it all from the hill, laughing out loud. Maybe now the Mexicans and the Americans would go back to war and he could return to the balancing act between them that had kept The People alive for so long. But to his disappointment, the shooting stopped, and the surviving leaders on both sides came forward to talk. He thought that perhaps the fight between the Mexicans and the Americans would convince the other leaders to continue fighting. But Chihuahua and the others said they still wanted to talk, and perhaps return to the reservation if Gray Fox would not punish them.[23]

So the Chiricahua leaders met with the *nantan* who took command of the scouts after Crawford died and agreed to meet with Crook at a place of their choosing. So they went all together to Canyon de los Embudos, just below the border, to meet once again with Gray Fox.

Geronimo went with a heavy heart and many forebodings. He wanted still to fight. He would never again trust the White Eyes, not even Gray Fox—especially not Gray Fox. But he could not fight alone. He must go along with the others, especially Naiche, who still had the largest personal following. He must go and see what Gray Fox would say, knowing he must somehow turn the words of Gray Fox to his advantage so he would not lose the hearts of the other leaders and of the warriors, who must each make their own decision.

So Geronimo went once again to face his great enemy, the only White Eye whose Power he feared.

14

Crook

CONFRONTATION WITH AN OLD FOE

CROOK UNDERSTOOD perfectly the risk he ran in meeting with Geronimo and the others in the rugged and remote Canyon of the Tricksters, which he feared was all too aptly named. He had sifted every possible clue and bit of information out of scouts like Chato and Kaytennae, who had returned now much subdued from his time in Alcatraz and his intimidating tour of San Francisco. He knew that the hostiles could continue to raid along the border for many months, even years, if they fought it out to the end. The territorial press was already in an uproar. He didn't so much mind the press—the coyotes could yip all they pleased. But generals all up the chain of command all the way to the president were much less sanguine. Crook knew that he had to report some greater success than seizing the hostiles' horses and supplies. So he knew that talking Geronimo and his cutthroats into surrendering remained his best tactic. However, his options were limited in this regard as well. He knew the absurd accusations that the Chiricahua in the Sierra Madre had captured him and forced him to grant them generous surrender terms had circulated throughout the territory. These rumors had reached the ears of his superiors, and provided ammunition for the jackals at the Indian Bureau in their political struggle to regain control of the reservation. Therefore, he could not afford to been seen as weak or overly generous in these crucial negotiations. On the other hand, if he adhered to terms that were too uncompromising, the renegades would simply scatter and resume their frustrating war of hit and run. The key, he realized, lay in the old maneuver of divide and conquer. Geronimo remained the key. He could be relied upon to wheedle, manipulate, threaten, coax, and resist surrender on any terms likely to prove acceptable to Crook. But all of Crook's information suggested that most of the other leaders were ready to surrender. If he could drive a wedge between Geronimo and the rest, they would all give way.

Resolved to rely on his time-honored tactics of confidence, bluff, and personal force, Crook assembled a small detachment, including a photographer from Tombstone who pleaded for a chance to record the negotiations. When they finally arrived at the canyon, Crook noted that the Chiricahua had picked the meeting place with their typical caution and adroit strategic sense. The Chiricahua had placed themselves on a rocky hill, with a multitude of escape routes. They remained absolutely safe from surprise or treachery. He would have to talk them out of the rocks—bullets would be useless.

Once he had settled into camp, taking care to protect himself against possible surprise, Crook went to meet with the leaders of the Chiricahua, desperate men in a hopeless cause.

Geronimo presented his grievances, his remarks carefully recorded, as was Crook's custom.

"I want to talk first of the causes which led me to leave the reservation," he said. "I was living quietly and contented, doing and thinking of no harm, while at the Sierra Blanca [Reservation]. I don't know what harm I did to those three men, Chato, Mickey Free, and Lieutenant Davis. I was living peacefully and satisfied when people began to speak badly of me. I should be glad to know who started those stories. I was living peacefully with my family, having plenty to eat, sleeping well, taking care of my people, and perfectly contented," he explained. "I hadn't killed a horse or man, American or Indian. I don't know what was the matter with the people in charge of us. They knew this to be so, and yet they said I was a bad man and the worst man there." He sought to shift responsibility for his decision to leave. "I did not leave of my own accord. . . . Some time before I left an Indian named Wadiskay [Nodiskey] had a talk with me. He said, 'They are going to arrest you,' but I paid no attention to him, knowing that I had done no wrong; and the wife of Mangus, Huera, told me that they were going to seize me and put me and Mangus in the guard-house, and I learned from the American and Apache soldiers [scouts], from Chato and Mickey Free, that the Americans were going to arrest me and hang me, and so I left."

Geronimo then sought to put Crook on the defensive. "I want to know now who it was ordered me to be arrested. I was praying to the light and to the darkness, to God and to the sun, to let me live quietly there with my family. . . . I have several times asked for peace, but trouble has come from the agents and interpreters. I don't want what has passed to happen again."

Geronimo continued in the manner of Apache oratory, invoking the spirits that watched, and judged—and acknowledging Crook's Power. "The Earth-Mother is listening to me and I hope that all will be so arranged that from now on there will be no trouble and that we shall always have peace. Whenever we see you coming to where we are, we think it is a God[1] . . . you must come always with God . . . Whenever I have broken out, it has always been on account of bad talk. Very often there are stories put in the newspapers that I am to be hanged. I don't want that any more. When a man tries to do right, such stories ought not to be put in the newspapers. There are very few of my men left now. They have done some bad things but I want them all rubbed out and let us never speak of them again."

He spoke then of his relatives on the reservation, showing how powerfully such considerations loomed in his motivations. "We think of our relations, brothers, brothers-in-law, fathers-in-law, over on the reservation, and from this time on we want to live at peace just as they are doing, and to behave as they are behaving. Sometimes a man does something and men are sent out to bring in his head. I don't want such things to happen to us. I don't want that we should be killing each other."

Geronimo then shifted to a personal appeal to Crook. "I have not forgotten what you told me, although a long time has passed. . . .

I want this peace to be legal and good. Whenever I meet you, I talk good to you, and you to me, and peace is soon established; but when you go to the reservation you put agents and interpreters over us who do bad things. Perhaps they don't mind what you tell them, because I do not believe you would tell them to do bad things to us. . . . I want to have a good man put over me. While living I want to live well. I know I have to die some time, but even if the heavens were to fall on me, I want to do what is right. I think I am a good man, but in the papers all over the world they say I am a bad man; but it is a bad thing to say so about me. I never do wrong without a cause."

Finally, Geronimo shifted to an appeal to morality and a sense of the spiritual Power that pervaded all things. "Every day I am thinking how I am to talk to you to make you believe what I say; and, I think, too, that you are thinking of what you are to say to me. There is one God looking down on us all. We are all children of the one God. God is listening to me. The sun, the darkness, the winds, are all listening to what we now say. . . . To prove to you that I am telling you the truth, remember I sent you word that I would come from a place far away to speak to you here, and you see us now. Some have come on horseback and some on foot. If I were thinking bad, or if I had done bad, I would never have come here. If it had been my fault, would I have come so far to talk to you . . . I am glad to see Ka-e-a-tena [Kaytennae]. I was afraid I should never see him again. That was one reason, too, why I left. I wish that Ka-e-a-tena would be returned to us to live with his family. . . . Now I believe that all told me is true, because I see Ka-e-a-tena again . . . as I was told I should."

Crook listened patiently to Geronimo's long self-justification, but then dismissed Geronimo's attempts to explain his actions. Geronimo objected to Crook's brusque manner, calculated to humiliate Geronimo and divide him from the other listening leaders. Crook often spoke to the others, pointedly ignoring Geronimo, whom he rightly saw as the chief obstacle to the surrender of the Chiricahua.

Geronimo asked, "What is the matter that you don't speak to me? It would be better if you would speak to me and look with a pleasant face; it would make better feeling; I would be glad if you did. I'd be better satisfied if you would talk to me once in awhile. Why don't you look at me and smile at me? I am the same man; I have the same feet, legs, and hands, and the Sun looks down on me a complete man; I wish you would look and smile at me. The Sun, the Darkness, the Winds, are all listening to what we now say."

Geronimo then challenged Crook directly, asking, "I want to ask who it was that ordered that I should be arrested."

Crook snorted, "That's all bosh. There were no orders for any-one to arrest you."

Geronimo feinted, sliding away from a direct confrontation with a sly compliment. He suggested someone else issued the arrest orders, arguing as much to convince the other Chiricahua leaders as to impress Crook. "There is no other captain so great as you. I thought you ought to know about these stories, and who started them."

But Crook only again accused Geronimo of lying.

"If you think I am not telling the truth," Geronimo responded, "then I don't think you came down here in good faith."

But Crook refused to be drawn into Geronimo's rhetorical net. "I have heard what you have said. It seems very strange that more than forty men should be afraid of three; but if you left the reservation for that reason, why did you kill innocent people, sneaking all over the country to do it? What did those innocent people do to you that you should kill them, steal their horses, and slip around in the rocks like coyotes? What had that to do with killing inno-cent people? There is not a week that passes that you don't hear foolish stories in your own camp but you are no child, you don't have to believe them. You promised me in the Sierra Madre that peace should last, but you have lied about it. When a man has lied to me once, I want better proof than his own word before I can believe him again. . . . You must make up your own mind whether you will stay out on the warpath or surrender unconditionally. If you stay out, I'll keep after you and kill the last one, if it takes fifty years." Seeing an opportunity to undercut Geronimo with the other leaders, Crook questioned Geronimo's sincerity in expressing satisfaction at seeing Kaytennae, who had become Crook's secret weapon in winning over the other leaders. "Over a year ago I asked you if you wanted me to bring Ka-e-a-tena back but you said no," he said, delivering a telling blow to Geronimo's credibility with the other leaders. Crook then demanded which of the Chiricahua leaders had been threatened, moving once again to isolate Geronimo from the others.

"All of us," Geronimo replied. "If you don't want to believe me I can prove it by all the men, women and children of the White Mountain Apaches . . . They wanted to seize me and Mangus."

"Then why did Naiche and Chihuahua go out?" Crook countered, displaying his old genius for the strategy of divide and conquer.

"Because they were afraid the same thing would happen to them," Geronimo answered.

"Who made them afraid?" Crook persisted.

"The only thing I told them was that I heard I was going to be seized and killed, that's all," Geronimo answered.

Crook asked why Geronimo had sent people to kill Davis and Chato, but Geronimo denied sending them, noting if it were true "these Indians would say so."[2]

"You reported that they were killed and that is the reason so many went out with you," Crook insisted.

But Geronimo said that even the White Mountain Indians among Crook's own scouts would vouch for him. "Well, there is a White Mountain sergeant, a man like that won't lie; ask him . . . Whenever I wanted to talk with Lieutenant Davis, I spoke by day or by night. I never went to him in a hidden manner. Maybe some of these men know about it. Perhaps you had better ask them."

But Crook sensed that he had driven a wedge between Geronimo and the others, and declined to engage in a back-and-forth argument. "I have said all I have to say. You had better think it over tonight and let me know in the morning."

"All right," said Geronimo, realizing that he had to confer with the other leaders to determine whether Crook had damaged his standing. "We'll talk tomorrow. I may want to ask you some questions too, as you have asked me some."

The Chiricahua leaders conferred most of the next day, as Kaytennae and Alchise circulated among them. They sent messages back and forth to Crook, who told them they must surrender unconditionally, but that he would spare their lives. He explained that all of the warriors, except Nana, whom Crook perhaps inaccurately considered to be too old and feeble to pose a threat, would face imprisonment in the East. However, he promised that they would be quickly reunited with their families, and that within two years they could return to the reservation.

Crook's strategy proved successful in the end. Chihuahua yielded first, followed after endless councils and talks by the others, until Geronimo stood isolated. On March 27, the five chief leaders returned to talk again with Crook.

Chihuahua spoke first, demonstrating the trust Crook had engendered and the sense of Power he exuded. "I am anxious to behave. . . . I surrendered myself to you because I believe in you and you did not deceive us. . . . You must be our God. . . . You must be the one who makes the green pastures, who sends the rain, who commands the winds. You must be the one who sends the fresh fruits that appear on the trees every year. . . . Everything you do is right . . . you send my family with me where ever you send me. . . . I ask you to find out if they are willing to go or not."[3]

Then Naiche stepped forward, seeming relieved to surrender the burden of resistance and leadership his father had placed on his never-eager shoulders. "When I was free I gave orders, but now I surrender to you. . . . You now order and I obey. . . . Now that I have surrendered I am glad. I'll not have to hide behind rocks and mountains; I'll go across the open plain . . . there may be lots of men who have bad feelings against us. I will go wherever you may see fit to send us, where no bad talk will be spoken of us. . . . I surrender to you, and hope you will be kind to us."

Finally Geronimo stepped forward, compelled to surrender by the deep-seated Apache respect and need for consensus. He no longer had the trust in Crook that the others expressed, but he had no choice. He could not fight on alone. His Power had brought him to this place, but now it seemed that he was alone.

General Crook (second from right) meets with Apache leaders at Canyon de
los Embudos to negotiate their surrender. Geronimo (third from left) initially
agreed to surrender but then slipped away, which led to Crook's resignation.
(*Courtesy Arizona Historical Society, Tucson*)

"Two or three words are enough. We are all comrades, all one
family, all one band. What the others say I say also," he said with
simple dignity. "Once I moved about like the wind. Now I surrender to you and that is all," he said, stepping forward to shake
Crook's hand gravely. "My heart is yours, and I hope yours will be
mine. . . . Whatever you tell me is true. We are all satisfied of that.
I hope the day may come when my word shall be as strong with
you as yours is with me. That's all I have to say now, except a few
words. I should like to have my wife and daughter come to meet
me at Fort Bowie or Silver Creek," he said, revealing in that
moment the yearning that still haunted him when he thought of
Zi-yeh and her baby and of his grown daughter Dohn-say, all captured by the soldiers months earlier.

Crook reassured them, seeing triumph now almost within
grasp. "Don't worry about bad talk," he told them, aware of the
almost obsessive concern among the Apache leaders about what

others said about them, the outcome of an intimate culture whose code of behavior was enforced almost entirely by social pressure. "There are some people who can no more control their talk than the wind can," Crook concluded.[4]

Geronimo, even then struggling to understand the shape of the trap into which he had delivered himself, called on Alchise and Kaytennae to "speak a few words. They have come a long way and I want to hear them speak."

But Kaytennae pleaded a sore throat, perhaps ashamed to speak for Crook in front of the warriors, and helpless finally to convey the overwhelming power of the White Eyes he had seen while wandering the foggy streets of San Francisco. But Alchise, one of the leading men of the White Mountain Apache, spoke for the Chiricahua, in the process reminding Crook that the other groups would observe his treatment of the Chiricahua. "They have surrendered. I don't want you to have any bad feelings toward them. They are all good friends now . . . because they are all the same people—all one family with me; just like when you kill a deer, all its parts are of the one body. . . . No matter where you send [them] we hope to hear that you have treated them kindly. . . . I have never told you a lie, nor have you ever told me a lie, and now I tell you that [they] really want to do what is right and live at peace. I want to carry away in your pocket all that has been said here today."[5]

Crook listened imperturbably, understanding better than anyone that these warriors responded to force of personality. One of the greatest successes of his career now lay in his palm, achieved principally through his shrewd understanding of the strengths and weaknesses of his enemy. He fully understood the near impossibility of hunting down even a small force of warriors freed from the need to care for their families. Ulzana, Chato, and Geronimo himself had demonstrated that a war party could elude thousands of soldiers, kill dozens of people, and escape unscathed. Crook knew also that the warriors camped warily on the nearby hill could scatter in a moment, and elude his best efforts to corner them. If he could not convince them to surrender voluntarily, he could spend years chasing this handful of warriors while the press roared for his scalp. But he also understood by what a thin thread of confidence, threat, and bluff he held them. So he maintained an attitude of studied indifference to whether they surrendered or not, by his every gesture indicating that it made little difference to him personally whether they surrendered to him or compelled him to hunt them down, killing them one warrior at a time. He knew that charisma and a sense of personality and power held them, dominated them.

That night, Crook was startled awake by the sound of shooting in the camp of the renegades. Alchise and Kaytennae soon hurried into Crook's camp, saying that Chihuahua had sent them to Crook to explain the shooting. They said that a whiskey seller named Tribolett had sold the Chiricahua a large quantity of bad whiskey, and the depressed and anxious Chiricahua had promptly become roaring drunk. Crook debated his options. If he rode into the Apache camp at this juncture, it could provoke drastic and unpredictable reactions. Crook told Alchise to drive off Tribolett, although several officers advocated taking the whiskey peddler out and shooting him. Such traders, who often had good relationships with the renegades, had consistently spurred trouble—and profited from every breakout. Crook believed that they operated as a semiorganized conspiracy directed by some of the major Army contractors in Tucson, who profited handsomely from the millions of dollars the army spent in the territory every year and who had everything to lose should peace break out. "For them, peace kills the goose that lays the golden egg," said Crook.[6]

Crook awoke the next morning to find a stuporous silence had settled over the Apache camp. Mules wandered back and forth, some topped by a drunken warrior. Geronimo and another warrior, seemingly nearly blind drunk, rode about their camp on a single mule. Again, Crook considered the alternatives. He could rush the camp, probably capturing most of the Chiricahua. However, some would certainly escape. On the other hand, they had agreed to surrender. Besides, he had given his word and accepted their promise, and so had no pretext for turning and attacking their camp. Therefore, he decided to rely once again on the appearance of supreme confidence that had so successfully cowed the warriors until now. Taking once again a bold gamble, he packed up his camp and headed back to Arizona to deal with the political complexities of the surrender he had coaxed out of the reluctant Chiricahua. He left Lieutenant Marion P. Maus in command of an escort of soldiers and scouts to bring in the Chiricahua and their families after the warriors had sobered up enough to travel.

Unfortunately, Crook had finally overplayed his hand.

His gambler's confidence was about to go bust against Geronimo's Power, and the fear and suspicion that had long dominated Geronimo's world.

15

Geronimo

THE TRIUMPH OF FEAR

THE CHIRICAHUA ROSE shakily from their hangovers to face a fearful future. Tribolett had sold them much more than bad whiskey. They had known him a long while, and he had come and gone freely from their camps even when the soldiers had hunted for them everywhere. Tribolett had provided a crucial source of trade. That night in their camp he had moved among them, going from one to the other with his whiskey and with a warning. He told Geronimo Crook intended to seize him and hang him as soon as they crossed the border into the United States.

Nonetheless, as soon as they all were able, they gathered their things and rode with Maus along the same trail as Crook. But they were full of troubles. They did not know whether they should believe Tribolett's warnings, and took care to shield their discussions of the matter from Kaytennae and Alchise. Even Naiche now had doubts, saying that even if Crook did not hang them as Tribolett said, he might take them to some bad place, some place worse even than San Carlos. Did not their children die already in great numbers from the diseases of the whites? Who could tell what terrible place awaited them now. Perhaps in two years no one would be left alive to return to their homes.[1] Geronimo saw the bad feelings growing, and wondered how to direct them. He even went to Maus, who rode right among the warriors, and suggested that it would be safer for the *nantan* if he rode apart from the warriors.

He should stay with the scouts, who rode apart, watching the still-armed Chiricahua warily.

They did not cover much distance that day (March 27, 1886), but stopped then and made camp, the Chiricahua setting up away from the scouts. The Chirichaua kept hold of their guns, and arranged their camp so that the scouts could not surprise them. That night the leaders conferred again, worried they were making a great mistake. Naiche especially had grown fearful, increasingly convinced they would all die far from home in a strange place, even the women and the children. They brought out more whiskey Tribolett had sold them, and soon the alcohol began to cloud their minds. Naiche's wife, E-clah-heh, heard them talking and saw that Naiche might not surrender after all. But she said that she wanted to go to the reservation, and would no longer live like a deer sur-rounded by hunters. E-clah-heh was Geronimo's sister (second cousin) and the great-granddaughter of Mahko and the sister (first cousin) of Fun, and a woman respected by the warriors because she had been through so much fighting with them. But now she said that she would not go out again, and so began to run away, back toward the soldiers' camp. Naiche, who was drunk already, took up his gun and shot her as she ran, afraid that many others would go with her. But the shot frightened them all. Geronimo and Naiche and eighteen other men and fourteen women and six children slipped away into the darkness with two horses and a mule, unwilling to gamble their lives on Gray Fox's words. But Chihuahua and his brother Ulzana and even old Nana stayed, see-ing that they had no choice but to trust Gray Fox, who had never lied to them before. Even Geronimo's two wives and three chil-dren would not go with him, and he did not make them come, knowing what lay ahead of him.

The next morning Maus discovered that Geronimo and Naiche and his followers had gone, and sent Chihuahua and Nana after them. Two warriors later came back, saying that they had been afraid, but that they didn't want to go out after all. But Geronimo and the others slipped away, leaving no trace, like wind in the grass that bends, and springs back, revealing nothing. Having lit-tle choice, Maus continued along with the rest of the Chiricahua,

This photo of Geronimo, also taken by C. S. Fly at Canyon de los Embudos, is one in a series of the only known photos of Apache warriors in the field. The Chiricahua, led by Geronimo and Naiche, camped on an easily defended hill well apart from Crook during the negotiations. (*Courtesy Arizona Historical Society, Tucson*)

which included fifteen men, thirty-three women, and twenty-nine children.

Geronimo had no illusions now. Juh had been right. They could not win. They could not even live. They could only die as warriors. After that, the last few warriors of a free people began to call themselves Indeh—the dead. The whites, they called Indah—the living.

They had only the eighteen warriors, and no one to help them, no place left to go.

So they went where they pleased, and killed whom they pleased.

Naiche said that they had no recourse to mercy. Everyone who saw them would seek to kill them, and so they killed everyone that they saw. They must do this in order to live.[2]

They were reckless with their lives, because every man's hand was turned against them. If they returned to the reservation, they knew that they would be put in prison and killed. If they stayed in Mexico, their enemies would continue to send soldiers against them as long as they lived. So they gave no quarter to anyone and asked no favors.[3]

And so Geronimo, who had been favored by Power all of his life, came finally to this—a hopeless war against an unbeatable enemy, with the end never in doubt. His Power still protected him, although it seemed now he was only the shell of what he had been. With almost all the women and children on the reservation now, the purpose of the fighting had been hollowed out and cast away. Geronimo had started out holding Power in his hand like a rifle, but now he was only the smell of gunpowder in the barrel of Power's gun. Still, he could only go forward, seeking the warrior's death his Power pushed him toward, and denied him.

Still, had he known, he might have found one small comfort in this dark path.

He had at least brought his enemy low. They were knife fighters bound together. They were caught in the same flood.

Gray Fox had met his match.

16

Crook

GERONIMO, GERONIMO, ALWAYS GERONIMO

THE NEWS that Crook had brought back most of the hostiles, but not Geronimo, touched off a firestorm of criticism. The *Silver City Enterprise* of June 13, 1885, intoned: "The general's great hobby is his Apache scouts that he expects to run down the renegades. Who are these scouts? Why they are mostly Apache Indians, friends, and relatives of Geronimo's band . . . This scouting is simply a training school for hostile leaders. . . . If it gets too hot for the renegades, they can surrender and are assured good treatment. . . . In reality the Indians are about the ugliest and filthiest brutes on the globe—lying, thieving, gambling cut throats, who when a beef is cut up and distributed among them, will quarrel over the entrails, and eat the filthy stuff raw or half-cooked." The editorial writer all but called for a massacre. "The citizens of these territories are at last thoroughly aroused. Our local press without exception are publishing the storm of indignation against Crook and the War Department, and every paper contains offers of prominent citizens to arm and furnish men to exterminate the occupants of the reservation be they good or bad. The government has been appealed to year after year to stop this annual butchery. What the citizens demand is: that the scouts be discharged; that every hostile found off the reservation and captured shall be turned over to the civil authorities; that the Indians at San Carlos be completely disarmed or that the reservation be abandoned. If not, the San Carlos Reservation will be raided and thousands of good Indians will be made."[1]

Others rallied to Crook's defense, including Charles Lummis, a *Los Angeles Times* correspondent dispatched initially to cover the anticipated surrender of Geronimo, and then to cover Crook's renewed efforts to hunt down Geronimo's band.

Lummis noted that the news trumpeted on the front pages of newspapers throughout the country had been based almost entirely on exaggerated, secondhand stories, gathered by wire service reporters who had never interviewed anyone actually present at the events they reported. "As a result of the farcical 'news' that has been furnished the nation throughout we have heard nothing but Geronimo, Geronimo, Geronimo. One would fancy that old Jerry was the only Apache who had been off the reservation; and there is not much question that it would have made a bigger impression on the public if instead of the seventy-six prisoners now rolling toward Fort Marion, Geronimo alone had been captured and all the rest were still at large. The fact is, Geronimo is only one of seven chiefs who have been off the reservation with their families and followers. He is not even a number one chief, but merely a war chief."

Lummis attacked the almost mythical focus already centered on Geronimo. "Geronimo has not been the biggest fighter, the cleverest schemer, nor the bloodiest raider in the outfit at any time. The only claim Geronimo has to his unearned pre-eminence of newspaper notoriety is that he is one of the originators of the outbreak. He is no greater and no worse than several of his co-renegades. History is so fashioned, however, that he will be remembered when his more important colleagues are forgotten."

Lummis defended Crook as fulsomely as the general's critics attacked him. "Since the Civil War, no prominent commander has been more persistently, more savagely, more cruelly hounded by jealousy, opposition and many another masked influence as has George Crook. Almost without exception the territorial papers have damned him—not with 'faint praise' but with the bitterest invective. He has been cursed, belittled, and lied about, his policy misrepresented, his acts distorted, and alleged acts of his have been made up out of whole cloth. Some of these lies—such as the one about his surrendering to the Apaches in the Sierra Madre—have already been nailed. Others have not; some never will be."

Lummis's description of Crook reflects the fierce loyalty the general could inspire.

> He is a soldier, not a war correspondent. Let the lying go as it will, telegraphed from end to end of the country—he never opens his mouth. He is here to fight, not to justify himself. No man whose heart quickens to honor and courage can but admire the grim old General. There is that in him that makes one want to take off one's hat. There never was a soldier who fought with a stiffer lip against heavier odds. He has the same patient, persistent, uncomplaining and unapologetic doggedness that was Grant's fundamental characteristic. Today the most prominent figure in the army—the only army in the field—he occupies a larger place in public discussion than any other general. And in this exposed condition, one of the fiercest fires is centered on him that ever whistled about a soldier's ears. It is the old story of political chicanery, greed, and intrigue. It is like pulling teeth to get anything out of him, however, and in his own defense he will not utter a word. He feels it, no doubt. He would be more than a man if the poisoned shafts did not sting.[2]

However, despite the staunch defense of journalists like Lummis, Crook soon found himself in deep political difficulties. His failure to bring back Geronimo—the most famous of the renegades—triggered events which led directly to his resignation.

Even before Crook learned that Geronimo, with about twenty warriors, had escaped, he was in trouble with his superiors. Crook telegraphed General Sheridan, his old commander from the Civil War years, that he had accepted the surrender of the remaining Chiricahua on the promise they would be reunited with their families and imprisoned in Florida for not more than two years before being allowed to return to the reservation.

But Sheridan's reply demonstrated that Crook had placed himself in a politically impossible situation, his independence having exposed his flank. Crook had simply ignored the implications of the near hysteria Geronimo and the others had evoked among the settlers and newspapers, once again disdaining to bend to those with whom he disagreed. But the far more politically astute Sheridan saw that allowing the Chiricahua to return to the reservation was a near political impossibility. "The President cannot assent to the surrender of the hostiles on the terms of imprisonment in the East for two years, with the understanding of their return to the reservation," he wired Crook on March 30, 1886. "He instructs you to enter again into negotiations on the terms of their unconditional surrender, only sparing their lives. In the meantime, and on the receipt of this order, you are directed to take every precaution against the escape of the hostiles that must not be allowed under any circumstances. You must take at once such disposition of your troops as will insure against further hostilities, by completing the destruction of the hostiles, unless these terms are agreed to."

The message put Crook in an ethically impossible position. He had already obtained the surrender of most of the renegades based on his promise that they would eventually be allowed to return to the reservation. His orders now seemed to require him to violate the bedrock code of personal honor on which Crook had founded his career, although in truth the vacillation and bad faith of his superiors had repeatedly transformed Crook's well-intentioned promises into lies. Crook protested that he had acted within the scope of his orders, since Sheridan had previously ordered him not to offer terms "unless necessary to secure their surrender." Crook pointed out that the Chiricahua had been well fortified in a position impossible to surprise and only surrendered because of the terms offered. Now faced with his lose-lose choice, Crook decided to simply not tell the Chiricahua who had already surrendered that his superiors had rejected the terms he had offered and they had accepted. "To inform the Indians that the terms on which they surrendered are disapproved would, in my judgment, not only make it impossible for me to negotiate with them, but result in their scattering to the mountains, and I can't at present see any way to prevent it."

Then Geronimo's escape had touched off another bitter round of telegraphs. On March 31, Sheridan wired, "It seems strange that Geronimo and his party could have escaped without the knowledge of the scouts," thereby echoing the questions about Crook's judgment and loyalty that had inspired such vicious headlines in the territorial press. Crook staunchly defended the loyalty of the scouts, saying that they had achieved almost every success in the long campaign.

> There can be little doubt that the scouts were thoroughly loyal, and would have prevented the hostiles leaving had it been possible. When they left their camp with our scouts, they scattered over the country so as to make surprise impossible and they selected their camp with this in view, nor would they all remain in camp at one time. They kept more or less full of mescal. To enable you to clearly understand the situation, it should be remembered that the hostiles had an agreement with Lieutenant Maus that they were to be met by me twenty-five miles below the line, and that no regular troops were to be present. While I was very averse to such an agreement, I had to abide by it as it had already been entered into. We found them in a camp on a rocky hill in such a position that a thousand men could not have surrounded them with any possibility of capturing them. . . . Even had I been disposed to betray the confidence they placed in me, it would have been simply an impossibility to get white troops to that point either by day or by night without their knowledge, and had I attempted to do this the whole band would have stampeded back to the mountains.[3]

Sheridan replied, "I do not see what you can do now except to concentrate your troops at the best points, and give protection to the people. You have in your department 46 companies of Infantry and 40 companies of Cavalry, and ought to be able to do a great deal with such a force."

That response outraged Crook and suggested that Sheridan had no conception of the problem Crook faced in protecting settlements and isolated ranches scattered over a vast area from an elusive band of twenty warriors determined to avoid any direct fighting with soldiers or scouts. All previous attempts based on the use of troops of cavalry, forts, and patrols had failed miserably. Only a relentless pursuit by units led by Apache scouts and supplied by pack trains so that they could remain in the field for months had any hope of success.

Crook responded:

It has been my aim throughout present operations to afford the greatest amount of protection to life and property interests, and troops have been stationed accordingly. Troops cannot protect property beyond a radius of one-half mile from their camp. If offensive movements against the Indians are not resumed, they may remain quietly in the mountains for an indefinite time without crossing the line, and yet their very presence there will be a constant menace, and require the troops in this department to be at all times in position to repel sudden raids; and so long as any remain out they will form a nucleus for disaffected Indians from the different agencies in Arizona and New Mexico to join.

That the operations of the scouts in Mexico have not proved as successful as was hoped is due to the enormous difficulties they have been compelled to encounter from the nature of the Indians they have been hunting, and the character of the country in which they have operated, and of which persons not thoroughly conversant with both can have no conception. I believe that the plan upon which I have conducted operations is the one most likely to prove successful in the end. It may be, however, that I am too much wedded to my own views in the matter, and as I have spent nearly eight years of the hardest work of my life in this department, I respectfully request that I may now be relieved from its command.[4]

Crook received the orders relieving him the next day, April 2.

After a career graced by courage and triumph, George Crook had been defeated by a warrior no less determined, fighting in a hopeless cause.

17

Geronimo
THE FINAL SURRENDER

THE LAST WARRIORS fought on for six months, giving no quarter. They remained mostly in the Sierra Madre, coming down when they had need of bullets, and supplies, to spread terror among the huddled villages of the Mexicans. Sometimes they went into the United States, moving as they pleased while more soldiers than they could believe existed chased the rumors of their passing. They saw sometimes flashes of light, like signal mirrors, from the mountaintops as they passed. Later they learned that this was a system like the talking wires that allowed the White Eyes to talk to one another over great distances. But still, the soldiers could not find them. Geronimo noticed that the soldiers came alone now, not with the scouts as they had before when Gray Fox had charge over them. Geronimo did not understand this change, since the soldiers could rarely find them without help from the scouts. Sometimes the soldiers came close enough for a little shooting, but the warriors and their women and their children had only to abandon their horses and run up into the mountains where the soldiers and their big horses could not follow them.

Still, they grew wan and weary, always hunted. Every time they heard a noise in the darkness, they jumped up and moved their camp. They could not risk a fire, and could not stay in one place long enough even to cook mescal in the fire pits.

Finally, Geronimo decided that perhaps they could offer to make peace with one of the Mexican towns, as they had done in the old days. He did not trust the Mexicans; he had seen too much death for that, but he thought perhaps the Mexicans would give them some supplies to try to get them to come into the town where they would no doubt try to slaughter them—as they had always done. So Geronimo sent Lozen and another woman to Fronteras to see if the Mexicans there would make a peace.[1] The Mexicans said they would make peace if Geronimo and the others came in. The women came back to the camp carefully, but the lookouts watching them coming saw that riding along behind on their trail was a small party with a white flag tied to the stalk of a century plant. The warriors gathered on a high place[2] to watch these other men coming, debating what they should do.

Geronimo said that no matter who they were, the warriors should kill them. They had no friends in the world now, and no need to stay their hands.

But when they had come close enough, Kanseah recognized that the riders were Martine, a Nednai who had been trained by Juh himself, and Kayihtah, the brother of Yahnozha, one of Geronimo's best warriors.[3] With them also were Long Nose, called Lieutenant Charles Gatewood, and George Wratten, a white man who had married a woman of The People and had always been a good friend.

It does not matter who it is, if they come closer they will be shot, said Geronimo, fearing that the words of these ones would take more warriors from him than the bullets of all of the soldiers who sought them.

But Yahnozha said, They are our brothers. Let us find out why they come. They are brave men to risk this.

Geronimo protested.

We will not shoot, insisted Yahnozha. The first man who lifts a rifle, I will kill you.

Fun moved up behind Yahnozha and said, I will help you.

Seeing that even the strongest of his warriors could turn against him, Geronimo relented. Let them come, he said, seeing the risk, but not knowing how to make this thing turn aside.

Kayihtah came and talked to them, saying that the soldiers would keep after them, coming from all directions, even if it took fifty years. He said that Geronimo and his warriors must eat their meals on their horses, and run whenever they heard a stick break, but that back on the reservation they could go wherever they pleased, and sleep all they liked, so long as they did as the white people told them to do. And even though Geronimo did not want to do it, the other warriors said they would talk with Gatewood, who had brought a message to them from the new *nantan* of the White Eyes, a general named Miles who had replaced Crook.

So they met the next day with Long Nose, who was a good man, and a strong one, who had fought a long time with the scouts and who was a truth-speaker. Seeing the end of things coming for him now, Geronimo had drunk all of the whiskey he had that night. He felt bleak and shaky when he greeted Long Nose, his hands trembling as he accepted the tobacco Long Nose offered and as they both rolled smokes in oak leaves.

They talked a long while. Long Nose said they could surrender and join their families in a place called Florida, as Crook had promised. They must accept these terms, or fight to the very end.

But Geronimo said they would surrender only if they could go back to live on the reservation. Then the warriors went aside to talk. Geronimo could see the warriors were doubtful, and many eager to take this one last opportunity to save their lives.

So they returned and talked to Long Nose for a long time more. Geronimo asked Long Nose every question he could about Miles. Long Nose said he was a good man, and an honest man.

We want your advice, said Geronimo to Long Nose, who was a man he respected. Consider yourself one of us and not a white man. Remember all that has been said today, and as an Apache, what would you advise us to do?

I would trust General Miles, said Long Nose, and take him at his word.[4]

And then Long Nose told them one more thing. He said that they could not go back to the reservation, because all of their families had already been sent to Florida.

Geronimo's heart fell then, seeing that they were lost. He felt a sudden terrible yearning for his wife, and his children, and for all of the children of The People. He saw the same feeling pass

General Nelson A. Miles deployed thousands of troops to try
to corner Geronimo and his small band of warriors after
Crook resigned. However, Miles eventually had to turn to
Apache scouts to convince Geronimo to surrender on terms
that he could not fulfill. Crook and Miles became bitter
rivals in the years to come, as Crook campaigned for the
release of the Chiricahua prisoners of war and criticized
Miles's surrender terms that were never honored. (*Courtesy
Arizona Historical Society, Tucson*)

among the other warriors as the strength flowed from them, like blood from a wound. The small hope of a return to the reservation, and to their loved ones, had sustained them more than he knew. Now it was gone. That night, the talk among the warriors showed Geronimo that sending all of their families to Florida had killed the hearts of the warriors. There seemed little point in continuing.

So they agreed the next day to go back to the border and to meet with General Miles to see what kind of a man he was and to hear the promise from his own mouth. They traveled with Long Nose to the border, eighteen warriors and ten women and children. The soldiers who had been hunting Geronimo all this time joined them also, and the two sides kept a wary eye one on the other, with Long Nose riding alongside Geronimo. On the third day, they encountered a force of two hundred Mexican soldiers and the warriors would have fought them, but Long Nose put himself in the middle and convinced the Mexicans that Geronimo and the others were returning to the United States to surrender.

Several days later, they came to a place where the warriors had killed some soldiers. The soldiers who were riding with them nearly started a fight then, thinking about their dead friends. But once again Long Nose rode in among them, and stopped the fighting.

They came at last to the place set for their meeting with General Miles, and waited there for him, taking care that the soldiers could not attack them by surprise.

Geronimo rode forward to meet General Miles, seeing that he was a tall, handsome man, who spoke smoothly and with warmth. His words were honeyed, not like Gray Fox, whose words were blunt as blows. They shook hands, and Geronimo wondered whether he had finally found a white man he could believe and who would hold to his words.

The general is your friend, said the translator.

I never saw him, but I have been in need of friends, said Geronimo. Why has he not been with me?

The officers who were listening broke out in laughter when they heard this, but Geronimo only looked at them, not understanding the cause of their laughter.

Chiricahua Apache prisoners of war pose in front of the train that would take them into twenty-eight years of confinement. Geronimo is in the center, third from the right, and Naiche sits in the center of the first row. Lozen, the sister of Victorio and the remarkable warrior-woman of the Apache, is third from the right in the second row. J. McDonald took the picture in 1886. (*Courtesy National Archives*)

So Geronimo and Miles talked awhile together. Miles said the president had sent him to make peace with Geronimo, and that all of his past crimes would be wiped clean—smooth as the sand beneath his palm. They would be taken to a reservation in Florida, with lots of trees, and lots of game, and lots of good land for growing things, where they would be reunited with their families. Miles promised they would have horses, and wagons, and cattle, and plows—everything that they would need to live in the beautiful land to which they would be sent.

And so it was agreed, because Miles talked so friendly, where Gray Fox had talked so ugly.

They rode together then to Fort Bowie.

They came finally to the fort in Apache Pass where Cochise, and Mangas Coloradas, and Victorio, and Geronimo had all fought the soldiers for the first time—and had lost so much for the first time. Geronimo stopped and looked up into the hills, which had known him, and which remembered his name still.

This is the fourth time I have surrendered, he said.

I think it will be the last time, said Miles quickly.

And so it was.

Of course, Miles did not keep his promises.

He put them all on a train, like cattle.

Geronimo looked out the window as the train moved away from the land that knew him. He counted the mountain ranges as they traveled, keeping careful track in his head so that he could find his way home. But soon there were too many mountains to remember, and he knew that he had passed beyond hope of home.

They took the warriors to a place so far from home that the wind was different, and the air was thick, and not one coyote could be heard. They held them in a prison, with great stone walls for a long time—away from their families. Crowds of White Eyes came to look at them, excited and fearful as children.

Stranger yet, they also brought to the prison Chato and the other Chiricahua who had helped them, just as if they had been with Geronimo to the end. Geronimo took grim satisfaction in it, seeing Chato's bewilderment and seeing also the hatred that the others had for Chato and the scouts who had helped to destroy them.

18

Crook

To Redeem His Honor

Ever the good soldier, George Crook had left his command quietly after his exchange of telegrams with General Sheridan.

Before he left, Chihuahua came to him, saying,

> When a man thinks well, he shows it by his talk. I have thought well since I saw you. Ever since you were so kind to me in the Mountains, my heart has quieted down. My heart is very quiet now. Geronimo has deceived me as much as he did you. I was very glad when I saw my sons and wife. I think well of my family, and want to stay with them. I am a man that whenever I say a thing I comply with it. I have surrendered to you. I am not afraid of anything. I have to die sometime. If you punish me very hard, it is all right. I am much obliged to you for your kindness. I surrender to you, and ask you to have pity on me. I hope you will not punish me very hard, but pity me. I was sleeping very quiet and happy with my family at Camp Apache, but Geronimo came and deceived me, played a trick and made me leave. Wherever you put me, keep me away from Geronimo and his band. I want nothing to do with them. People will talk bad about me and get me into trouble, I don't want anything to do with him.[1]

But Crook could do so little for him; for any of them. He could not bear, in the end, even to tell them that his promises to them had been turned to lies by his superiors, by circumstances beyond his control.

Crook gathered the leaders just before he left, talking to them like children. "I am going to leave you, another officer is coming in my place. I want to thank you for the good work you have done. You have been very faithful. I have made many enemies among my own people by being honest and square with you. After I am gone, probably some will tell you lies about me," he said, sounding surprisingly like Geronimo. "But you must judge me by my acts. Talk is cheap. I hope you will remember the good advice and teachings I have given you. Do everything to stop this *tizwin* drinking. You get it in your stomachs, and there is no sense left. Then you go and gamble away all your money, and the next day there is nothing to show for it but a swelled head," he said, and they all laughed. "Go to raising stock, as well as the farming you have already learned. You will do better to raise sheep than cattle. To get anything out of a steer you have to kill him, but you can sell the wool off your sheep and still have the sheep," he said, and the intent warriors looked at one another saying "Hu! Hu!" in appreciative affirmation. "Also the sheep, though they have to be watched, will not wander off great distances as the cattle will. Besides, you know if thieves come and run off a few of your cattle, it is hard to get them again; but when a few sheep go, they travel very slowly, so you can easily catch them and the thief," and the warriors again grunted "Hu! Hu!" knowing this well since they had stolen so many cattle in their free days.

Crook continued to fight the Apache wars for the remaining years of his life, now fighting with words on the side of the Apache. Angered by the government's decision to imprison all of the Chiricahua, even the scouts who had fought so loyally for the army, Crook was drawn into advocacy for the Indians by groups like the Indian Rights Association. In a January 5, 1885, letter to the association he wrote, "The Indian is at this moment capable with very little instruction, of exercising every manly right; he doesn't need to have so much guardianship as so many people would have us believe; what he does need is protection under the law; the privilege of suing in the courts, which privilege must be founded upon the franchise to be of the slightest value."

He spoke highly of the ability of the Indians to govern themselves, in the teeth of a blizzard of racism and prejudice. "The vast majority of Indians are wise enough to recognize the fact that liquor is the worst foe to their advancement. Complaints have frequently been made by them to me that well-known parties had maintained this illicit traffic with members of their tribe, but no check could be imposed or punishment secured for the very good reason that Indian testimony carries no weight whatever with a white jury. Now by arming the red men with the franchise, we remove this impediment, and provide a cure for the very evil which seems to excite so much apprehension; besides this, we would open a greater field of industrial development."

Crook continued indignantly to ignore the political realities of the white attitudes toward the Indians, and speak out against the government's Indian policies. Lummis, the *Los Angeles Times* reporter who was with him in the midst of his war of words with his superiors and his pillorying by the territorial press, recorded Crook's views on Indian policy. But despite Crook's respect for his foes, and his disdain for the most outspoken white critics of the Indian, he remained deaf to the contradictions in his own views and locked into the racist parentalism of even those whites most sympathetic to the Indian's plight. "It is a poor sort of honor, though a popular one, which holds that decency is to be used only toward white folks, and that when you lie or swindle an Indian, it doesn't count," he told Lummis. "No one else in the world is so quick to see and to resent any treachery as is the Indian. You can do nothing toward his management unless you have his confidence. True of all men, this is particularly true of him. I have known one of these Apaches to go sixty miles out of his way to ask a man the same question he had asked a month before, and see if he would get the same answer." But in spite of his respect for many Indians as individuals, he could not bring himself to question his own assumptions of cultural superiority. "Eventually all their tribal organizations will be broken up. It cannot be done in a moment, it takes time to uproot the institutions of centuries, but it is the inevitable outcome."

However, he continued to argue for justice and compassion—on practical, if not moral, grounds. "Now, of course if you have ten thousand troops and one Indian tied down in the middle of them, you don't need any Indian policy. But when you have to catch your Indian, there's where the policy begins to be useful. If we could always put our hands on these fellows, the question of managing them would be simple enough. You can bulldoze a lion when you have him in a stout cage and a red hot iron in your hand, but when he is on his native heath the proposition is different. You can't bulldoze these fellows either, when they are loose in a wilderness as big as Europe."

He stood ready to consider matters from an Indian point of view, although he knew the criticism this would call down on his head. "In dealing with the question, I would not lose sight of the fact that the Apache represents generations of warfare and bloodshed. From his earliest infancy he has had to defend himself against enemies as cruel as the beasts of the mountains and forests. In his brief moments of peace, he constantly looks for attack or ambuscade, and in his most constant warfare no act of bloodshed is too cruel or unnatural. It is, therefore, unjust to punish him for violations of a code of war that he has never learned, and which he cannot understand." He even mitigated the atrocities he'd seen committed—perhaps because he had seen so many terrible things done by his own troops. "He has, in almost all of his combats with white men, found that his women and children were the first to suffer, that neither age nor sex is spared. In pursuing attacks on camps, women and children are killed in spite of every precaution; this cannot be prevented by any foresight or order of the commander any more than shells fired into a beleaguered city can be prevented from killing innocent citizens or destroying private property. Nor does this surprise the Apache, since it is in accordance with his own mode of fighting. With this fact before us, we can understand why he should be ignorant of the rules of civilized warfare."

Therefore, he called upon policy makers to put aside the past, and start afresh, even as he had so often urged the Indians to do. "All that we can reasonably do is keep him under such supervision that he cannot plan new outbreaks without running the risk of immediate detection; for these new acts of rascality, punish him so severely that he will know we mean no nonsense. As rapidly as possible, make a distinction between those who mean well and those who secretly desire to remain as they are. Encourage the former and punish the latter. Let the Apache see that he has something to gain by proper behavior and something to lose by not falling in with the new order of things. Sweeping vengeance is as much to be deprecated as silly sentimentalism."[2]

It gave Crook some satisfaction to see the abject failure of General Miles's campaign against Geronimo in the six months after Crook left to resume his old command on the Great Plains. Miles massed nearly five thousand troops against Geronimo's handful, and took Sheridan's advice to scatter garrisons of troops across the country to protect settlements. Miles also built heliographic stations on mountaintops, so he could flash messages from one end of the state to the other. However, Miles also discharged the Apache scouts. This satisfied the press and his superiors, but crippled his attempts to actually find Geronimo. Miles made strenuous efforts, but despite the deployment of nearly one-quarter of the standing army and the efforts of handpicked units that remained in the field for months, Miles's men didn't kill a single warrior in some six months of trying. In the end, Miles turned to Lieutenant Gatewood and two former Apache scouts to convince Geronimo to surrender for the final time. Miles also tricked the Chiricahua remaining peacefully on the reservation into coming in for a headcount, whereupon they were arrested and put on a train for Florida. Crook decried the move as base treachery, but the discovery that their families had already been sent to Florida helped convince Geronimo's band to surrender. Even so, Miles could only induce Geronimo to surrender by lying to him about the surrender terms, thereby sowing the seeds of a bitter debate that would pit him against Crook.

It rankled Crook that Miles received credit as the man who beat Geronimo and ended the Apache wars. As Lummis noted in defense of Crook, "What a nation of ingrates we are. Here is a man who has done more for the frontiers of the United States than any other man living—probably more than any two men. For more than a generation he has been in the active military service of his country, and always successfully. But all this is lost sight of because in this little campaign he has captured only four-fifths of the hostiles! It makes me ashamed of my country."[3]

In the meantime, Crook assumed command of the Department of the Platte and directed the final mopping-up operations against the few Indian bands that had not dispiritedly accepted their fate. In August 1887, he was called upon to deal with an uprising of the Ute Indians that had been settled in Utah at the Uintah and Ouray agencies. Each year, the Ute sent hunting parties into their old homeland in Colorado. One Ute hunting party had encountered a game warden with a posse who attempted to arrest them for hunting out of season. The warriors resisted and three were wounded. The warden then raised a second posse, served a warrant for horse theft, and again exchanged shots with the Ute hunting party. At this point, the sheriff appealed to Crook for troops, but Crook demurred, saying it was a civil matter. The sheriff then raised a one-hundred-man posse and fought another battle with the twenty-five warriors in the hunting party. The fight resulted in the deaths of three whites and at least four Indians, including a young girl and three boys. The Utes abandoned four hundred horses and twenty-five hundred sheep and fled back to their reservation. Crook then intervened, extracting a promise that the sheriff return the Ute's livestock. "The governor's outfit have been trying all day to get me to relieve them from their dilemma by making me their scapegoat," Crook observed. "The whole transaction of this affair has been a disgraceful job from beginning to end."

In the spring of 1888, Crook was promoted to major general upon the retirement of General Alfred Terry. Crook then assumed command of the Division of the Missouri, which included the departments of the Platte, Dakota, Missouri, and Texas, the largest and most active command in the army with 13,045 men, about half of its strength.

Crook moved to Chicago, where for the first time in his life he lived a relatively settled, domesticated life. His wife, Mary, hosted dances and parties for the officers, fulfilling the substantial social obligations of a high-ranking general. He didn't care much for such affairs, and usually soon repaired to a back room with a few old comrades, where they whiled away the evening playing cards and telling stories about their days on the frontier. He rarely wore a uniform, would tolerate no orderly dogging his heels, and maintained a quiet, informal atmosphere in his headquarters. He escaped Chicago whenever possible for extended hunting trips. During one bear hunt in September of 1889, Crook and his party bagged eighty-six antelope, thirty-eight deer, five bears, five sheep, two wildcats, one skunk, one porcupine, one coyote, one elk, two badgers, six sage hens, and four rattlesnakes. The hunt ended on a tragic note, however, when one private was accidentally shot and killed. Ironically, the days of such hunting trips were already numbered, the abundant game of the West dwindling in the face of the settlement which Crook's destruction of so many Indian bands had made possible.

Crook continued to advocate a shift in Indian policy, first supporting the movement to give Indians the vote, and then supporting the breakup of the reservations in favor of land allotments for individual Indians. Crook supported the 1887 Dawes Act, which was to prove an almost unmitigated disaster for Indian tribes nationwide. The Dawes Act was supported by an unlikely combination of liberal reformers like Crook, who were convinced that the Indians had been abused and swindled and betrayed, and western congressmen and interests, who saw opportunities for profit in parceling out the reservations to individual Indians. In the end, the Dawes Act cost the surviving Indian tribes nearly half of their remaining land, without materially bettering their condition.

However, Crook supported the act with the best of intentions and agreed to serve on a presidential commission charged with convincing the still-proud Sioux to agree to the breakup and distribution of their reservation. Once again, the honest, forthright, and affectionate relationships Crook's courage and personal honor had forged with the beleaguered Indian leaders was turned against the Indians that he so sincerely respected. Crook went with the other commissioners to a series of meetings with the Sioux and Cheyenne on the various reservations, urging many of the leaders who had served him loyally during the Sioux wars to accept this latest proposal from the whites. The proposal he presented would grant each individual a large tract of land and then sell off a large chunk of the reservation to white settlers for about seventy-five cents an acre. The Sioux at first resisted, with opponents threatening to kill anyone who signed. But Crook addressed the gathering, skillfully playing one faction off against another. "They were very undemonstrative, and inclined to be a little sullen. They showed little desire to hear me talk, saying they all understood the bill, which was a lie. After explaining the benefits of the legislation to them, they said they would talk over the subject amongst themselves, but didn't want to be pushed. I told them we could not wait much longer, and that if they did not sign soon we would take it for granted that they were not going to sign, and we wanted to go away, as we had much work elsewhere, that we had no personal interest in their signing, etc. After I left they broke up in a row which reacted in our favor."[4] Most of the Sioux ultimately agreed to sign the agreement—many convinced by the arguments of Crook, who had always been honest with them. As American Horse observed, "When I am laying on my deathbed, I will have the satisfaction of knowing that I can leave a piece of land to my children, so that they will not have to say that for my foolishness I deprived them of lands they might have had."

The discussion with the Cheyenne proved even more explosive. The argument dragged on for hours, whereupon Crook broke off the talks and said that anyone who wanted to sign the agreement should start. A warrior named Black Fox jumped up waving his war club, saying he would kill the first one who signed. "I looked for a club," said Crook, an old warrior whose blood was roused. "Finding none and noticing the chairs had a thick wooden bottom, I took a seat near him, where I could see all his movements, intending on felling him on his first hostile movement." But Black Fox was ousted by the police, and taken to the guardhouse. In the end, the Cheyenne refused to sign.

The agreement proved a disaster for those tribes that accepted it. Among the Sioux, many families that received individual allot-

ments leased the land to whites, and through assorted legal maneu-
verings lost it altogether. In the next thirty-three years, the policy
Crook believed would turn the Indians into independent yeoman
farmers cost them half their land and left them mired in poverty.

Crook's fervent advocacy on behalf of the imprisoned Chiricahua also proved a frustrating failure. This underscored the bitter
lesson of his career, as politics and economics once again betrayed
the rationalizations by which Crook fought. The army had sent a
total of 498 Chiricahua to prison in Florida, most of them people
who had remained quietly on the reservation, and many of them
scouts who had helped the army hunt down the hostiles. The 17
warriors who had fought to the end with Geronimo were first confined at Fort Pickens, Florida, for an extended period, although
Miles had promised they would be reunited immediately with their
families. The Indian Rights Association, with Crook's support, had
helped pressure the army into moving the entire band to the
Mount Vernon barracks near Mobile, Alabama, reuniting them all
there by May of 1888. Of the Apaches sent to Florida, 120 had
died by 1890–including 30 children who died at the Carlisle board-
ing school. Of the adult males, only 30 of 79 were considered able-
bodied, the rest weakened by disease and disability.

General Howard, Crook's old political opponent, was now commanding general of the Division of the Atlantic. Crook and Howard conferred about how to help the Chiricahua. Howard sent his
son to prepare a report, which was issued in December 1889. It
documented the plight of the Chiricahua and recommended that
they be moved to a more healthful location. The secretary of war
ordered Crook to inspect a location in North Carolina as a possible reservation. Crook ultimately recommended moving the Chiricahua to Fort Sill, in Indian Territory, arguing it was much more
like their native land.

In the course of preparing his report, Crook visited his old
friends and enemies at the Mount Vernon barracks one last time.
Along with Crook was Lieutenant Lymon Kennon, who wrote about
the January 1, 1890, meeting between Crook and the Chiricahua
in his diary.

A young Indian with long, black hair saw the general, and before we had finished breakfast, Chihuahua was outside, waiting. He seemed overjoyed to see the General. Kaetena joined him, and we walked over to the Indian village, which was just outside the gate of the fort. They lived in little log cabins, which had been built for them. At the gate was a considerable number of Indians waiting for us. Chato came out, and went up to the General and gave him a greeting that was really tender. He took him by the hand, and with his other made a motion as if to clasp him about the neck. It was as if he would express his joy, but feared to take such a liberty. It was a touching sight. The Apaches crowded around the General, shaking hands, and laughing in their delight. The news spread that he was there, and those about us shouted to those in the distance, and from all points they came running in until we had a train of them moving with us.

But the atmosphere changed when Crook came face-to-face with his old nemesis, Geronimo. He was accompanied by Wratten, who served as translator. "We went to the school. A young woman was in charge. Old Geronimo had come up, but the General had not noticed him at all. He was in the schoolroom with a stick with which he threatened the youngsters who misbehaved, and turned to us for some mark of approbation. The children were called upon to recite. A few words of one syllable were written on the black-board, and they read it off. They were so bashful that they did not look at the board when reading, having learned it by heart. Soon the school was dismissed, and we had a council outside. The General asked some of them to tell him about the last escape in March '86. Geronimo pressed forward to speak, but the General said to Wratten, 'I don't want to hear anything from Geronimo. He is such a liar that I don't believe a word he says. I don't want to have anything to do with him.' Geronimo stood back."[5]

It was the final, bitter, unconsciously ironic meeting between Crook and the one warrior he could neither kill, nor convince, nor outlast. Crook would not live out the year. He would die with his last battle unwon, and the Chiricahua still prisoners.

He disdained Geronimo as a liar, but the same twist of forces that had made Geronimo had also made Crook. In the end, those forces betrayed the promises Crook had made, and so made of him the liar he saw in Geronimo.

They were, in the end, more alike than different—although they would each have bitterly disputed the parallels. They were the ultimate warriors of their respective cultures, believing without flinching in honor, courage, endurance, determination, and the ultimate destruction of their enemies. They each fought for noble ends, but were betrayed by their own means. And they each remained finally mired in their cultures, in their circumstance, in their times.

Crook died, finally, in the deep shadow of his contradictions.

He was an honorable man, whose career was devoted to a grave injustice. He remained throughout his life steadfast, unflinching, courageous, dutiful, resourceful, stoic, and duty bound. He eschewed politics, did his duty no matter what the cost, and won the admiration of those who knew him best. And yet his best qualities were turned against themselves by some bewildering political alchemy. Lesser men rose to greater honors, he found himself always the tool in the hands of others, and he helped bring about the ultimate destruction of the West that he so loved. In the end, he died estranged from the times that he had helped bring about—as uprooted from his place as the Indian warriors he had admired, and killed, all his life.

And when he died, his many friends among the Sioux and among the Apache mourned his loss. They keened at the passing of a good enemy—a man who had tried to keep his word.

19

Geronimo

A Long Time in a Cage

GERONIMO LIVED a long time after Gray Fox died, which was only small satisfaction to him. Even though Geronimo lived many years in the cages of the White Eyes, he never came to understand them.

After a while, the soldiers moved the warriors—putting them back together with their families in a new place. But they had little to do, and no land to farm, and no cattle to watch. They merely waited, yearning for their home. The trees pressed in so close that they could not see to the horizon, could not pray to the sun at the edge of all things, could not smell the desert after the rain.

The People died steadily of the diseases of the White Eyes.

The soldiers even came and took the children, sending them off to a school where they would learn to become like White Eyes. But mostly the children died there, put all together where the sickness could find them more quickly, far from the healing ceremonies that might have saved them. Later (in 1905), the soldiers moved them again, to Fort Sill, in Oklahoma, where they lived near other Indians. This was a better place, where they could see the sky and sometimes hear coyotes calling. But it was still not their home, and still The People sickened and died—knowing not even where to find the plants and the places that would make them whole and heal their spirits.

Geronimo saw many wonders. Sometimes the soldiers took him to great cities, and showed him magical things that all testified to the Power of the White Eyes, who had seized all of the gifts of Slayer of Enemies with such greedy hands.

And still, the White Eyes never made sense to him. He did not understand their laughter. He did not understand their curiosity about him. He did not understand why they could never tell the truth, and could never keep their word. He did not understand how they could be enemies, and friends, and enemies again—all without reason or sense.

But he understood at last that they had far more Power than The People, and that he had been as a child before it.

Once he even met the Great Father, riding in a great parade (in March 1905) with everyone shouting and calling his name. He spoke to President Theodore Roosevelt with quiet dignity.

Great Father, said Geronimo, I look to you as I look to God. When I see your face I think I see the face of the Great Spirit. I come here to pray you to be good to me and my people. . . . Did I fear the Great White Chief? No. He was my enemy and the enemy of my people. His people desired the country of my people. My heart was strong against him. I said that he should never have my country. I defied the Great White Chief, for in those days I was a fool. . . . I ask you to think of me as I was then. I lived in the home of my people. . . . They trusted me. It was right that I should give them my strength and my wisdom. When the soldiers of the Great White Chief drove me and my people from our home, we went to the mountains. When they followed us we slew all that we could. We said we should not be captured. No. We starved but we killed. I said that we would never yield, for I was a fool . . . so I was punished, and all my people were punished with me. The white soldiers took me and made me a prisoner far from my own country.

As always, he made his case with dignity and eloquence. Great Father, other Indians have homes where they can live and be happy. I and my people have no homes. The place where we are kept is bad for us. . . . We are sick there and we die. White men are in the country that was my home. I pray you to tell them to go away and let my people go there and be happy. . . . Great Father, my hands are tied as with a rope. My heart is no longer bad. I will tell my people to obey no chief but the Great White Chief. I pray you to cut the ropes and make me free. Let me die in my own country, an old man who has been punished enough and is free.

But Geronimo's words could find no place in the president's heart to root. The Great Father replied, I have no anger in my heart against you. I even wish it were only a question of letting you return to your country as a free man, but I could not do that because the people there still hated you. I should have to interfere between you. There would be more war and more bloodshed . . . it is best for you to stay where you are.[1]

So Geronimo returned to the place where they kept the Chiricahua, still struggling to understand what had happened, and whether in all his struggles to protect his people he had brought about their destruction.

Geronimo tried to keep the old ways. He could still perform healing ceremonies for Ghost Sickness, and for Coyote Sickness, although they were now so far from home that you could not in a week of searching find a single coyote track, or in a year of listening hear a single coyote call. Still, people called him to help him when they had problems with Dogs and with Foxes and with Wolves. He could still heal people, so that it seemed his Power had not deserted him after all. Geronimo was still a strong singer, and knew more songs and more ceremonies than almost any other person. Sometime he would sing;

O, ha le
O, ha le
Through the air
I fly upon a cloud
Toward the sky far, far, far,
O, ha le
O, ha le
There to find the holy place
Ah, now the changes come o'er me![2]

But the song made his heart ache, because he was so far now from the holy place that he could not find it even if he could fly upon a cloud.

And still, those he loved died, dropping like leaves that left the branches of his heart bare. Nana died in 1896, his sister Na-doste in 1907, Chihuahua in 1901, Mangus in 1901, and Loco in 1905. Geronimo's two wives died in captivity and so did his three children—Chappo in Alabama and Fenton and Lulu at Fort Sill. Even Geronimo's grandson died in 1908, at the age of 18.

And still Geronimo lived on, so that he wondered what evil had come upon his family, to destroy everyone else and leave him alive. His Power had promised that no bullet could kill him and that he would live to be an old man. Then, it had seemed a great gift. Now, it seemed a curse—a trick played on him because he had not paid enough attention. He had been cheated now out of a warrior's death and made to watch everyone he loved die, even The People.

So he went to Lot Eyelash, thinking to discover the one who had witched him. But Lot Eyelash only pointed his long finger at Geronimo, and spoke the things Geronimo's own heart had most feared.

Geronimo thought that perhaps the White Eyes had the greater Power, and so he studied their religion. Many others, like Naiche, embraced the Jesus Way and would no longer perform ceremonials and would go to the church and listen to the preachers.

Once, after Geronimo took a bad fall from a horse, Naiche convinced him that he should also take the Jesus Way. Geronimo wrestled with Naiche's words, seeing that his old friend had himself gained great peace, even joy, on the Jesus Way. Geronimo thought back on his life and all of the things he had done. He could see now from the point of view of the Jesus Way that he had done many terrible things. He remembered one time when he had gone into the house of an enemy, having already killed many of the people there. Inside, he found a baby in its bed. He had picked up that baby, playing with him for a moment until the baby was laughing in the way babies do. Then, as if moved by the hands of something else, Geronimo had taken out his long knife, and tossed the baby into the air, and caught the baby on the blade of his knife.[3] It had made sense to him at the time. He had thought of Alope and of his little children, butchered by the Mexicans, with their scalps cut away. He had been thinking of all of the babies the White Eyes and the Mexicans had thrown into the bonfire of a burning wickiup, or had dashed against the stones. He had been thinking about the soldiers who had cut off the private parts of the women, and made purses of them. He had been thinking of all of those things, and so it had seemed just and fair to make the baby laugh and then impale the little one on his knife. But the memory of it had come back to him in all the years since—sometimes in his dreams. Now he thought maybe he could make sense of the things he had done and the way things had turned out if he went down along the Jesus Way as Naiche had done.

So Geronimo went into the church. He said, I am old and broken by this fall I have had. I am without friends, for my people have turned from me. I am full of sins and I walk alone in the dark. I see that you missionaries have got a way to get sin out of the heart, and I want to take that better road and hold it till I die.

But he could not hold to that road, because still he liked to gamble, and to drink, and to sing the old songs. So after awhile they kicked him out of the Jesus Way, and told him not to come back anymore.

So he was left then with the same problem, the knot that he had never been able to cut or loosen. He said to himself, We are vanishing from the earth. But it makes no sense that The People were useless, or Usen would not have created us. The People and their homes had been created by Usen himself. But now they were taken away from these homes, so that they sickened and died. How long would it be until it is said that there are no more Apache?[4]

But he had no answer.

His Power had fallen silent.

So he only went on, as he had always done. But he wished he had never surrendered. He wished that he had stayed in the Sierra Madre until his enemies finally found him, and killed him, even if

Geronimo became one of the most-photographed Indian
warriors, in part because he lived so long as a prisoner of
war in Florida, Alabama, and Oklahoma. He remained a
healer, a farmer, and a storyteller among the Chiricahua
during his long exile, as well as a curiosity for tourists.
(*Courtesy National Archives*)

he had stayed alone. He wished that he had died a warrior's death—although his Power had denied that to him.

Geronimo had seen many people die and seen many people laying dead, but he had never seen a man's spirit rising up and going away, leaving the husk of the body behind. He hoped, in the end, that the old ways were correct, and that after he died he would go to The Happy Place where he would go on doing what he had always loved to do. He would go raiding again, riding against the Mexicans. He remembered one time he had gone partway to The Happy Place, lying injured after a fight with the Mexicans. Or perhaps he had only dreamed it. Or maybe it was another warrior who had done that, and come back to tell him about it. He had gone into a cave, passing the guard there, and descended into the cave world, going past snakes, and bears, and mountain lions, who waited there along the way to make sure that only a fearless man could pass through to The Happy Place. Maybe that is how it would be for him, and he would see Mangas Coloradas, and Victorio, and Cochise, and best of all Alope and his children, still playing with the small things he had made for them.

So he waited.

And ignored the talk about him.

And ceased finally even to wonder at the riddle of the White Eyes, who were, in the end, like fire, or lightning, or any other thing beyond understanding.

One day in February of 1909, he went into town and bought some whiskey and drank it all down, the only sure way he had ever found to believe that none of it mattered anymore. Riding back to his home, he fell from his horse, and lay all night in the cold, an old man who had lost his way a great long ways from home.

He was already sick by the time a friend found him, laying partly in the water. His friends sat by his bed as he died. He recalled the warpath in his singer's voice, now rattling with the fluids that filled his lungs. One boy who loved him came to him and said that he had had a vision that Geronimo should become a Christian. But Geronimo shook his head, saying that he could not follow the Jesus Way in his life, and it was too late now in death.

He died quietly, an old man in his bed, just as his Power had promised. But he died on the wintry plains of Oklahoma, where the rocks had never learned his name.

Strangely enough, he achieved by his death what he could not accomplish in his life.

His enemies had always feared him, and had punished his people with that fear for all the years of his life. But now, after his death, his old enemies looked around and decided they did not need to hold Geronimo's people any longer in this great prison so far from the place where the Mountain Spirits danced.

So they let them finally go home, after twenty-eight years as prisoners. And the 261 people left alive went to live with the Mescalero in New Mexico just four years after Geronimo died.

For his part, he had passed finally beyond care and loss. He had only to confront the guards, and the snakes, and the bears, and the angry cries of his enemies—waiting always to be sure that only a brave man could go all the way through to The Happy Place.

Notes

Part One: Prologue

Chapter 1. Geronimo: The Price of Power

1. Interview with James Kaywaykla in Angie Debo, *Geronimo: The Man, His Time, His Place* (Norman: University of Oklahoma Press, 1976), 437.

Chapter 2. Crook: The Cost of Duty (1890)

1. Nelson A. Miles, *Personal Recollections* (Chicago: Werner, 1897), 496–497.
2. John G. Bourke, *On the Border with Crook* (New York: Charles Scribner's Sons, 1891), 485.
3. George Crook, *General George Crook: His Autobiography*, ed. Martin F. Schmitt (Norman: University of Oklahoma Press, 1960), 298.
4. Ibid., xx.
5. Ibid., xii.
6. Bourke, *On the Border with Crook*, 486.

Part Two: Early Conflicts (1828–1861)

Chapter 3. Geronimo: The Making of a Warrior (1827–1850)

1. *Geronimo, His Own Story*, as told to S(tephen) M(elvil) Barrett (New York: Duffield, 1906). This is a shortened version of the creation myth with which Geronimo starts his own autobiography. It differs in several important respects from other versions of the Apache creation myths recorded by Grenville Goodwin and others. For instance, Goodwin's informant in *The Myths and Tales of the White Mountain Apache* (Tucson: University of Arizona Press, 1996) indicates that the first monster killed by the cultural hero was "Big Owl." Geronimo may have used the embellishment of a dragon knowing that the tale was intended to be read by whites.
2. Identified in various other accounts as the brother of Child of Waters, who is also referred to as "Slayer of Monsters."

3. Geronimo, in *His Own Story*, said that the cultural hero's name was "Apache," which is probably the result of the translation. Actually, the Apache called themselves "The People." The summary of the mythological events in the Apache creation stories offered here is taken from Goodwin and other sources. The details of the creation myths differ from band to band. They variously identify the father of Child of Waters as the sun, the rain, or the wind.

4. Many translators indicate Goyathlay means "one who yawns," but Angie Debo, in *Geronimo: The Man, His Time, His Place* (Norman: University of Oklahoma Press, 1976), notes that it might mean "intelligent or clever."

5. Geronimo puts his birth date at 1829 in his autobiography, but he was probably born a few years earlier, because he had a wife and three children by 1850, among other evidence.

6. The Chihenne, or Red Paint, people are often also referred to as the Ojo Caliente or Warm Springs. I opted for Chihenne because that is the term that Eve Ball's Warm Springs informants, who are descendants of Victorio and the other Chihenne leaders, use most often in referring to themselves. Ball spent decades living on the Mescalero reservation with the survivors of the Chihenne and Chiricahua, recording their accounts.

7. The Tonto Apache occupied the Verde Valley and the Mogollon Rim country. This put them beyond the range of contact for most of the Chiricahua groups. After Crook defeated the Tonto Apache, many served as scouts against the Chiricahua.

8. Angie Debo, in *Geronimo*, notes that Geronimo was born in the early 1820s near the Upper Gila Mountains near the present Arizona–New Mexico border near present-day Clifton.

9. Morris Opler, in *An Apache Lifeway* (1941; reprint, Chicago: University of Chicago Press, 1996), 10, reports that adults commonly rolled to the four directions when they returned to the spot of their birth.

10. Ibid., 16.

11. Ibid., 27.

12. Ibid., 67. This is a speech one of Opler's informant's fathers delivered to him. I took the liberty of attributing it to Geronimo's father, although Geronimo was not one of Opler's informants.

13. Geronimo, in *His Own Story* (70), puts the year at about 1846, but many of Geronimo's dates are probably wrong.

14. As Geronimo said in *His Own Story* (71), "Then I was very happy, for I could go wherever I wanted and do whatever I liked. I had not been under the control of any individual, but the customs of our tribe prohibited me from sharing the glories of the warpath until the council admitted me. When opportunity offered, after this, I could go on the warpath with my tribe. This would be glorious. I hoped soon to serve my people in battle. I had long desired to fight with the warriors."

15. The Apache had a difficulty understanding the political structure of the Mexicans and Americans. They believed that each Mexican town functioned like an Apache band, free to make its own arrangements with outsiders. The Apache often concluded peace agreements with one village while raiding nearby villages

or provinces. The Mexicans took this as evidence of Apache treachery, and retaliated. The Apache considered this retaliation base treachery.

16. In fact, most historians believe both the Apache and the Navajo migrated into the Southwest not long before the Spanish arrived. Both Apache and Navajo began raiding the settled, agricultural peoples who had occupied the river valleys for eons. The Apache quickly adopted the horse to expand their raids, which brought them into conflict with the expanding Spanish empire in the 1600s.

17. The first Americans to show up were fur trappers who mostly maintained peaceful relationships with the bands they encountered. The first significant military presence came in 1846 when the war between the United States and Mexico prompted Brigadier General Stephen Watts Kearny to occupy Santa Fe. He encountered the Apaches near the Rio Grande before continuing on to California. After the Treaty of Guadalupe Hidalgo was concluded in 1848, a well-armed border survey under John Russell Bartlett camped for a prolonged period in April 1851 at the Santa Rita Copper Mines near the chief campsite of Mangas Coloradas. The initially friendly relations soured when the Americans freed two Mexican boys held captive and then refused to turn over a Mexican teamster who murdered an Apache warrior. The Apache then stole most of the expedition's livestock, and Bartlett departed. There is no evidence that Geronimo was present during this first, momentous encounter between the Americans and the Apache, although he must have heard the details from friends and kinsmen.

18. Geronimo, in *His Own Story* (71), notes that they "had been lovers for a long time" when he was granted the privileges of a warrior at the age of seventeen and immediately presented his case to Alope's father.

19. The Apache referred to the town as Kas-ki-yeh, according to Jason Betzinez's account in *I Fought with Geronimo*, edited and annotated by Wilbur Sturtevant Nye (Harrisburg, Pa.: Stackpole, 1959), 47. This might have been the Mexican town of Ramos, but was probably Janos, according to Debo's comment in Betzinez's version.

20. *Geronimo, His Own Story* and other Apache accounts depict the attack in which Alope was killed as an act of Mexican treachery. However, Geronimo and other warriors had been raiding actively throughout the area, although they may have preserved a peace with one town or another. Historians differ as to the details of the attack, including the timing. For instance, Geronimo's autobiography puts the year at 1858, but it was probably actually in 1850. The most plausible version suggests that various Apache bands rebuffed attempts by the province of Chihuahua to make peace, although they did maintain peaceful relationships with towns in neighboring Sonora. The warriors raided Chihuahua and sold the plunder to merchants in Sonora. A Chihuahuan force under General Carrasco entered Sonora and attacked a band of Apaches trading near Janos, killing twenty-five and capturing fifty or sixty, who they promptly sold into slavery. Sonora protested the Chihuahuan expedition, but the federal government supported Carrasco. I have presented Geronimo's version of events, taken from *His Own Story*.

21. Betzinez, in *I Fought with Geronimo* (78), wrote that the warriors were sleeping off a binge near Janos when the soldiers attacked the camp, killing the women and children. This is plausible, since Apaches in general and Geronimo in particular never seemed to learn that getting drunk in a Mexican town could easily prove a fatal mistake. The text here reflects the version offered by Geronimo in his autobiography.

22. *Geronimo, His Own Story*, 78.

23. Geronimo, in his autobiography, says he observed the stringent Apache aversion to the dead, and did not go to the camp to recover the bodies of his wife, children, and mother. However, Debo, in *Geronimo*, reports that in later years Geronimo said that he had stolen away and gone to the scene of the massacre, where he found his family lying in a pool of blood.

24. Debo, *Geronimo* (38), based on an interview with Sam Haozous. Known accounts don't make it clear where Geronimo was at the time of the vision, although he was reportedly alone. Geronimo doesn't mention the voice at all in his autobiography, not surprising since the Apache rarely spoke of matters of spiritual power, especially with whites. I took the liberty of assuming it might have occurred at the time of his reported return to the scene of the massacre.

25. This is a description of his eyes borrowed from the account of a journalist who met Geronimo in captivity in later years and quoted by Debo in *Geronimo*, 379.

26. *Geronimo, His Own Story*, 86.

27. The summer of 1859 in *Geronimo, His Own Story*, but the summer of 1851 in Betzinez's version, which is a more likely date.

28. Apache accounts identify the site as Arispe, although it's unclear how the Apache selected that Sonoran town for their revenge. Typically, the Apache were not very legalistic in selecting the objects of their revenge and so killed anyone affiliated with the band or group which committed the original wrong. It probably sufficed that Arispe was then the capital of Sonora. Mexican accounts make note of conflicts with Apaches at roughly the same time and same place, but disagree in many details.

29. The soldiers might have been calling on Saint Jerome, which the Apaches heard as "Geronimo."

30. As Geronimo commented in *His Own Story* (83), "All the other Apaches were satisfied after the battle of Kas-ki-yeh, but I still desired more revenge." Geronimo's account of this pivotal battle is supported by Betzinez, and other oral Apache traditions, but does not closely coincide with any known written Mexican accounts. However, it remains plausible. Apache had contempt for a warrior who would exaggerate his accomplishments in battle, and throughout his autobiography Geronimo provided a surprisingly evenhanded account of his successes and setbacks in warfare.

CHAPTER 4. Crook: Early Years (1828–1861)

1. George Crook, *General George Crook: His Autobiography*, ed. Martin F. Schmitt (Norman: University of Oklahoma Press, 1960), xxii.

2. Ibid., xxi.

3. Ibid., 16.
4. Ibid., 41.
5. Ibid., 68.

Part Three: Taking Command (1861–1871)

CHAPTER 5. Geronimo: The Unquenched Flame (1851–1861)

1. This description of the gun ceremony comes from Morris Edward Opler, *An Apache Lifeway* (1941; reprint, Chicago: University of Chicago Press, 1996), 311. Opler noted that Geronimo knew a gun ceremony. He did not attribute this particular gun ceremony to Geronimo and so Geronimo's actual ceremony might have differed somewhat.

2. The summer of 1861 in *Geronimo, His Own Story*, as told to S(tephen) M(elvil) Barrett (New York: Duffield, 1906), although it was likely earlier.

3. My suggestion that Alope's death left Geronimo fixed on vengeance and death is based, in part, on his curious silence about Nana-Tha-Thtith and his other wives in his autobiography. Nana-Tha-Thtith's death apparently had much less impact on him than Alope's.

4. *Geronimo, His Own Story* puts the date at the summer of 1862, but, again, it probably occurred some years earlier.

5. From the account of a victory celebration by Opler, *An Apache Lifeway*.

6. Ibid., 200. "Geronimo got political power from the religious side. He foresaw the results of the fighting, and they used him so much in the campaigns that he came to be depended upon. He went through his ceremony, and he would say 'You should go here; you should go there.' That is how he became a leader."

7. This discussion of Power derives largely from Opler's informants, on pages 207–208 of *An Apache Lifeway*.

8. Ibid., 209.

9. In the late 1850s and early 1860s, Geronimo's autobiography presents persistent problems in chronology, since he assigns incorrect dates to some events, and provides a confusing chronology for other well-documented events like the battle of Apache Pass and Cochise's battles with the Americans.

10. The Apache often got roaring drunk on mescal, even in perilous situations like during a visit to a Mexican town. Perhaps that's because they usually drank a mild corn beer of their own making, which spoiled so quickly that they usually made big batches which they drank quickly on special occasions. The same drinking pattern applied to the much more potent mescal, resulting in a drunken binge.

11. *Geronimo, His Own Story*. The responsibility of leadership probably kept him from getting drunk on this occasion, but Geronimo clearly loved to drink and sometimes indulged this weakness in dangerous circumstances. He never apparently had the inclination or the authority to enforce the ban on drinking in questionable circumstances enforced by leaders like Victorio and Cochise.

12. The Gulf of California.

13. There remains some uncertainty about this fourth marriage; accounts conflict.

14. The United States acquired the Mimbreno and Chiricahua homelands as a result of the $10 million Gadsden Purchase in 1853, and began a long, futile effort to forbid Apache raiding into Mexico. Dr. Michael Steck, agent to the Mescalero, Chiricahua, Mimbreno, and Warm Springs Apaches, reported that the Indians were generally cooperative and peaceful. He endeavored to convince them to give up much of their land and move away from settlements and travel routes, but Congress then rejected his efforts to concentrate the Apaches on a large reservation along the Gila. Nonetheless, the Apache made few depredations against the Americans, although Steck reported that many of the eight thousand to nine thousand Indians he supervised were destitute and close to starvation. A gold strike in 1859 northwest of Santa Rita and Piños Altos led to increasing frictions.

15. This occurred in the spring or summer of 1860. Perhaps the miners thought Mangas Coloradas intended to lure them out of town and into an ambush.

16. I have generally opted for the current, American names of topographical features for the convenience of modern readers.

17. January 1861.

18. Geronimo's autobiography does not indicate he was present, although he was evidently living with Cochise's band at the time. He might have been off raiding, or might have overlooked it in dictating his recollections decades later.

19. Second Lieutenant George Bascom provoked a war with Cochise as a result of his bungling of the confrontation in Apache Pass. Bascom was reinforced by a detachment commanded by Bernard Irwin, who had seized three Coyotero Apache prisoners of his own, and was further reinforced by two companies of dragoons. The commander of the dragoons, a Lieutenant Moore, executed six Apache prisoners once Cochise killed his hostages. Bascom released the woman and the child he had taken prisoner, evidently Cochise's wife and his son, Naiche. Some Apache accounts insist the army killed its hostages first.

20. Geronimo's autobiography leaves no mention of his participation in these events, but as a leading warrior of Cochise's band he would certainly have been involved. The Apache assumed they forced the abandonment of the forts in the area, but it was actually the outbreak of the Civil War in 1861 that prompted the Union to shift its troops to the East. The outbreak of the war also prompted the Union to abandon the Butterfield Stage route through Apache Pass in favor of a northern route.

CHAPTER 6. Crook: The Politics of Death (1861–1871)

1. Whitelaw Reid, *Ohio in the War*, 2 vols. (Cincinnati: n.p., 1868–1872), 235.

2. George Crook, *General George Crook: His Autobiography*, ed. Martin F. Schmitt (Norman: University of Oklahoma Press, 1960), 119.

3. Rutherford B. Hayes. *Diary and Letters of Rutherford B. Hayes* (Columbus, Ohio: 1922–1926), 5:477–478.

4. *The War of the Rebellion: A Compilation of the Official Records of the Union and Confederate Armies* (Washington, D.C.: Government Printing Office, 1880–1901), ser. I, vol. 37, pt. 1, 287–288.

5. Hayes, *Diary and Letters*, 514.

6. Crook, *Autobiography*, 141.

Chapter 7. Geronimo: The Americans Return (1861–1871)

1. This describes the battle of Apache Pass in July 1862, involving the 122-man advanced detachment of California Volunteers commanded by General James Henry Carleton assigned to retake Arizona and New Mexico from the Confederates commanded by Colonel John Robert Baylor.

2. Geronimo's autobiography omits reference to this battle, although both logic and tradition suggest he was present.

3. The Apache were caught between the Union and the Confederate forces, which spent more time fighting the Apache and the Navajo than they did each other. Baylor, the confederate commander, at one point ordered his men to execute without warning any warriors and to sell as slaves any women or children they captured. The Union commander, Carleton, also ordered his soldiers to kill any warriors, even encouraging his commanders to lure in the warriors by promising negotiations. Carleton put the famous scout Kit Carson in command of a punitive expedition that within two years had rounded up the Navajo and the Mescalaro Apache and confined them to a disease-ridden concentration camp on the Rio Grande. However, these events had only an indirect impact on Geronimo, who remained in the Dragoons between raids into Mexico.

4. On his way to Piños Altos in response to peace overtures, Mangas Coloradas was seized under a flag of truce by a party of thirty miners under Joseph Reddeford Walker. The miners then encountered a detachment led by General J. R. West, who confiscated their prisoner. West placed two guards on his prisoner and suggested he would be happy if the Apache chief were killed "trying to escape." The guards tormented Mangas Coloradas with heated bayonets, then killed him when he protested, according to one of the miners' sentries. The chief's skull was later sent to the Smithsonian Institution, where surprised phrenologists declared that the 7'5" tall chief had a greater cranial capacity than Daniel Webster. In his autobiography, Geronimo termed it the worst thing the whites ever did to the Apaches. See *Geronimo, His Own Story*, as told to S(tephen) M(elvil) Barrett (New York: Duffield, 1906), 116.

5. In Geronimo's autobiography, he says he was elected tribal chief after the death of Mangas Coloradas. This was probably a translator's error, as most accounts agree Geronimo never acted as a chief. On the other hand, perhaps he did take charge of a Bedonkohe band for a time before it was absorbed into a larger group.

6. Victorio and Loco met with First Lieutenant Charles E. Drew in the summer of 1869 and again in October 1870 with agent William Arny in an attempt to convince the government to establish a reservation at Warm Springs. Cochise and one hundred Chiricahua joined this second conference, and appeared willing to settle with the Chihenne and Mimbreno at Warm Springs. However, the

government persisted in trying to convince the Indians to move to one of several alternative sites.

7. The Apache term for late fall.

8. The Apache despised liars, but made an exception for lies told to an enemy. The Apache culture imposed more sanctions on a liar than did white culture. However, Geronimo and others frequently violated promises made to whites, killed people under flag of truce, and embraced deception as a useful tool in dealing with their enemies.

9. Several sources report this incident in the winter of 1869 or 1870. Morris Edward Opler's informants reported that Geronimo had both Coyote and Ghost Power; therefore, I made the assumption here that Geronimo diagnosed Coyote Sickness before undertaking to cure Ishton. Some shamen had specific Power in pregnancy, but there is no mention beyond this incident of Geronimo having such Power. The account of the healing ceremony he used here is based on a description from one of Opler's informants who observed one of Geronimo's ceremonies later, while living on the reservation. See Opler's *An Apache Lifeway* (1941; reprint, Chicago: University of Chicago Press, 1996), 41.

10. Apache tradition says Ishton labored for four days, which is the Apache sacred number. The recollection of the incident may have been adjusted to match the requisite number.

11. Angie Debo, *Geronimo: The Man, His Time, His Place* (Norman: University of Oklahoma Press, 1970), 77.

Part Four: A Fight to the Death (1871–1883)

Chapter 8. Crook: The Coming of the Fox (1871–1875)

1. John G. Bourke, *On the Border with Crook* (New York: Charles Scribner's Sons, 1891), 101.

2. Ibid., 110.

3. Ibid., 112.

4. Charles Lummis, *General Crook and the Apache Wars* (Flagstaff, Ariz.: Northland Press, 1966), 33.

5. Bourke, *On the Border with Crook*, 140.

6. Ibid., 139.

7. Ibid., 148.

8. George Crook, *General George Crook: His Autobiography*, ed. Martin F. Schmitt (Norman: University of Oklahoma Press, 1960), 171.

9. Ibid., 177.

10. Bourke, *On the Border with Crook*, 181.

11. Ibid., 183.

12. Ibid., 185.

13. Crook, *Autobiography*, 178.

14. Crook's secondhand account does not quite match the topographyo of Turret Peak. For instance, there's no cliff off which the warriors could have hurled themselves, and the shell casings which undoubtedly mark the battle site

are at the base of the peak itself, in a plateau between the canyons cut by two creeks. Moreover, it would be out of character for the warriors to commit suicide. Officers making their report to Crook may have embellished the account he presented in his autobiography.

15. Dan Thrapp, *The Conquest of Apacheria* (Norman: University of Oklahoma Press, 1967), 185 n.

16. Bourke reports that Cha-lipun represented some twenty-five hundred people in surrendering. But two years later when the Tonto and Yavapai were relocated, only about fifteen hundred made the journey. Either far fewer than twenty-five hundred surrendered initially, or the survivors suffered a horrendous death rate before the relocation.

17. Bourke, *On the Border with Crook*, 215.

18. Thrapp, *Conquest of Apacheria*, 210.

19. The spelling of Apache names varied widely in contemporary accounts.

20. The first part of the quote comes from Crook, *Autobiography*, 185. The second part is from Bourke, *On The Border with Crook*, 228.

21. Bourke, *On the Border with Crook*, 222.

22. Ibid., 230.

23. William Corbusier, *Verde to San Carlos* (Tucson: Arizona Historical Society, 1971).

CHAPTER 9. Geronimo: Making Peace with the White Eyes (1871–1883)

1. Cochise's speech comes from accounts left by Howard and by Captain Joseph Sladden, his aide, in O(liver) O(tis) Howard, *Famous Indian Chiefs I Have Known* (New York: Century, 1907).

2. Geronimo does not mention this incident in his autobiography, although he describes General Howard as the greatest friend the Apache ever had among the whites. General Howard, in *Famous Indian Chiefs I Have Known*, recalls Geronimo riding behind him and trembling "with fear." It seems more likely Geronimo was poised to fight, and perhaps rode behind Howard to make sure that the general did not survive should he prove treacherous.

3. Arizona Governor Anson Safford wrote that "so far as the people of Arizona are concerned, I believe that Cochise has kept his word," although he noted that the government's stated intention of cutting off Chiricahua raiding into Mexico could well spark renewed fighting. See Angie Debo, *Geronimo: The Man, His Time, His Place* (Norman: University of Oklahoma Press, 1976), 91.

4. Jeffords did his best to manage the reservation under increasingly difficult conditions. He proved unable to curtail Apache raiding into Mexico. Jeffords realized that the Chiricahua would be hard-pressed to support themselves on the reservation if denied supplies from Mexico. He also understood that Cochise prevented turbulent souls like Geronimo from attacking the whites only with some difficulty and that his authority might not survive an effective ban on raiding down into Mexico.

5. Cochise died in 1874.

6. The government instituted its disastrous concentration policy after transferring Crook to the Department of the Platte to fight the Sioux.

7. The incident touched off a firestorm of protest. Governor Safford, who had praised Cochise's efforts to keep the peace, wired Washington and demanded that the reservation be closed down. The *Tucson Citizen* editorialized on April 15, 1876, that "the kind of war needed for the Chiricahua Apaches is steady, unrelenting, hopeless, and undiscriminating war, slaying men, women, and children & until every valley and crest and crag and fastness shall send to high heaven the grateful incense of festering and rotting Chiricahua." Debo, *Geronimo*, 97.

8. Debo, ibid., reports that the scouts, Taza, and Naiche attacked the camp of the dissidents. In *Geronimo: A Biography* (New York: Da Capo Press. 1971), 82, Alexander Adams reports that the dissidents, including Juh and Geronimo, attacked Taza's camp.

9. June 7 or 8, 1876.

10. Jeffords reported twenty deaths and the theft of 170 head of livestock between the closing of the agency in June and the following summer. See Dan L. Thrapp, *The Conquest of Apacheria* (Norman: University of Oklahoma Press, 1967).

11. Clum took Taza and other Apache leaders on an ill-conceived tour of the East, financed in part by an impromptu Wild West show. In Washington, D.C., Taza contracted pneumonia and died. Clum staged an elaborate funeral with General Howard in attendance, which reassured some of the White Mountain leaders that Taza's death had been unintentional, but Naiche maintained Clum had poisoned his brother.

12. This incident occurred on April 21, 1877. Clum left a vivid, somewhat suspect account. Geronimo barely mentions the incident; see *Geronimo, His Own Story*, as told to S(tephen) M(elvil) Barrett (New York: Duffield, 1906), 126. He said he agreed to a conference with the scouts, but was then arrested by soldiers. He and Victorio were both questioned and then Victorio was released while Geronimo was imprisoned, apparently for leaving the agency in Apache Pass and joining Victorio's people. He said he was kept in chains for four months, and then released, apparently as a result of another trial at which he was not present.

13. Apache accounts insist Geronimo was not captured in this public and humiliating confrontation. However, Clum's report is detailed and plausible and backed by official documentation. In this case, I chose his version of the confrontation over the vague Apache accounts. See Woodworth Clum, *Apache Agent: The Story of John P. Clum* (Boston: Houghton Mifflin, 1936).

14. The number of chained warriors varies in different accounts. Geronimo put it at seven plus himself.

15. Clum insisted the government hang Geronimo. However, Clum soon found himself locked in such bitter conflict with the army that his recommendations were largely ignored. Clum insisted that he could supervise all of the Apaches in Arizona without the assistance of the army by relying on his Indian police force and judicial system. He instituted an enlightened administration

that provided work and relative autonomy for the huge, growing concentration of Indians under his charge. However, Clum clashed repeatedly with the army, and quit in a huff when the Bureau of Indian Affairs refused to boost his salary after he concentrated five thousand Apaches at San Carlos and consolidated five agencies, at a savings to the government of $25,000 for each agency. Clum later founded the *Tombstone Epitaph* and played a role in the conflict between the Earps and the Clantons. The new agent, Henry Lyman Hart, released Geronimo, apparently fearing that an execution would spark an outbreak from the seething San Carlos Reservation. Clum maintained that Geronimo had at that point murdered one hundred men, women, and children and that hanging him would have saved five hundred more lives and $12 million. Clum wrote that his shackles "never should have been removed except to permit him to walk untrammeled to the scaffold." Debo, *Geronimo*, 114.

16. James Kaywaykla made this suggestion to historian Eve Ball, in *In the Days of Victorio: Recollections of a Warm Springs Apache* (Tucson: University of Arizona Press, 1970), 158. He recalled his mother's horrified reaction to a can of deviled ham which bore the picture of a very human-looking devil on the label.

17. Geronimo makes no mention of this incident in his autobiography. It is recounted by his cousin, Jason Betzinez, in *I Fought with Geronimo*, edited and annotated by Wilbur Sturtevant Nye (Harrisburg, Pa.: Stackpole, 1959), 89.

18. April 4, 1878.

19. Betzinez, in *I Fought with Geronimo*, 53, reports that Geronimo was also accompanied by his third wife, Ih-tedda, but he probably married her later.

20. Many sources indicate Geronimo had great Power, and was considered primarily a religious leader. Several also suggest he was a respected and sought-after singer. I have assumed he also played a role in organizing the dances, and preparing the dancers as Edward Morris Opler describes in *An Apache Lifeway* (1941; reprint, Chicago: University of Chicago Press, 1996), 108.

21. These songs are described by Opler's informants on pages 119 and 120 of *An Apache Lifeway*. I have taken the liberty of attributing them to Geronimo to illustrate the nature of Apache singing, of which Geronimo was a renowned practitioner.

22. Dan Thrapp, *Juh: An Incredible Indian*, Southwest Studies, monograph no. 39 (El Paso: Texas Western Press, 1973), 15.

23. Many officers, including Bourke, denounced as criminal stupidity the Indian Bureau polices that drove Victorio into open warfare. Ironically, the Indian Bureau was evidently about to accede to Victorio's request when the Chihenne chief learned that a judge, a prosecutor, and several others were approaching his camp. Victorio assumed they had arrived to serve a murder warrant previously issued by civilian authorities, and so bolted with several hundred followers, including about eighty warriors, on August 21, 1879. Tragically, the judge and prosecutor were on a hunting trip and not seeking Victorio's arrest. Victorio then raged back and forth across Arizona, New Mexico, and Mexico for the next two years. See Dan L. Thrapp, *Victorio and the Mimbres Apaches* (Norman: University of Oklahoma Press, 1974).

24. Some accounts by American officers suggested Juh and Geronimo joined Victorio's band and raided with him. Subsequent conflicts between the Chiricahua and the Chihenne argue against that suggestion. Most tellingly, James Kaywaykla, who as a boy traveled with Victorio's band, makes no mention of Geronimo or Juh joining the band.

25. Colonel Joaquin Terrazas surprised Victorio's force at Tres Castillos on October 14, 1880, killing and scalping for the bounty 78 Indians—62 of them warriors. The Mexicans also captured 68 women and children, 120 horses, 38 mules, and 122 burros. Only 17 members of the band escaped, including Nana, who had been off looking for ammunition, and Kaywaykla and his mother, Guyan. Apache accounts say Victorio was vulnerable to the surprise attack because his sister, Lozen, was not with the group at the time. Nana led the survivors on a remarkable revenge raid, covering more than a thousand miles, killing 50 Americans, and stealing hundreds of horses and cattle, while pursued fruitlessly by 10 companies of cavalry and infantry.

26. Noch-ay-del-klinne attended a school run by white missionaries before coming up with a strange amalgam of traditional Apache belief and a quasi-Christian belief in resurrection and a day of judgment. He was presumably influenced by the Ghost Dance that originated with the Paiute a few years earlier. Another version of the Ghost Dance arose among the Sioux a decade later, leading to the massacre at Wounded Knee and the death of Sitting Bull.

27. Donald Worcester, *The Apaches, Eagles of the Southwest* (Norman: University of Oklahoma Press, 1979), 237. The dialogue is taken from an account of the incident from one of the Indian participants, later recounted to Lieutenant Cruse.

28. The ability of the Ghost Dance to unite the bickering Apache bands thoroughly alarmed the corrupt San Carlos agent Joseph Tiffany and Colonel E. A. Carr, the commander of the garrison at Fort Apache in the nearby White Mountains. Tiffany insisted that the army either kill or arrest the Prophet, and the army reluctantly agreed—noting that the Prophet even made the normally reliable White Mountain Apache scouts restive, resentful, and reluctant. Carr set out with 117 men, including 23 scouts, to make the arrest.

29. The army's official version blames several of the scouts, for initiating the battle. Apache accounts generally blame the soldiers, but concede that no one knows for certain who fired the first round.

30. This version accords with an account left by a half-Apache, half-white witness who had worked for the army, and accords with the Apache version of events. The army accounts cited by Thrapp, in *Conquest of Apacheria*, and others claim that The Prophet called upon the warriors to fight, saying he would come to life again if the soldiers killed him.

31. Apache tradition suggests that Geronimo, Juh, Nana, and Lozen were all present at the battle, but Geronimo does not mention the fight at Cibicue Creek in his autobiography. It's possible that even when dictating his autobiography he decided to omit any reference to his participation at Cibicue for fear the Army would punish him. However, other evidence suggests he was not present. For instance, the Apache attack proved surprisingly ineffectual, especially since

most of the twenty-three Apache scouts turned against the soldiers in one of the only cases of mutiny on the part of the scouts on record. One officer commented that if the milling warriors had possessed a single effective leader, they would have wiped out the detachment, according to Thomas Cruse in *Apache Days and After* (1941; reprint, Lincoln: University of Nebraska Press, 1987). This argues against either Juh or Geronimo being present, since they were both gifted leaders in combat. On the other hand, perhaps they were present but could not take command because of the mixture of bands.

32. Ace Daklugie, Juh's son, later told historian Eve Ball that Geronimo and Nana and Juh all wondered at their own faith in the Prophet. They said the Prophet had convinced the leaders they should not fight, but allow Usen to take care of the whites. See *Indeh: An Apache Odyssey* (Provo, Utah: Brigham Young University Press, 1980).

33. A grand jury that later investigated Tiffany's administration found widespread evidence of corruption.

34. Geronimo offers this explanation in *His Own Story*, 129.

35. I rely here on the description of Chato's history and motivation provided to Eve Ball by James Kaywaykla and Ace Daklugie, members of the Nednai and Warm Springs (Chihenne) bands who considered Chato a traitor. Other descriptions of Chato, mostly from white officers he later served, presented a different picture. However, I have adopted the view that would most closely reflect Geronimo's perceptions.

36. Perico and Fun were both cousins of various degrees, but the Apache made little distinction between siblings and cousins, especially through the maternal line.

37. From *Geronimo, His Own Story*.

38. Apache accounts conflict as to whether Juh helped lead the expedition. Kaywaykla's secondhand report suggests Juh planned and led the expedition, and historian Dan Thrapp agrees in *Conquest of Apacheria*, 235. However, Betzinez's firsthand account (in *I Fought with Geronimo*) makes no mention of Juh; neither does White Mountain scout John Rope's secondhand account.

39. The army put the estimate at sixty warriors. The rancher, Stevens, put the number at seventy-six.

40. The foreman's name was Victoriano Mestas. This version of the incident is based on an account by Apache scout John Rope, a relative of some of those present, included in Keith H. Basso, ed., *Western Apache Raiding and Warfare: From the Notes of Grenville Goodwin* (Tucson: University of Arizona Press, 1971). Four somewhat conflicting accounts exist of the incident, but Rope's seems the most credible.

41. April 19, 1882.

42. Lieutenant Colonel George Forsyth commanded six companies of cavalry, but Geronimo's much smaller force drove them away.

43. I have accepted the Apache descriptions of Geronimo's exercise of Power throughout this account at face value to respect the Apache view of the history of these events. Several firsthand informants reported that Geronimo's songs delayed dawn for two or three hours. Perhaps a heavy overcast held back the light,

or perhaps it was a tradition added later to Geronimo's growing myth, or perhaps they mistook the time—or perhaps Usen did hold back the sun from rising.

44. Colonel Forsyth had decided to disregard international law and cross the border in pursuit with fifty Apache scouts and four hundred soldiers. An advanced contingent of forty-seven scouts and thirty-nine soldiers under the command of Captain Tullius Tupper and Al Sieber overtook Geronimo's group and decided to attack on April 27, 1882, before the main force arrived.

45. Several credible Apache accounts suggest that this advanced guard moved ahead of the main body without detecting the Mexican ambush and then sat smoking during the battle. These accounts remain difficult to reconcile with other documented behavior of these three warriors. Perhaps the accounts are wrong. Or perhaps the warriors had come into some conflict with Geronimo and so had left the group.

46. *Geronimo, His Own Story*, 110.

47. Geronimo provides a fairly detailed account of this battle in *His Own Story*, 109, but puts it in a somewhat different context and omits telling details provided by other Apache participants. For instance, Geronimo does not indicate that the Mexican attack surprised the column. I have used portions of Geronimo's account plus other firsthand Apache accounts that seem to provide a more complete version.

48. The officer's speech comes from *Geronimo, His Own Story*. Geronimo's emphasis on the soldiers' desire to kill him is plausible and is one of the few times he seems to personalize and magnify his role. His autobiography is otherwise remarkably restrained and willing to acknowledge his failures.

49. I am here accepting the account of Talbot Gooday, Loco's grandson, who gave this secondhand account to historian Eve Ball (*Indeh*, 114). However, it may simply reflect the bitter split between Apache factions that runs throughout Apache accounts of key events. Gooday was a member of Loco's band and bitterly resented the deaths Geronimo caused by forcing his people to leave the reservation. However, Geronimo on three occasions escaped from a battle in which his own wives and children were killed and so showed the preference for pragmatism over futile heroism that typified Apache warriors. After accepting Gooday's version, I speculated on Geronimo's motivations for an uncharacteristic desertion of other warriors under fire and a conflict with Fun, who remained with Geronimo for years to come.

50. The Mexican Commander, Colonel Lorenzo Garcia, lost about 19 soldiers and three officers out of a force of 250 in the daylong battle.

CHAPTER 10. Crook: Fighting the Sioux (1875–1883)

1. John G. Bourke, *On the Border with Crook* (New York: Charles Scribner's Sons, 1891), Chapt. 14.

2. Charles King, *Campaigning with Crook* (Lincoln: University of Nebraska Press, 1964).

3. J. W. Vaughn, *With Crook at the Rosebud* (Lincoln: University of Nebraska Press, 1956), 158.

4. Frank Gruard, *Life and Adventures of Frank Gruard.*

5. John Finerty, *War-Path and Bivouac: The Big Horn and Yellowstone Expedition* (Chicago: R. R. Donnelley & Sons, 1955).

6. Vaughn, *With Crook at the Rosebud*, 38.

7. Ibid., 80.

8. Annual Report of the Secretary of War, 1876, in George Crook, *General George Crook: His Autobiography*, ed. Martin F. Schmitt (Norman: University of Oklahoma Press, 1960), 500.

9. Vaughn, *With Crook at the Rosebud*, 133.

10. Quoted in ibid., 164 n.

11. Quoted in ibid., 163.

12. Quoted in ibid., 166.

13. Finerty, *War-Path and Bivouac*, 287.

14. Ibid., 285.

15. Jerome Green, *Slim Buttes, 1876: An Episode of the Great Sioux War* (Norman: University of Oklahoma Press, 1982), 112.

16. Ibid., 113.

17. Ibid., 112.

18. *Army and Navy Journal* 14, no. 11 (October 21, 1876): 166.

19. Annual Report of General Crook, Division of the Missouri, October 30, 1876, in Crook, *Autobiography.*

20. Bourke, *On the Border with Crook*, 413.

21. Ibid., 423.

22. Crook, *Autobiography*, 221.

23. *Army and Navy Journal* 15, no. 47 (June 29, 1878): 758.

24. Annual Report of the Secretary of War, 1876, cited in Crook, *Autobiography.*

25. Crook, *Autobiography*, 229.

Part Five: The Fox Faces the Whirlwind (1883–1909)

CHAPTER 11. Geronimo: The Last Days of a Free People (1883)

1. Eve Ball, *Indeh: An Apache Odyssey* (Provo, Utah: Brigham Young University Press), 172.

2. Probably Galeana. Angie Debo, *Geronimo: The Man, His Time, His Place* (Norman: University of Oklahoma Press, 1976), 156.

3. Lozen is not specifically mentioned in this period, but she probably would have gone along with the Warm Springs remnant following Kaytennae.

4. Apache accounts indicate Geronimo's Power warned him that the soldiers were coming near Oputo. The dialogue is speculative based on Morris Edward Opler's descriptions of the way people talk to Power in *An Apache Lifeway* (1941; reprint, Chicago: University of Chicago Press, 1996). Apache informants indicate that the relationship with Power is much like a relationship between two people, with conversations back and forth and a mutual play of egos and needs.

5. Juh's son, Ace Daklugie, recounted Juh's vision to historian Eve Ball, who recorded it in *Indeh*. I have assumed that Juh would have recounted that vision to Geronimo as well.

6. Apache sources don't often indicate which group Loco followed in this period; perhaps he was no longer highly regarded as a war leader. Logically, he would have remained with the Chihenne.

7. I have used specific numbers throughout Geronimo's account, although the Apache did not pay much attention to such numbers. Apache informants often said simply that a few, or many, people were killed, evincing disdain for the numbers game of the whites. Nonetheless, I have in many places included the numbers the whites collected regarding specific events.

8. The raiders killed federal judge H. C. McComas and his wife and kidnapped his son, Charlie. The murders and kidnapping inflamed public opinion, garnered national headlines, and played a role in Crook's decision to follow the raiders down into Mexico.

9. The Mexican commander, who had eighty-six federal troops and fifty auxiliaries, reported that on April 25, 1883, his command encountered the Indians in a strongly fortified position, attacked, and drove off the Indians, killing eleven warriors. The official Mexican accounts often differ dramatically from Apache accounts. However, if the Apache had suffered a fraction of the losses reported by various Mexican commanders, they would have been wiped out quickly. Moreover, Bourke, in *On the Border with Crook*, later reported that Crook's column came across traces of this battle that supported the Apache account.

CHAPTER 12. Crook: A Bold Gamble (1883)

1. John G. Bourke, *On the Border with Crook* (New York: Charles Scribner's Sons, 1891), 443.

2. Ibid.

3. Ibid., 439.

4. Quoted in ibid.

5. General Orders No. 43, Nov. 5, 1882, in George Crook, *General George Crook: His Autobiography*, ed. Martin F. Schmitt (Norman: University of Oklahoma Press, 1960).

6. Bourke, *On the Border with Crook*, 454.

7. John G. Bourke, *An Apache Campaign in the Sierra Madre* (New York: Charles Scribner's Sons, 1958), 21.

8. Ibid., 35.

9. Jason Betzinez, *I Fought with Geronimo*, edited and annotated by Wilbur Sturtevant Nye (Harrisburg, Pa.: Stackpole, 1959), 113.

10. Ibid., 114.

11. Bourke, *An Apache Campaign*, 83.

12. Charles Lummis, *General Crook and the Apache Wars* (Flagstaff, Ariz.: Northland Press, 1966), 95.

13. Bourke, *An Apache Campaign*, 85.

14. Lummis, *General Crook and the Apache Wars*, 106.

15. Keith Basso, ed., *Western Apache Raiding and Warfare: From the Notes of Grenville Goodwin* (Tucson: University of Arizona Press, 1971). This account comes from John Rope. It is not supported by Chiricahua Apache accounts and may represent a later oral tradition among the White Mountain Apache intended to make a hero of Dji-li-kine. However, Rope's account remains accurate in most respects and the incident rings true, given Geronimo's long struggle to convince his fellow warriors to continue fighting.

16. Bourke, *An Apache Campaign*, 95.

Chapter 13. Geronimo: Return to the Reservation (1884–1886)

1. The two men were a customs collector from Nogales who wanted to confiscate the cattle and a marshal who wanted to arrest Geronimo for murder. Lieutenant Davis argued with them, since his orders were to bring Geronimo safely to the reservation. The marshal deputized Davis, which meant he would have to choose between violating his orders or violating the law. The arrival of Lieutenant J. F. Blake from Fort Bowie gave him an out, since Blake could go with Geronimo while Davis remained with the marshal in compliance with the law.

2. Geronimo seemed set on locating his people on Eagle Creek, and insisted that Crook had promised him the right to settle there. Crook probably did not make that specific promise, but it is possible the translator made an implied promise. Problems with the reliability of translations haunted discussions between the Apache and the Americans.

3. National Archives Records Service 1601 AGO 1884, F/@ 1066 AGO 1883. This is from Crawford's report, shifted into first person. Angie Debo, *Geronimo: The Man, His Time, His Place* (Norman: University of Oklahoma Press, 1976), 193.

4. Geronimo made this statement to Crawford on March 21, 1884.

5. Crawford reported to Crook that McIntosh was diverting the supplies due to the Chiricahua, in the time-honored tradition of Indian agents. Crook, acting with his customary integrity, replaced his old scout, although McIntosh did rally the Apache leaders to his case. It is possible that they proved so supportive because he was providing payoffs to the leaders, giving them each a portion of the diverted supplies.

6. Primary Apache accounts date a bitter split in the ranks of the Chiricahua to this period. It is hard to sort out the truth from the bitterness. Geronimo's faction described Chato, Mickey Free, and Tsoe harshly, but Davis and others have described them as honorable, courageous, and motivated by a desire to help their people. For purposes of this account, I am adopting Geronimo's view of the matter.

7. Kaywaykla, the stepson of Kaytennae, provided this account to historian Eve Ball in *In the Days of Victorio: Recollections of a Warm Springs Apache* (Tucson: University of Arizona Press, 1970). Britton Davis, in *The Truth about Geronimo* (1929; reprint, Lincoln: University of Nebraska Press, 1976), does not

provide the specific source for the intelligence that Kaytennae was planning to kill him and spark a breakout.

8. June 22, 1884.

9. Kaytennae was sentenced to a month of hard labor in irons at Alcatraz, and then at Crook's recommendation was permitted to go into San Francisco so that he could glimpse the true extent of American power and the hopelessness of the Apache position.

10. Morris Edward Opler, "A Chiricahua Apache's Account of the Geronimo Campaign of 1886," *New Mexico Historical Review* 13, no. 4 (October 1938): 365.

11. October 1884.

12. Crook was battling the Interior Department to regain undivided control of the reservation. Crawford was particularly frustrated, since Interior Department officials had accused him of corruption. At one point, Crook threatened to resign if he wasn't given undivided control. Finally, Crawford asked for reassignment to field service. Crook approved the transfer and replaced him with the inexperienced Captain Francis Pierce at what proved just the wrong moment.

13. The Apache accounts do not indicate why the man beat his wife. I have made the assumption she had been unfaithful, although it is also possible he simply got drunk.

14. Davis, *The Truth about Geronimo*, 139–141.

15. Davis's telegram went to the newly appointed Captain Pierce, who showed it to Al Sieber, who was sleeping off a drunk. Sieber said it was nothing, and Pierce failed to forward it to Crook or to reply to Davis.

16. Opler, "A Chiricahua Apache's Account," 367.

17. They killed at least seventeen civilians on their May 15, 1885, flight from the reservation.

18. Opler's informants, in *An Apache Lifeway* (1941; reprint, Chicago: University of Chicago Press, 1996), who were generally critical of Geronimo, said Geronimo had tricked Chihuahua and Naiche into leaving the reservation. However, none of the principal figures ever mentioned this incident and the group they led later reunited and worked closely together. The detail rings true to me, since it seems consistent with Geronimo's drive and shrewdness and would account for Chihuahua's decision to break off from Geronimo's group.

19. The original army report claimed Nana and Geronimo's son had been killed and Geronimo wounded, none of which proved true. The army may also have captured Geronimo's wife, Shtsha-she, although it's possible that she was not his wife, and the accounts are confused. In any case, she is not mentioned again after this incident. Therefore, if she existed, she must have been either killed or captured. The children captured included Zi-yeh's infant son Fenton; a three-year-old girl; a two-year-old son who later died in captivity; and two other children.

20. This conversation between Geronimo and his Power is speculative, since it does not appear specifically in any of the Apache accounts of these events. However, the Apache accounts do indicate that Geronimo consulted his Power at every important juncture and was guided by its advice.

21. Ulzana's warriors, between November 23 and the end of December 1885, killed 38 people, captured 250 head of stock, and covered 1,200 miles with but a single casualty. The raid inflamed settlers and prompted the army's commander in chief, Phil Sheridan, to journey out from Washington to confer with Crook at Fort Bowie.

22. It's unclear whether it was Lozen or another woman who went to negotiate with Crawford, but Geronimo and the other leaders often used women as intermediaries in such negotiations, reasoning that the soldiers would not imprison or kill a woman.

23. The January 11, 1886, confrontation between the Apache scouts led by Crawford, Lieutenant Maus, and Tom Horn and a force of Mexican irregulars cost Crook one of his most able commanders, since Crawford died of a head wound shortly after the battle.

CHAPTER 14. Crook: Confrontation with an Old Foe (1886)

1. This is probably a reference to Geronimo's belief that Crook had Power, but this was the closest the translator could come to the concept.

2. It remains unclear whether Geronimo did send Chappo and Perico to kill Davis, and whether he stampeded Chihuahua and Naiche by telling them that he had already done so. It's possible this was just a manipulation of Davis by Chato and Tsoe, which Crook believed. It's also possible that Crook was at this point skillfully dividing Geronimo from Naiche and Chihuahua.

3. The abject nature of these surrender speeches seems curiously out of character for these hardened warriors. It probably reflects their belief that Crook had demonstrated substantial access to Power, and was the closest approach to these concepts the translators could muster.

4. The dialogue between Crook and the Chiricahua leaders comes from the transcript of the conference; Britton Davis, The Truth about Geronimo (1929; reprint, Lincoln: University of Nebraska Press, 1976), 200–212; John G. Bourke, On the Border with Crook (New York: Charles Scribner's Sons, 1891), 472–479; and Crook's report in the Annual Report of the Secretary of War, 1886 (Washington, D.C.: Government Printing Office), 153.

5. Angie Debo, Geronimo: The Man, His Time, His Place (Norman: University of Oklahoma Press, 1976), 263.

6. Ibid., 264.

CHAPTER 15. Geronimo: The Triumph of Fear (1886)

1. This was the reason for fleeing that Naiche offered to Crook on January 2, 1890.

2. Naiche provided this explanation to Crook in 1890. U.S. Senate, 51st Cong., 1 sess., Exec. Doc. 35, 33, cited by Angie Debo in Geronimo: The Man, His Time, His Place (Norman: University of Oklahoma Press, 1976).

3. Quoted from Geronimo, His Own Story, as told to S(tephen) M(elvil) Barrett (New York: Duffield, 1906), shifted into third person.

CHAPTER 16. Crook: Geronimo, Geronimo, Always Geronimo (1886)

1. Charles Lummis, *General Crook and the Apache Wars* (Flagstaff, Ariz.: Northland Press, 1966), xiv. This is a reference to the frontier belief that the only good Indian is a dead Indian.

2. Ibid., 13.

3. John G. Bourke, *On the Border with Crook* (New York: Charles Scribner's Sons, 1891), 483.

4. George Crook, *General George Crook: His Autobiography*, ed. Martin F. Schmitt (Norman: University of Oklahoma Press, 1960), 265.

CHAPTER 17. Geronimo: The Final Surrender (1886)

1. Apache tradition indicates Lozen was with Geronimo to the end and often served as the intermediary in peace discussions, but it is not certain she was one of the women who went to Fronteras.

2. August 23, 1886.

3. Actually his cousin, but the Apache terms for brother and cousin are the same.

4. This dialogue comes from Gatewood's account of the meeting, cited in *Geronimo and the End of the Apache Wars*, ed. C. L. Sonnichsen (Lincoln: University of Nebraska Press, 1986), 53.

CHAPTER 18. Crook: To Redeem His Honor (1886–1890)

1. Charles Lummis, *General Crook and the Apache Wars* (Flagstaff, Ariz.: Northland Press, 1966), 34.

2. Ibid., 123.

3. Ibid., 98.

4. George Crook, *General George Crook: His Autobiography*, ed. Martin F. Schmitt (Norman: University of Oklahoma Press, 1960), 285.

5. Quoted in ibid., 293.

CHAPTER 19. Geronimo: A Long Time in a Cage (1886–1909)

1. Angie Debo, *Geronimo: The Man, His Time, His Place* (Norman: University of Oklahoma Press, 1976), 422.

2. Morris Edward Opler, *An Apache Lifeway* (1941; reprint, Chicago: University of Chicago Press, 1996).

3. David Roberts, *Once They Moved Like the Wind: Cochise, Geronimo and the Apache Wars* (New York: Simon & Schuster, 1993), 313. Roberts seems to cite as the source for this incident Fred T. Corum, "When Geronimo Smiled," *Pentecostal Evangel* (December 11, 1988). It's possible this terrible incident is another of the exaggerations which have grown up around Geronimo, including the once widely believed newspaper claim that he had a blanket made of 100 scalps, although Geronimo rarely took scalps and would not have kept them,

given the Apache attitude toward death. Even if the specific incident involving the impalement of a baby is exaggerated, Geronimo certainly committed other atrocities of a similar nature that would have fueled such a speculation.

4. A slightly altered quote from *Geronimo, His Own Story*, as told to S(tephen) M(elvil) Barrett (New York: Duffield, 1906), 15–16.

BIBLIOGRAPHY

Adams, Alexander B. *Geronimo: A Biography*. New York: Da Capo Press, 1971.

Aleshire, Peter. *Reaping the Whirlwind: The Apache Wars*. New York: Facts on File, 1998.

Altshuler, Constance Wynn. *Starting with Defiance: Nineteenth Century Arizona Military Posts*. Tucson: Arizona Historical Society, 1983.

Ambrose, Stephen. *Crazy Horse and Custer: The Parallel Lives of Two American Warriors*. New York: Meridian, 1975.

Annual Reports of the Secretary of the Interior, 1858–1869, 1881, 1913, 1914. Washington, D.C.: Government Printing Office.

Annual Reports of the Secretary of War, 1882–1887, 1890, 1892, 1894–1896. Washington, D.C.: Government Printing Office.

Ball, Eve. *Indeh: An Apache Odyssey*. Provo, Utah: Brigham Young University Press, 1980.

——. *In the Days of Victorio: Recollections of a Warm Springs Apache*. Tucson: University of Arizona Press, 1970.

Barnes, Will C. *Apaches and Longhorns: The Reminiscences of Will C. Barnes*. Tucson: University of Arizona Press, 1941.

Basso, Keith H. *The Cibecue Apache*. Prospect Heights, Ill.: Waveland Press, 1973.

——, ed. *Western Apache Raiding and Warfare: From the Notes of Grenville Goodwin*. Tucson: University of Arizona Press, 1971.

Betzinez, Jason. *I Fought with Geronimo*. Edited and annotated by Wilbur Sturtevant Nye. Harrisburg, Pa.: Stackpole, 1959.

Bigelow, John. *On the Bloody Trail of Geronimo*. Edited by Arthur Woodward. Tucson: Westernlore Press, 1986.

Bourke, John G. *An Apache Campaign in the Sierra Madre*. New York: Charles Scribner's Sons, 1958.

——. *Apache Medicine-Men*. 1892. Reprint, New York: Dover, 1993.

——. *On the Border with Crook*. New York: Charles Scribner's Sons, 1891.

——. *With General Crook in the Indian Wars*. Palo Alto, Calif.: Lewis Osborne, 1968.

Bowman, John S., ed. *The Civil War Almanac*. New York: Facts on File, 1983.

Brown, Dee. *Bury My Heart at Wounded Knee.* New York: Holt Rinehart & Winston, 1970.

Browning, Sinclair. *Enju: The Life and Struggle of an Apache Chief from the Little Running Water.* Flagstaff, Ariz.: Northland Press, 1982.

Carr, Camillo Casatti Cadmus. *A Cavalryman in Indian Country.* N.p.: n.d.

Clum, Woodworth. *Apache Agent: The Story of John P. Clum.* Boston: Houghton Mifflin, 1936.

Colyer, Vincent. *Peace with the Apaches of New Mexico and Arizona.* Washington, D.C.: Government Printing Office, 1872.

Connell, Evan. *Son of the Morning Star: Custer and the Little Big Horn.* San Francisco: North Point, 1984.

Conner, Daniel Ellis. *Joseph Reddeford Walker and the Arizona Adventure.* Edited and annotated by Donald J. Berthrong and Odessa Davenport. Norman: University of Oklahoma Press, 1956.

Corbusier, William. *Verde to San Carlos.* Tucson: Arizona Historical Society, 1971.

Corle, Edwin. *The Gila, River of the Southwest.* Lincoln: University of Nebraska Press, 1951.

Cortes, Jose. *Views from the Apache Frontier: Report on the Northern Provinces of New Spain.* Edited by Elizabeth John. New York: Macmillan, 1938.

Cremony, John Carey. *Life among the Apaches.* 1868. Reprint, Glorieta, N. Mex.: Rio Grande Press, 1969.

Crook, George. *Address of General George Crook, U.S. Army at the Reunion of the Army of West Virginia at Cumberland, Maryland.* September 1884. N.p.: 1884.

———. *Address to the Graduates of the United States Military Academy, West Point, New York, Class 1884.* West Point, N.Y.: n.p., 1884.

———. *General George Crook: His Autobiography.* Edited by Martin F. Schmitt. Norman: University of Oklahoma Press, 1960.

Cruse, Thomas. *Apache Days and After.* 1941. Reprint, Lincoln: University of Nebraska Press, 1987.

Davis, Britton. *The Truth about Geronimo.* 1929. Reprint, Lincoln: University of Nebraska Press, 1976.

Debo, Angie. *Geronimo: The Man, His Time, His Place.* Norman: University of Oklahoma Press, 1976.

———. *A History of the Indians of the United States.* Norman: University of Oklahoma Press, 1970.

Du Pont, Henry A. *The Campaign of 1864 in the Valley of Virginia and the Expedition to Lynchburg.* New York: n.p., 1925.

Faulk, Odie B. *The Geronimo Campaign.* New York: Oxford University Press, 1969.

Finerty, John. *War-Path and Bivouac: The Big Horn and Yellowstone Expedition.* Chicago: R. R. Donnelley & Sons, 1955.

Foote, Shelby. *The Civil War: A Narrative.* 3 vols. New York: 1958, 1963, 1974.

Forbes, Jack D. *Apache, Navaho, and Spaniard.* Norman: University of Oklahoma Press, 1960.

Geronimo, His Own Story. As told to S(tephen) M(elvil) Barrett. New York: Duffield, 1906.

Goodwin, Grenville. "Experiences of an Indian Scout." Parts 1 and 2. *Arizona Historical Review* 7, no. 1 (January 1936); no. 2 (April 1936).

————. *The Myths and Tales of the White Mountain Apache.* Tucson: University of Arizona Press, 1996.

Green, Jerome. *Slim Buttes, 1876: An Episode of the Great Sioux War.* Norman: University of Oklahoma Press, 1982.

Haley, James L. *Apaches: A History and Cultural Portrait.* New York: Doubleday, 1981.

Hand, George. *The Civil War in Apacheland.* Edited by Neil B. Carmony. Silver City, N. Mex.: High-Lonesome, 1996.

Hayes, Rutherford B. *Diary and Letters of Rutherford B. Hayes.* 5 vols. Columbus, Ohio: n.p., 1922–1926.

Horn, Tom. *Life of Tom Horn.* Norman: University of Oklahoma Press, 1964.

Howard, Helen Addison. *The Saga of Chief Joseph.* Lincoln: University of Nebraska Press, 1941.

Howard, O(liver) O(tis). *Famous Indian Chiefs I Have Known.* New York: Century, 1907.

————. *My Life and Experiences among our Hostile Indians.* Hartford, Conn.: A. D. Worthington, 1907.

Johnson, Barry. *Crook's Resume of Operations against Apache Indians, 1882–1886.* London: n.p., 1971.

Josephy, Alvin M. *The Civil War in the American West.* New York: Random House, 1991.

King, Charles. *Campaigning with Crook.* Lincoln: University of Nebraska Press, 1964.

————. *Major-General George Crook, United States Army.* Milwaukee: n.p., 1890.

Knight, Oliver. *Following the Indian Wars: The Story of the Newspaper Correspondents among the Indian Campaigners.* Norman: University of Oklahoma Press, 1960.

Leermakers, J. A. *Great Western Indian Fights.* Lincoln: University of Nebraska Press, 1960.

Lockwood, Frank. *The Apache Indians.* Lincoln: University of Nebraska Press, 1938.

————. *Pioneer Portraits.* Tucson: University of Arizona Press, 1968.

Lummis, Charles. *General Crook and the Apache Wars.* Flagstaff, Ariz.: Northland Press, 1966.

Mails, Thomas. *The People Called Apache.* New York: BDD Illustrated Books, 1993.

Miles, Nelson A. *Personal Recollections.* Chicago: Werner, 1897.

————. *Serving the Republic.* Freeport, N.Y.: Books for Libraries, 1971.

Miller, David Humphreys. *Custer's Fall: The Native American Side of the Story.* New York: Meridian, 1957.

Moody, Ralph. *Geronimo, Wolf of the Warpath.* New York: H. Wolf, 1958.

Olge, Ralph Hedrick. *Federal Control of the Western Apaches, 1848–1886.* Albuquerque: University of New Mexico Press, 1970.

Opler, Morris Edward. *An Apache Lifeway.* 1941. Reprint, Chicago: University of Chicago Press, 1996.

——. "A Chiricahua Apache's Account of the Geronimo Campaign of 1886." *New Mexico Historical Review* 13, no. 4 (October 1938).

——. "Mountain Spirits of the Chiricahua Apache." *The Masterkey* 20, no. 4 (July 1946).

——. *Myths and Tales of the Chiricahua Apache Indians.* Lincoln: University of Nebraska Press, 1942.

——. *Myths and Tales of the Jicarilla Apache Indians.* New York: Dover, 1994.

Perry, Richard. *Western Apache Heritage, People of the Mountain Corridor.* Austin: University of Texas Press, 1991.

Redstorm, Lisle. *Apache Wars: An Illustrated Battle History.* New York: Barnes and Noble, 1990.

Reid, Whitelaw. *Ohio in the War,* 2 vols. Cincinnati: n.p., 1868–1872.

Rickey, Don. *Forty Miles a Day on Beans and Hay: The Enlisted Soldier Fighting the Indian Wars.* Norman: University of Oklahoma Press, 1963.

Roberts, David. *Once They Moved Like the Wind: Cochise, Geronimo and the Apache Wars.* New York: Simon & Schuster, 1993.

Sandoz, Mari. *Cheyenne Autumn.* New York: Avon, 1953.

——. *Crazy Horse: The Strange Man of the Oglala.* New York: MJF Books, 1942.

Santee, Ross. *Apache Land.* New York: Charles Scribner's Sons, 1947.

Schellie, Don. *Vast Domain of Blood: The Story of the Camp Grant Massacre.* Los Angeles: Westernlore Press, 1968.

Sheridan, Philip H. *Personal Memoirs of P. H. Sheridan.* 2 vols. New York: n.p., 1888.

Simmons, Marc. *Witchcraft in the Southwest.* Lincoln: University of Nebraska Press, 1994.

Sladen, Joseph Alton. *Making Peace with Cochise.* Norman: University of Oklahoma Press, 1997.

Smith, Cornelius C. *Fort Huachuca: The Story of a Frontier Post.* Washington, D.C.: U.S. Government Printing Office, 1981.

Smith, Sherry. *The View from Officer's Row: Army Perceptions of Western Indians.* Tucson: University of Arizona Press, 1990.

Sonnichsen, C. L. *Geronimo and the End of the Apache Wars.* Lincoln: University of Nebraska Press, 1986.

——. *The Mescalero Apaches.* Norman: University of Oklahoma Press, 1958.

Stockel, Henrietta. *Women of the Apache Nation: Voices of Truth.* Reno: University of Nevada Press, 1991.

Sutherland, Edwin Van Valkenburg. "The Diaries of John Gregory Bourke: Their Anthropological and Folklore Content." Ph.D. diss., University of Pennsylvania, 1964.

Thrapp, Dan L. *Al Sieber, Chief of Scouts.* Norman: University of Oklahoma Press, 1964.

——. *The Conquest of Apacheria*. Norman: University of Oklahoma Press, 1967.

——. *General Crook and the Sierra Madre Adventure*. Norman: University of Oklahoma Press, 1972.

——. *Juh: An Incredible Indian*. Southwest Studies, monograph no. 39. El Paso: Texas Western Press, 1973.

——. *Victorio and the Mimbres Apaches*. Norman: University of Oklahoma Press, 1974.

Tiller, Veronica E. Velarde. *The Jicarilla Apache Tribe: A History*. Lincoln: University of Nebraska Press, 1992.

U.S. Congress. Senate Executive Documents. 49th Cong. S. Doc. 73, 117.

Utley, Robert. *A Clash of Cultures: Fort Bowie and the Chiricahua Apaches*. Washington, D.C.: National Park Service, 1977.

——. *Frontiersmen in Blue: The United States Army and the Indian, 1848–1865*. Lincoln: University of Nebraska Press, 1967.

Vaughn, J. W. *With Crook at the Rosebud*. Lincoln: University of Nebraska Press, 1956.

Ward, Geoffrey. *The Civil War*. New York: Knopf, 1990.

Weems, John Edward. *Death Song: The Last of the Indian Wars*. New York: Indian Head Books, 1994.

Welch, James, with Paul Stekler. *Killing Custer: The Battle of the Little Bighorn and the Fate of the Plains Indians*. New York: W. W. Norton, 1994.

Wellman, Paul I. *The Indian Wars of the West*. Garden City, N.Y.: Doubleday, 1947.

Worcester, Donald. *The Apaches, Eagles of the Southwest*. Norman: University of Oklahoma Press, 1979.

ARIZONA

NEW MEXICO

N
W   E
S

C Cibecue
Salt R.
D
Ft. Apache
Globe •
SAN CARLOS RESERVATION

O
• Ojo Caliente
Cañada Alamosa

MESCALERO RESERVATION

E
Tucson •

San Pedro R.

Gila R.

Pinos Altos •

Rio Grande

Alamosa R.

STATES

A

F
Ft. Bowie
G

UNITED

TEXAS

H
Tombstone •
I
J
K

MEXICO

Ft. Buchanan

Janos • **B**

Bavispe •
Bacerac •
L

Casas Grandes
• Galeana

0   50
Miles

Bavispe R.

M

N

SONORA

CHIHUAHUA

©1999 by D. L. McElhannon

A Geronimo born near the headwaters of the Gila
B 1850–Mexican troops kill Geronimo's family
C Death of Prophet spurs Geronimo's outbreak
D Chiricahua stay near Turkey Creek
E Camp Grant massacre
F Battle of Apache Pass
G Chato kidnaps McComas boy
H General Howard meets with Cochise
I Geronimo delays dawn
J Geronimo surrenders to Miles, Sept. 1886
K Geronimo surrenders to Crook then reneges
L Geronimo negotiates with Gatewood, Aug. 1886
M Crook finds Geronimo in the Sierra Madre
N 1880–Mexican Army traps and kills Victorio
O Victorio's people plead for a reservation here

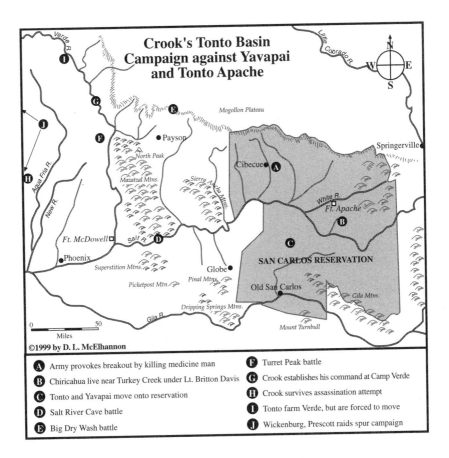

Crook's Tonto Basin Campaign against Yavapai and Tonto Apache

Verde R.

Little Colorado R.

N
W E
S

Mogollon Plateau

I

G

E

J

F

Payson

Springerville

North Peak

H

Agua Fria R.

New R.

Mazatzal Mtns.

Sierra Ancha Mtns.

Cibecue **A**

White R.

Ft. Apache

B

Ft. McDowell

Salt R.

D

SAN CARLOS RESERVATION

C

Phoenix

Superstition Mtns.

Globe

Pinal Mtns.

Old San Carlos

Gila Mtns.

Picketpost Mtn.

Dripping Springs Mtns.

Gila R.

Mount Turnbull

0 ——— 50
Miles

©1999 by D. L. McElhannon

A Army provokes breakout by killing medicine man

B Chiricahua live near Turkey Creek under Lt. Britton Davis

C Tonto and Yavapai move onto reservation

D Salt River Cave battle

E Big Dry Wash battle

F Turret Peak battle

G Crook establishes his command at Camp Verde

H Crook survives assassination attempt

I Tonto farm Verde, but are forced to move

J Wickenburg, Prescott raids spur campaign

Index

Ah-koch-ne, 62
Alchesay, 244
Alchise, 240, 241, 285, 287, 288, 291
alcohol
  army contractors and, 11, 145
  Crook's denouncement of, 310, 311
  Geronimo's weakness for, 71, 155–56, 228, 288, 303, 327, 333n.11
  prohibitions on Indian *tizwin* brewing, 242, 267, 270–71
Alope (Geronimo's wife), 28–34, 39, 159, 325, 327, 331nn.18, 20, 333n.3
American Horse, 212–13, 316
Antietam, battle of (1862), 82–84
Apache, 65, 82, 100, 319
  Camp Grant massacre of, 112–13, 120–21, 122, 123–24
  creation myth, 15–17, 329–30nn.1, 3
  Crook's death and, 12
  Crook's Mexico expedition and, 245–55
  despisement of liars, 106, 336n.8
  disease's impact on, 7, 152, 153, 227, 321
  fighting among, 145–47, 153

first encounters with Americans, 27, 331n.17
and horses, 29, 331n.16
and Janos (Mexico) massacre, 30–39, 331–32nn.20, 21, 23, 27, 28, 30
Mexican raids by, 62–69, 71–73, 105, 139, 143–44, 230, 235–38, 337n.4, 344n.9
Mexico as enemy of, 3, 5, 21–22, 26–27, 73–74, 103, 132, 181–85, 231–38, 254, 330–31n.15
peace treaties, 124–25, 140–43
reservations, 121, 124, 132–35, 143–44, 239–42, 255–57
schooling of children, 317, 321
treatment of unfaithful wives, 242, 267, 270
U.S. Army and, 101–6, 111–13, 119–37, 335–36nn.1, 3, 6
as U.S. Army scouts, 7–8, 10, 113, 114, 116–18, 126, 131, 134, 137, 165, 170, 172, 244–48, 253, 295, 299, 313, 340–41nn.29, 31
white settlers and, 74–75, 76, 101, 111–12
See also Geronimo; *specific bands and people*